Praise for Sydne T0201750

"Superbosses foster innovation and market domination through the strategic management of talent. Sydney Finkelstein shows you how to elevate your own leadership, superboss style, to create a lasting, impactful legacy."
—Marshall Goldsmith, author of *Triggers*

"If you've ever wondered how some mentors manage to spawn so many star protégés, this is a book well worth reading. Through case studies of legendary leaders across a range of industries, *Superbosses* highlights new strategies for attracting and developing talent."
—Adam Grant, Wharton professor; author of *Give and Take* and *Originals*

"In *Superbosses*, Finkelstein identifies the qualities that set great leaders apart. This fascinating look at the importance of encouraging innovation and the ability to motivate is useful for leadership not only in kitchens and restaurants but in all industries."
—Eric Ripert, chef and co-owner, Le Bernardin

"A groundbreaking and absorbing look into not only how to create the world's best talent but how and why you might be better off letting them go."
—Bill McNabb, chairman and CEO, The Vanguard Group

"Maybe you're a decent boss. But are you a superboss? That's the question you'll be asking yourself after reading Sydney Finkelstein's fascinating book. By revealing the secrets of superbosses from finance to fashion and from cooking to comic books, Finkelstein offers a smart, actionable playbook for anyone trying to become a better leader."
—Daniel H. Pink, author of *To Sell Is Human* and *Drive*

"Finkelstein combines rich storytelling with practical advice in this surprising exploration of great talents—and their superbosses."
—James M. Kilts, former chairman and CEO, The Gillette Company

"We have long recognized Sydney Finkelstein as one of the world's leading management thinkers. With *Superbosses*, he demonstrates why. It is a riveting, inspiring, and practical tour de force."
—Stuart Crainer and Des Dearlove, founders, Thinkers50

"Superbosses—and they are to be found in every industry and every market—are able to facilitate extraordinary innovation by attracting exceptional people and unleashing their full potential through their companies. This book shows you how to do it and then some."
—Eric Spiegel, president and CEO, Siemens Corporation

"Talented management is the key driver of business. Nurturing that talent makes businesses sustainable winners. In *Superbosses*, Finkelstein reveals how the best of the best succeed at it and offers guidance any manager can follow to be a great leader."
—Michael Ward, managing director and COO, Bain Capital

"This book could make some bosses angry—and that's a good thing. Finkelstein's examination of what actually makes a legendary leader goes against the grain of much standard management 'best practice' and offers a whole new way to think about talent."
— Kevin Roberts, executive chairman, Saatchi & Saatchi Worldwide

"This is a great book that not only identifies the skills of the best leaders across a number of industries but gives readers clear, practical guidance on how they can develop and practice the skills of a superboss."
— Ken C. Hicks, retired chairman and CEO, Foot Locker, Inc.

"Sydney Finkelstein sheds light on an unexplored topic in management with careful research and insightful storytelling."
— Akira Uehara, president, Taisho Pharmaceutical Holdings Co., Ltd.

"Finkelstein performs a valuable public service in analyzing how corporate leaders can educate and nurture others to be successful. This is required reading for all those executives interested not only in their own performance but in developing and promoting superstar talent in their businesses."
— Kenneth Feinberg, director, September 11th Victim Compensation Fund

"A fascinating study of extraordinary leaders we all know of but few have access to. Sydney Finkelstein's surprising findings offer insight into how great talent is developed and nurtured."
— Ed Haldeman, former CEO, Freddie Mac and Putnam Investments

"Sometimes great wisdom comes in simple truths: how a leader uniquely creates, manages, and activates his 'personal' network matters. For leaders, entrepreneurs, and all those people who want to get there, *Superbosses* is an inspiring and engaging must-read."
— Blair B. LaCorte, executive vice president, Business Rockstars Network

"Finally an answer to the millennial leadership puzzle at work. Simply break all the rules about what you thought you knew regarding identifying their potential and unleashing their talent to impact the broader team! Finkelstein has created a compelling road map for great leadership."
— Jim Weber, chairman and CEO, Brooks Running

"*Superbosses* is not a career book, yet it will entirely transform the way you think about your career and that of everyone around you. With riveting stories and deep insight into how standout successes in a number of fields treat talent, Finkelstein offers a whole new framework to turbocharge your career."
— Tom McInerney, president and CEO, Genworth Financial

"How better to learn about talent than to study the bosses who developed the most talent in their industries? In the process, Sydney Finkelstein discovered the remarkable similarities across a wide variety of industries in the actions these bosses take to produce talent. The result is a playbook that any and all business leaders can follow to identify, inspire, and develop talent in a way that brings the best out of people. It's an inspirational reminder that great business leaders don't just produce results, they create an environment focused on a compelling vision where great people believe they can achieve the impossible—and they do!"

—Sherri C. Oberg, cofounder and former CEO, Acusphere, Inc.

"Finkelstein offers tremendous insight into an unexplored area of management with his extensive study of superbosses. A truly important read."

—Philip Hanlon, president, Dartmouth College

"*Superbosses* offers all managers—no matter where they are in an organization—a blueprint for success. It's always about people, and Finkelstein's original examples, stories, and insights will stick with you long after you put this pathbreaking book down."

—Jeremy Reitman, CEO, Reitmans

"Most of us have worked for good bosses at some point in our career. Most of us have also admired from afar great bosses in industry. And most of us aspire to be great bosses. *Superbosses* adroitly articulates through examples from multiple industries and endeavors the attributes that make for great bosses who create winning teams. It will change the way you think about talent—how you hire, foster innovation, and even view attrition. An enlightening, and often surprising, look at the real well of success for any industry."

—Charles L. Harrington, chairman and CEO, Parsons Corp.

"We always remember that one boss who made a difference in our lives by helping us accomplish more than we ever thought possible. *Superbosses* explains how each of us can become that boss."

—Greg Maffei, president and CEO, Liberty Media Corporation

"*Superbosses* is a concrete study of the mind-sets, behaviors, and habits defining outstanding leadership practices. Great leaders inspire the extraordinary from people and create unforgettable environments. A must-read for leaders who want to accelerate growth, engagement, and purpose in others."

—Bruno Vinciguerra, former COO, Sotheby's

"Distilling more than a decade's research and probing across dozens of sectors, America's preeminent leadership scholar, Sydney Finkelstein, proves that the ability to uncover and nurture talent matters far more than the mastery of metrics. Superbosses are transformational for more than their companies, teams or nonprofits; they instill in their protégés techniques that often revolutionize whole industries. Whether you run a company or dream of doing so, *Superbosses* will change the way you think about the talent around you—and your own."

—C. Richard Allen, CEO, SnagFilms, Inc.

SUPERBOSSES

How Exceptional Leaders Master

the Flow of Talent

Sydney Finkelstein

PORTFOLIO / PENGUIN

PORTFOLIO / PENGUIN

An imprint of Penguin Random House LLC

penguinrandomhouse.com

The Library of Congress has cataloged the hardcover edition as follows:

Names: Finkelstein, Sydney, author.
Title: Superbosses : how exceptional leaders master the flow of talent / Sydney Finkelstein.
Description: New York : Portfolio, 2016.
Identifiers: LCCN 2015041563 (print) | LCCN 2016004481 (ebook) | ISBN 9781591847830 (hardback) | ISBN 9780698192836 (ebook)
Subjects: LCSH: Leadership. | Executives—Psychology. | Personnel management. | Management. | BISAC: BUSINESS & ECONOMICS / Leadership. | BUSINESS & ECONOMICS / Management. | BUSINESS & ECONOMICS / Human Resources & Personnel Management.
Classification: LCC HD57.7 .F5567 2016 (print) | LCC HD57.7 (ebook) | DDC 658.4/092--dc23
LC record available at http://lccn.loc.gov/2015041563
International edition ISBN 9780399564079

First Portfolio/Penguin hardcover edition: February 2016
First Portfolio/Penguin trade paperback edition: February 2019
Portfolio/Penguin trade paperback ISBN: 9780525537328

Printed in the United States of America

Set in Fairfield LT Std
Designed by Alissa Rose Theodor

To the first superboss I ever knew, Anna Dunajec Finkelstein

CONTENTS

Introduction   *1*

1   Iconoclasts, Glorious Bastards, and Nurturers   *11*

2   Getting People Who "Get It"   *37*

3   Motivating Exceptional People to Do the Impossible   *61*

4   Uncompromisingly Open   *81*

5   Masters and Apprentices   *103*

6   The Hands-On Delegator   *127*

7   The Cohort Effect   *149*

8   Networks of Success   *171*

9   Superbosses and You   *197*

Acknowledgments   *221*

Notes   *225*

Index   *253*

INTRODUCTION

Some years ago, a family of New Yorkers came in for dinner at Alice Waters's legendary Chez Panisse restaurant in Berkeley, California. According to longtime cook Seen Lippert, the family—Mom, Dad, a little boy, and a little girl—claimed not to have been aware of the restaurant's practice, then unheard of in the United States, of changing its menu daily to feature the freshest locally sourced and organic ingredients. The family agreed to stay for the meal, giving the restaurant a list of items they didn't like and didn't want to be served. One of the items on their list was peas. As it happened, the restaurant had gotten its hands on "these beautiful, sweet, fresh peas" and the staff had spent the afternoon shucking them by hand. Waters, who loved superior ingredients and always evangelized on their behalf, insisted that a dish of peas be presented for the family to try. The staff reminded Waters of the family's wishes, but she was unmoved. "I don't care. I just want them to try it. I just want them to try *one*."

The peas were brought out, and the family loved them. "I'm telling you," Lippert related in an interview, "that little boy, he smiled and looked, like, 'WOW. I've never tasted a pea before. I've never tasted *anything* like this before.'" Soon, the family had eaten the whole bowl. "They were so excited and so happy at the end of that dinner."[1]

It was a small victory for Waters, one of countless that she's had. Many Americans now expect to see organic produce at supermarkets and enjoy ordering dishes prepared with fresh ingredients at local "farm-to-table" restaurants. But when Waters opened Chez Panisse in 1971, the nation's culinary scene was very different. Americans didn't know much about fresh peas; their diets consisted largely of a limited array of mass-produced, frozen, and processed foods—hard, unripe tomatoes shipped clear across the country, "mystery meat" raised on industrial farms, shelf-ready baked goods whose ingredient list seemed straight out of a chemistry lab. In France, Waters had discovered the joys of simple cooking and fresh fruits, vegetables, and meats readily available at local farm markets. At Chez Panisse, she pioneered a new American cuisine that incorporated these elements and benefitted from close personal relationships with local producers. As celebrated chef Thomas Keller told me in an interview, it wasn't just a restaurant but a "phenomenon" and "something that cannot possibly be duplicated anywhere else."[2] *Gourmet* magazine named Chez Panisse the best restaurant in America in 2001, one of an endless number of such honors for Waters and her restaurant.

Through this success and other high-profile projects, such as her Edible Schoolyard and her efforts to improve food quality at Yale University, Waters has emerged as a leading advocate for the organic, local, and "slow food" movements in the United States. Industry insiders will tell you that Waters is also known for something else: spawning the country's best culinary talent. Over the years, her restaurant has served as an informal school, incubator, and launching pad for a generation of aspiring chefs. Dozens of employees passed through Chez Panisse before opening establishments of their own, gaining fame as some of the country's most creative culinary figures. These former employees include such stars as Judy Rodgers, the late chef at San Francisco's Zuni Café and winner of two James Beard Awards (known as the "Oscar" of food) for best chef; Jeremiah Tower, another James Beard Award winner, who came out of retirement to take over New York's famed Tavern on the Green restaurant in 2014; Joyce Goldstein, yet another James Beard Award winner; award-winning cookbook author and cooking teacher Joanne Weir; and award-winning pastry chef David Lebovitz, to name a few. "I mean, how many of my chef colleagues came through her kitchens or worked for her, I can't count them," renowned chef Eberhard Muller told me. "I don't even know all of the people who came out of her circle of chefs or people who worked with her or interacted with her."[3]

When I first learned about Alice Waters, I was fascinated that a single person could foster such a disproportionate share of top talent. Some years back I had written a book (*Why Smart Executives Fail*) exploring how overconfidence, complacency, inaction, and lack of curiosity prevented otherwise intelligent leaders from adapting to changing business conditions. Companies were wilting under the weight of unimaginative, close-minded strategies and cultures; they lacked the talent required to shake things up and evolve. How interesting, I thought, that a lone creative genius who apparently possessed no special training in management had somehow nurtured precisely the kind of curious, energetic, open-minded people companies need to adapt to change and compete at a world-class level. How curious as well that in our world of Big Data, close, personal relationships played such an outsize role in channeling top talent into an industry.

I investigated further and found that sous-chefs often move on after a period of time to start their own restaurants. But I wondered if other industries worked this way, with genealogical "trees" of talent germinating from one or a few legendary innovators. I started exploring a number of industries—including professional football, advertising, consumer foods, real estate, hedge funds, comedy, and fashion—and was surprised to find that the same basic pattern held true. If you looked at the top fifty people in these industries, you would find that perhaps fifteen or twenty had once worked for or had been mentored by one or a few talent spawners—or "superbosses," as I came to call them. Likewise, these very same superbosses were responsible for a remarkable share of innovation in their industries.

Football was a great example of why working for a superboss paid off. During the 1980s and 1990s, five coaches dominated the NFL: Bill

Walsh, Joe Gibbs, Bill Parcells, Jimmy Johnson, and Marv Levy. But the one coach of these five who spawned the largest "tree" of talent was Bill Walsh. Between 1979 and 2015, Walsh or coaches in his lineage appeared in thirty-two Super Bowls, winning seventeen of them. Johnson and his protégés appeared in only six Super Bowls; Levy, Gibbs, and Parcells and their protégés did better, appearing in twenty-three, twenty-one, and twenty-four Super Bowls, respectively. Of the ten head-coaching changes in the NFL in 2005, six were filled with members of Walsh's tree. As of 2008, the year after Walsh's death, coaches trained by Walsh led twenty-six of the league's thirty-two teams.

Walsh's success and that of his protégés derived from an important innovation of his, the "West Coast offense." This strategy allowed teams with nontraditional players to win games through better execution. Teams following the West Coast offense focused on making quicker, more precise passing plays. It wasn't about being bigger or badder but using what you had in a more disciplined fashion. Walsh also innovated in ways less obvious to football fans. Whereas many coaches left to others the minutiae of leading an organization, Walsh broke down the minute-to-minute progression of team practices, defined responsibilities for coaches and players, and set rules for how to handle business matters such as negotiating contracts and dealing with the media. He also dispensed with an authoritarian style of leadership and empowered individuals by teaching them to think independently. These innovations amounted to a comprehensive new approach to coaching, one adopted and refined by a generation of Walsh's successors.

The more I looked at people like Walsh, the more I wanted to understand what made them tick. Why have innovators such as Ralph Lauren and Calvin Klein enabled so many heavy hitters in the fashion and lifestyle businesses to make it to the top of their fields, while other luminaries such as Giorgio Armani, Martha Stewart, or former Gucci chief executive Patrizio di Marco have not? How did Julian Robertson spawn a generation of acolytes in hedge funds, unlike other rich and famous investors such as Eddie Lampert and Steven Cohen? What techniques did the superbosses mobilize? What were their secrets?

I consulted the business literature, but to no avail. The pattern of a superboss's giving rise to a "tree" of talent just didn't appear in conventional business management. Human-resources consultants weren't talking about it, executives weren't devising talent management strategies around it, and my colleagues and I weren't teaching it at business schools. Yet superbosses were behaving in ways that energized promising individuals, inspired their very best performance, and launched them into high-powered careers. They knew something that the rest of us didn't—and they used that knowledge to achieve extraordinary results.

In 2005, I embarked on a full-blown research project, scouring business, sports, fashion, and the arts to find potential superbosses and map out their genealogical trees. In the end, I spent ten years conducting more than two hundred interviews; sifting through thousands of articles, books, monographs, and oral histories; and writing three dozen case studies in the most extensive and rigorous research project of its kind. I compiled, dissected, and analyzed stories about the lives and careers of eighteen primary superbosses: Lorne Michaels, Ralph Lauren, Jay Chiat, Larry Ellison, Bill Walsh, Jorma Panula, Bob Noyce, Bill Sanders, Miles Davis, Michael Milken, Michael Miles, Alice Waters, Norman Brinker, Roger Corman, Julian Robertson, Gene Roberts, George Lucas, and Tommy Frist. I also collected materials on a few dozen likely superboss figures such as Hillary Clinton, Stan Lee, Oprah Winfrey, and David Swensen. I wound up finding superbosses in fields as diverse as casual dining (Brinker), hospitals (Frist), comic books (Lee), politics (Clinton), nonprofit endowment investment (Swensen), filmmaking (Corman), hedge funds (Robertson), newspapers (Roberts), and special effects (Lucas), among others.

Looking for recurring themes and patterns, I discovered that superbosses differ considerably in their interpersonal styles; but the ways in which they identify, motivate, coach, and leverage others are remarkably consistent, highly unconventional, and unmistakably powerful. Superbosses aren't like most bosses; they follow a playbook all their own. They are unusually intense and passionate—eating, sleeping, and breathing their businesses and inspiring others to do the same. They look fearlessly in unusual places for talent and interview candidates in colorful ways. They create impossibly high work standards that push protégés to their limits. They engage in an almost inexplicable form of mentoring and coaching, one that occurs spontaneously with (apparently) no clear rules. They lavish responsibility on inexperienced protégés, taking risks that seem foolish to outsiders. When the time is right, superbosses often *encourage* star talent to leave, after which these acolytes usually become part of the superboss's strategic network in the industry.

As my research progressed, the differences between superbosses and traditional managers became increasingly obvious. The worst bosses out there tend to demotivate employees, slow their growth, and erode performance by engaging in any number of behaviors that are far from "best practice": gossiping, backstabbing, inappropriately claiming credit for others' success, and so on. Superbosses are clearly miles ahead of these bosses; there is no comparison. Another, somewhat more successful breed of boss is what I call Bossy Bosses: outsize, Donald Trump–style personalities who crack the whip and push employees to their limits. They lord it over their reports, standing as remote, godlike figures, people to be admired but never, ever equaled. Superbosses easily surpass these Bossy Bosses. Superbosses can be fierce or gentle, belligerent or self-deprecating, but whatever their style, they do a much better job inspiring and teaching because they get in the trenches with protégés, leading by example and giving them the personalized attention they require to move up quickly. Bossy Bosses may achieve great personal success for a time, but eventually they lose it all as their house of cards collapses. Superbosses enjoy more lasting success and they also spawn a generation of protégés who become movers and shakers in their own right.

Now, what about all those good bosses, those managers whom we typically recognize as competent, well meaning, and effective? It turns out that even these bosses don't match up to superbosses, for two reasons: superbosses embrace certain practices that good bosses don't, and they do even more of the productive things that good bosses do. For instance, good bosses give employees opportunities to move up, even using "career ladders" to define opportunities. Superbosses also create opportunities for employees to move up, but they personalize those opportunities rather than organize them in a standard or lockstep way. Good bosses measure engagement formally, using standard metrics; superbosses don't need to rely on the standard metrics, because they're living the workplace experience *with* their employees. Likewise, good bosses are very big on best practices. They want to know what works and they want to *do* what works. Superbosses have little interest in best practices. For them, such practices amount to codification of the past that implicitly reduces openness to new ways of doing things. Would hedge-fund titan Julian Robertson have funded so many apparently inexperienced Tiger Cubs, as his successful protégés are called, if he followed a textbook approach to selecting fund managers?

Much of the difference between good bosses and superbosses comes down to mentality. Many of the best bosses today tend to think of themselves as professional managers. They do the basics well and strive to get better, as most professionals do. What these bosses sometimes lose is the intuition, the innate curiosity, and the rough-and-tumble entrepreneurial energy that characterize superbosses. It's not that professional managers don't exist among the ranks of superbosses; they do, and in fact this book will feature several. Yet superbosses don't limit their sense of self to that of a professional manager, no matter how professional they might in fact be. Superbosses always add something more to the equation. And on this account they exercise a uniquely powerful and beneficial effect on their employees.

As the secrets of superbosses became visible, I realized I had stumbled upon a veritable holy grail for business managers and professionals. Despite human-resources specialists' best efforts, surveys show that most workers remain unengaged and unhappy at work. Studies by McKinsey and others reveal that organizations don't "get" how to develop strong, self-motivated leaders—even though most executives regard talent as absolutely vital to their organization's survival.[4] Superbosses yield a fresh set of answers, practices that anyone can borrow to nurture others and create an inexhaustible pipeline of rising stars. These answers seemed especially relevant for the challenge of inspiring, developing, and engaging millennial employees. If even *some* of these practices are widely disseminated, careers could become more meaningful—and more lucrative. Professionals could do more good, get more satisfaction out of their work, and make their organizations nimbler and more resilient. Workplaces could be transformed from dull, dreary places to powerhouses of innovation.

But the stakes are greater than that. Ultimately, *more companies may survive* if superbosses' practices become widespread. As a kid growing up in Montreal, I used to visit our neighborhood bakery every week. It was the center of the community—a warm, lively place redolent with the smell of fresh baked bread. Years later, I returned to my old neighborhood and discovered, to my dismay, that the bakery had folded. It left me thinking: Why do perfectly good companies have to die? They don't. Companies can avoid or overcome almost any business challenge with the right talent. It's when organizations don't regenerate their talent— and with it their supply of new ideas, approaches, and solutions—that they flounder. The wisdom of superbosses isn't merely *useful* for the rest of us in business—it's life or death. The primary path to winning is via great talent fully immersed in creating value.

As a professor at Dartmouth's Tuck School of Business and director of the Center for Leadership there, I've had the privilege of consulting to dozens of the world's largest companies, from Boeing and General Electric to JPMorgan Chase and Deutsche Bank. I've written nineteen books on leadership, including several bestsellers, and more than eighty articles. The biggest discovery I've made over the course of studying organizations is also the simplest: it really is about the people. Executives often prioritize strategy, assuming that if they get that right, everything else will fall into place. They think they can ignore their people or, at any rate, treat them as secondary. Bad idea. People are an essential part of any strategy, and regenerating the talent pool is the single most important thing any leader can do to survive and prosper. Superbosses understand this, and for this reason they're able to achieve unparalleled influence and business success in their respective fields.

Superbosses explores the characteristic behaviors of the world's most effective bosses, upending conventional best practices and presenting a new, comprehensive paradigm for developing talent. This book is the first to offer a systematic, empirically based study of what *really* motivates, inspires, and enables others to achieve their full potential. It teaches professionals how to be better bosses so that they can unleash unprecedented creativity, engagement, and accomplishment in their teams, generating and regenerating the world's best talent. And it shows employees in any field how to identify superbosses in their industry so that they can get hired and advance their careers.

The first chapter of *Superbosses* defines superbosses and provides a more complete account of my research journey. The following seven chapters present "the superboss playbook"—the techniques, mind-sets, philosophies, and secrets that the world's best bosses use and others don't. Chapter 9 concludes the book, addressing how managers and leaders can incorporate the larger superboss approach into their own careers, management practice, and organizations. Throughout, readers will observe that the clear majority, although not all, of the superstar bosses discussed, are white men. This isn't by choice; rather, I have simply presented my research findings, which reflected white men's traditional dominance of top leadership roles. I expect (and hope) that if I were to look into superbosses a decade or more in the future, I would find a much more balanced gender and racial representation.

Many books have been written about talent, applying everything from common sense to psychology to Big Data, but nobody has studied those few individuals who, with their seemingly strange, idiosyncratic practices, grow human capital better than anyone else. We desperately need new approaches to nurturing people so that they're primed for success and are in turn driving the success of managers and organizations. Superbosses, exceptional and colorful as they are, offer wisdom that all of us can apply to build meaningful careers for others. And when we help others make their way, the benefits we reap are equally great. What could be more fulfilling than knowing that we've helped others achieve their dreams? What could be more satisfying than having legions of protégés proclaim to the world that we *mattered*?

Larry Fink, CEO and founder of BlackRock, one of the world's biggest and most influential financial institutions, was once asked what he would remember most about his career. His answer: "The legacy of the people who will run the firm after I'm gone."[5] As you apply the lessons of *Superbosses* and change how you behave, I think you'll agree: the only thing better than working for one of the world's most effective bosses is *being* one yourself.

CHAPTER ONE

Iconoclasts, Glorious Bastards,
and Nurturers

A nondescript white truck chugged through the streets of downtown Philadelphia, passing the Beaux-Arts Rodin Museum building and the Community College of Philadelphia before arriving at the iconic structure located at 400 North Broad Street. The front of this building, known locally as the "Tower of Truth," bore the insignia of the town's leading newspaper, the *Philadelphia Inquirer*.[1] Eighteen stories tall, it housed editorial offices and, at one time, giant newspaper presses whose operation sent vibrations coursing through the entire building.[2] On this day in 1978, the van skirted the front entrance and continued around the building to the back. Normally trucks came here to load newspapers hot off the presses, but not this van. It was there to unload.

The driver and other workers walked around to open the van's rear door. Out came a long, spindly leg. Then another. In the end there were four legs, as well as a hump, a sizable torso, and a serenely smiling face: a camel, rented from a local circus.[3] More legs followed, shorter ones—a goat, thrown in by the circus, an *Inquirer* employee remembers, "at no additional charge."[4]

The animals' handlers and *Inquirer* staff who had come to meet the creatures led them through a door to a freight elevator that unfortunately went no higher than the fourth floor. When the doors opened, the animals were led through the building—through the cafeteria, in fact— onto a passenger elevator and up to another floor. Employees in the cafeteria stared in astonishment. Some got up to follow the animals, eager to see what was going on (these were reporters, after all).[5]

A gaggle of spectators darted up the stairs, arriving in time to see the camel exit the passenger elevator and cross the newsroom. At the time, editor in chief Gene Roberts was meeting with architects and interior decorators, discussing plans for the "newsroom of the future" to be built for the *Inquirer*. Roberts didn't jump or shriek or laugh as the animals entered. "Without batting an eye," former associate managing editor– news editor Jim Naughton recalls, "he turned to these experts and said, 'Oh, yes, we'll need the newsroom to be near the freight elevator.'"[6]

Longtime staffers told this story thirty years later, gathering together in 2008 to celebrate their time working for Roberts. The camel was meant to celebrate the recent Pulitzer awarded to *Inquirer* journalist Richard Ben Kramer for his Middle East reporting, as well as Roberts's ability to parley that success into increased corporate funding from the *Inquirer*'s owners for foreign correspondents. Any number of other colorful stories also revealed how the *Inquirer*, led by Roberts, pulsed with energy and creativity. On his forty-sixth birthday, Roberts came into the bathroom by his office to find forty-six frogs croaking in his honor. On an employee's birthday, Roberts arranged for a live elephant to show up at his house. On Roberts's fiftieth birthday, a number of people on staff got together to plan something *really* memorable. A staff member explains: "A clandestine committee plotted how to suitably call maximum attention to the event. Yes, we could put together a kazoo band from within our ranks. Yes, we could get the city to barricade the 1000 block of Clinton Street on which Gene and Sue Roberts had an elegant old brownstone." The committee also arranged for a Goodyear blimp to fly over Roberts's house with its giant electronic sign proclaiming, "The Frog Is 50."[7]

What's with the frogs? It was Roberts's nickname, bestowed on account of his distinctly amphibian facial features. It was meant affectionately, not derisively. When I spoke with Roberts's protégés, I discovered that they didn't merely respect and admire him as a leader—they revered him. Every person I contacted immediately got back in touch and said they'd love to share stories about the Roberts era. Working for Gene Roberts clearly wasn't just another job for them. It was the job of a lifetime. And Roberts wasn't just another boss. He was one of a kind. A force of nature. *The Frog.* As investigative reporter Don Barlett put it, "If you were a reporter and you didn't love him, there was something wrong with you."[8]

There may also have been something wrong with you if, upon leaving Roberts's nest, you didn't claim a place for yourself at the apex of American journalism. At the reunion, attended by more than three hundred people, there were sixteen Pulitzer Prize winners, a National Book Award winner, and the authors of the bestselling books *Friday Night Lights* and *Black Hawk Down.*[9] Other former staffers of Roberts's have gone on to head the *Los Angeles Times,* the *Baltimore Sun,* the *Akron Beacon Journal,* and the Poynter Institute (the leading in-service school for journalists). Not to mention others who became investigative reporters for top papers and magazines across the country.

Every industry has its leading lights, its superstars, its innovators. Gene Roberts fell into this group. But unlike other equally successful and prominent peers, Roberts had something special: he knew how to help talented people accomplish more than they ever dreamed was possible, and in the process developed a talent machine that made almost everyone who entered his orbit a star. Roberts was that rare boss who made it his business to push people out of their comfort zones with new and challenging assignments; who provided personal guidance and support that made a difference; and who demanded that his staff make their own creative decisions rather than rely on him. Reporters and editors in his employ came away transformed. They put out their best work, and had fun doing it. During Roberts's eighteen years at the *Inquirer*, the paper won an incredible seventeen Pulitzer Prizes.[10] Today, in newsrooms across America, insiders know him as the man who produced a generation of world-class journalists.

Talent spawners like Roberts aren't exclusive to the newspaper business. If you've been paying attention to the movers and shakers in your industry, you may have noticed that a surprising number of them, at some point, have all worked for the same person. You may also have noticed that colleagues and others in the industry mention this name with a strange mixture of familiarity and awe, and that some even make a habit of referring to this person in passing, expecting listeners to know whom they mean, and treating them as if they have failed a test if they don't. Gradually, you come to realize that having contact with this person, especially if you've worked for him or her, seems to put people on a fast track to success. Log some time with this person, and you're likely to go places. Remain far away, and you will forever be at a disadvantage, compared with those who were close.

It's important to recognize how absolutely extraordinary this "superboss effect" is. Most bosses have trouble ensuring a steady stream of talent for their own teams and companies, even with the assistance of world-class human resources. By contrast, superbosses fuel the talent pool for an entire industry. Likewise, most employees are not holding twenty-year reunions to reminisce about the good ol' days. If recent surveys serve as any indication, they're happy to forget working for their bosses.[11] Superbosses are looked upon by protégés as pivotal figures in their careers and, indeed, their lives.

Superbosses are the great coaches, the igniters of talent, and the teachers of leadership in most industries. In effect, superbosses have mastered something most bosses miss—a path to extraordinary success founded on making *other* people successful. That such a path exists is surprising, even counterintuitive, but it's also wonderful news for anyone trying to live a life of impact. What does this path look like? Who are these superbosses? What makes them tick? And where have they been all this time?

The Makings of a Superboss

One paradox of superbosses (one of many we'll encounter in this book) is that these bosses, although frequently overlooked for their talent-spawning prowess, don't hide in the background. On the contrary, they practically scream out for our attention. By the time of the camel incident, Gene Roberts was already attracting serious notice in the newspaper industry for having turned around the *Inquirer*.[12] The paper he inherited when he took it over in 1972 hardly merited offices in the "Tower of Truth"; it was corrupt through and through. Previous owner Walter Annenberg reportedly had a curious rule: if he didn't like you, you didn't make it into the paper.[13] Every photo in which certain local leaders appeared had to be cropped to eliminate Annenberg's antagonists. Further, the paper's chief investigative reporter, Harry Karafin, was unmasked by *Philadelphia* magazine as blackmailing subjects of his reporting. He was convicted of extortion and sent to prison.[14] The *Inquirer* was clearly the number two paper in the city behind the *Philadelphia Bulletin*—it had less staff, less budget, and less clout. It also wasn't making any money.[15]

Roberts, a former bureau chief and editor at the *New York Times,* was energized by the challenge of turning the *Inquirer* around. He wanted to make it one of the top papers in the country and truly his own. He succeeded brilliantly, beating the *Bulletin* in a competition so fierce it was covered by *Time* magazine.[16] After effectively putting the *Bulletin* out of print in 1982, the *Inquirer*'s daily circulation rose to over 500,000 and its

Sunday circulation soared to well over a million.[17] The paper became known nationally for its investigative journalism. Even today, numerous stories that the *Inquirer* produced are astonishing—like the one about crooked homicide detectives who put phone books on the heads of suspects and then beat the books with baseball bats until a confession was proffered, a method that accounted for two-thirds of the resolved murder cases in Philadelphia.[18] Or the one about blood donation in which a reporter discovered that a pint of blood donated in Philadelphia would be sold in Miami for $700. The fallout from stories like these helped elevate the profile of the *Inquirer* far higher than what it had been before.[19]

As impressive as Roberts's success was, you couldn't as an industry outsider simply look at it and know instantly that a superboss's hand was at work. Early on, Roberts was successful at luring some established journalists to work for him—Steve Lovelady of the *Wall Street Journal*, Gene Foreman of *Newsday*, and others from the *Boston Globe* and *Washington Post*.[20] Later, as word spread of the paper's quality and work environment (and all those Pulitzers), the *Inquirer* became inundated with applications. Clearly, Roberts was doing something right. Yet unless you worked in the newspaper business or closely followed it, you likely wouldn't have noticed any of this. You wouldn't have known about all the successful reporters at other publications who had started with Roberts, and you certainly wouldn't have known about those who had grown up inside Roberts's organization and stayed there for much of their careers. All you would have seen was a successful paper fronted by a determined, inventive, highly regarded leader.

Identifying and studying superbosses can be a subtle art. If you're on the hunt for superbosses, you can sometimes create comparative quantitative analyses that demonstrate clearly who the superboss of an industry is. In football, for instance, a quick count reveals that, as of 2015, Bill Walsh produced almost twice as many active NFL coaches as the next most prolific talent spawner.

	WALSH	PARCELLS	JOHNSON	GIBBS	LEVY
2008	26	20	6	11	15
2009	25	21	8	10	17
2010	25	19	10	10	14
2011	27	17	12	8	12
2012	27	15	14	10	10
2013	22	12	10	8	9
2014	21	13	10	5	9
2015	20	13	10	5	10

Count of how many coaches in the entire NFL come from five top legendary coaches (2008–2015). Football fans will notice that the totals in any given year will inevitably exceed the number of teams in the league. That's because some coaches worked on multiple coaching staffs.[21]

It would be nice if we could perform such a straightforward analysis in every industry to tease out the superboss figures, but football is actually a fairly special case. Football teams are all the same size and they compete in highly structured ways, allowing for meaningful comparisons between coaches. Also, there are tons of public data in football and clear ways to measure success. Most other industries aren't so neat and tidy. Often companies generate more talent in absolute terms on account of their size, culture, or pedigree; it may have nothing to do with specific leaders in those companies. For instance, Roberts achieved an outsize level of talent production, but more distinguished and much larger papers, such as the *New York Times,* spawned more talent. Of course, the *New York Times* might also have produced lots of underperformers. If we could calculate the "hit rate" of Gene Roberts and the *Inquirer* in producing great talent, it would almost certainly dwarf that of the *New York Times*.

In general, the size and scope of industry goliaths do confer certain advantages as far as talent spawning goes. Most notably, great talent will often seek to work at such places simply because of their reputation. Yet superbosses can make *any* organization attractive as a talent magnet, not just those blessed with size, scope, and prestige. Most of the things superbosses unleash to develop all-star talent—motivation, inspiration, innovation, opportunity creation, apprenticeships, coaching—are often not available to the same extent in the largest, most prestigious organizations. An industry-leading paper such as the *New York Times* may not have to work so hard to attract great talent, but if it *did* have a superboss at the helm, it would do even better.

In any case, because of the complexities of analyzing and comparing organizations, the most reliable way to identify a superboss required attending to both quantitative measures (e.g., tallying successful protégés) and qualitative indicators (e.g., assessing the boss's reputation). This is also the most credible way, since the insiders in any industry are the ones who really know what's going on. As this method revealed, Roberts was definitely the superboss of newspapers in a way that nobody else was. I first became aware of Roberts in 2010 during a conversation with journalist Rob Gurwitt, a longtime writer for *Governing* magazine. Gurwitt said Roberts not only attracted a lot of talented writers and editors but was known for allowing writers to develop areas of expertise and to report on them as they saw fit. My research team and I followed up, interviewing other industry insiders. Again and again, people referenced Roberts—and nobody else—as a key progenitor of talent in the newspaper industry. Insiders also explicitly distinguished between Roberts and other contemporaries, such as Abe Rosenthal of the *New York Times*, who had not had the same impact on their staffs.

Identifying a superboss, then, requires that we proceed *inductively,* amassing insider stories and other evidence while counting as many of their successful protégés as possible. In some cases, I became curious about an industry and then worked from there to find the main talent spawners. Other times, I became interested in a prominent person, wondered if he or she was a superboss, and followed up with exploratory research. On still more occasions, I got a hot lead on a talent spawner from a protégé and decided to map out the industry in depth. Regardless of what industry I studied, the identity of superbosses became indisputably clear as the evidence accumulated.

I eventually identified the eighteen primary superbosses listed in the introduction, as well as two to three dozen other likely superbosses. To my surprise and delight, I found these figures *everywhere*, not just in corporate contexts. I'm sure you've already thought of superbosses in your own industry who match my definition. You may also have spotted them in the middle management of organizations for which you've worked. Many superbosses assuredly do exist at the middle levels, but since they are not in the media spotlight, they're much more difficult to identify and document than those at the highest levels. For this reason, I resolved early on to limit my study to superbosses who lead organizations, as well as to their protégés.

For each of the superbosses, I compiled a partial list of successful protégés the superboss has nurtured. These protégés usually succeeded in the superboss's industry, although not always in the specific niche the superboss had carved out. Take Hollywood filmmaker Roger Corman. Over the course of some five decades, Corman produced dozens of sex-ploitation movies based on a well-worn and proven formula of gratuitous nudity, excessive violence, and a roller-coaster plot. But the man who became known as "King of the B's" became famous for another, and perhaps even more fascinating, reason: he produced an impressive list of world-class directors and actors. There was Robert De Niro, who as a young man played the part of drug addict Lloyd Baker in Corman's 1970 small-budget flick *Bloody Mama,* a full three years before he came to fame in Martin Scorsese's *Mean Streets.*[22] And there were also Jack Nicholson, Peter Bogdanovich, Francis Ford Coppola, James Cameron, Ron Howard, Gale Ann Hurd, Jonathan Demme, and literally dozens of others.

Real estate offers another example. Mogul Bill Sanders is often considered the personal-contact cornerstone for the industry, as his network extends to a near majority of real estate's big players. One magazine, remarking on how many industry figures Sanders had spawned, spoke of a "six degrees of Bill Sanders" theory.[23] R. Scot Sellers, chairman and CEO of Archstone, worked with Sanders as a senior vice president. Constance Moore, president and CEO of Broadway Real Estate Properties (BRE), served as a former managing director for Sanders. C. Ronald Blankenship, president and CEO of the Verde Group since 2003, served as vice chairman for one of Sanders's companies from 1998 to 2003. Mary Lou Fiala, president and COO of Regency Centers Corporation, was formerly managing director at another of Sanders's companies. And the list goes on. Ask people who worked for Sanders, and like Roberts's protégés, you'll find that they credit their former boss for providing them with a tremendous training ground. Sanders's protégés still keep in touch, both professionally and personally; some have even teamed up to form their own companies.

In the early days of my research, I never anticipated just how widespread the fundamental pattern of the superboss would turn out to be. Indeed, as the years passed, I even found new superbosses popping up in industries I'd already studied. In comedy, Steve Carell delighted fans as a not-so-great boss in the TV show *The Office,* and later had them cringing as he had his chest-hair forcibly removed in the movie *The 40-Year-Old Virgin.* But before all of this, Carell worked for an extended period on Jon Stewart's hit program *The Daily Show.* Stephen Colbert created his conservative alter ego for Stewart as well, leaving to host his own show *The Colbert Report* before taking over in 2015 as host of CBS's *The Late Show with Stephen Colbert* (Stewart departed the show himself in 2015). A surprising number of other *Daily Show* alums have also gone on to successful careers in comedy and acting, including John Oliver (who left to host HBO's *Last Week Tonight*), two-time Emmy winner Rob Corddry (who appears in the hit TV show *Happy Endings*), and Ed Helms (star of the *Hangover* movies and another regular on *The Office*). Lorne Michaels may still sit atop the most prolific talent-spawning machine in comedy, but in a relatively short time Stewart has emerged as a super-boss in his own right. His example suggests that the terrain of talent is fluid and new superbosses are always evolving, and can evolve, even in fields where dynamic superbosses already exist.

Regardless of where you are in your career or what you do in and out of work, superbosses are the people whose businesses you should study, not least because the protégés of a superboss will usually determine where the industry is going next. If you're tasked with managing talent, these are the role models whose example will guide you to become good at producing, finding, and developing all-stars yourself. If you're a senior leader interested in creating a never-ending pipeline of world-class em-ployees, these are the kinds of bosses you want to seek out, support, and multiply in your organization. If it's early in your career, these are the people whom you want to work for. If you're an investor, these are the people whose ventures you want to keep an eye on. If you're going to participate in an industry, superbosses will matter—whether you like it or not.

Miles Apart

Imagine you're in a high-end jazz club in a large metropolitan city. It's a small, intimate place with seating for perhaps fifty or sixty people. Well-heeled patrons sit clustered around small, round cocktail tables, taking sips from their martini glasses and tapping their feet to the rhythm. They're listening with rapt attention as a quintet performs, led by a trumpet player who turns his back to the audience and seems primarily engaged with the other musicians. The music tonight is incredible, the groove intense. These world-class musicians are utterly locked in with one another, finishing one another's phrases, building off one another's musical ideas.

As the group continues to play, you notice that the drummer, bassist, saxophonist, and pianist all seem to take most of their cues from the trumpet player. They're listening intently to every note he plays and watching every gesture. He's not just their leader; he's a dominant, almost entrancing presence. When he deems it appropriate to pay special attention to one of them, whether by a glance or by echoing a musical phrase, they seem to spark up. Throughout the show, his energy brings out their energy.

This scene was repeated hundreds of times, over many years, by legendary trumpeter Miles Davis and his band. As a creator of modern jazz, Davis is widely regarded as one of the most important musical influences of the twentieth century. He developed a generation of top talent, including John Coltrane, Herbie Hancock, Wayne Shorter, Cannonball Adderley, Lee Konitz, J. J. Johnson, Dave Holland, Chick Corea, Keith Jarrett, and Tony Williams.

Contrast Miles Davis with Michael Miles, who was considered one of the leading executives in the food industry in the late twentieth century. As CEO of Kraft Foods, he was credited with turning around the largest American food company through new product introductions, aggressive marketing, and cost cutting. Executives who worked for Miles went on to become the CEOs of Nabisco, Campbell Soup, Mattel, Young & Rubicam, Gillette, and other top consumer-facing organizations.

Here are two revered innovators and prolific talent spawners from entirely different worlds, yet they are both superbosses. In fact, considering the social context of mid- to late-twentieth-century America, it's hard to think of two figures more different than a marketing titan and a jazz artist. The jazz subculture of the 1950s to the 1970s explicitly defined itself *against* corporate America, seeing itself as a countercultural, largely African American art form. Meanwhile, African Americans were few and far between in the corporate boardrooms that Michael Miles dominated.

Glancing briefly at the lives of these two men brings to life the sharp differences between them. Davis had a string of tumultuous relationships and marriages, served jail time for domestic violence, and suffered periods of depression. Like other jazz musicians of his day, he struggled with drug addiction—heroin, alcohol, cocaine, and prescription drugs.[24] In contrast, Michael Miles enjoyed a relatively stable personal life. At the time of his death in 2013, he had been married to his college sweetheart, Pamela, for fifty-two years.[25] His daily habits were also unusually disciplined. John Tucker, who served as senior vice president of human resources at Kraft under Miles, recalls that early on in his tenure, he would come into work at six thirty in the morning. Miles, whose office was a couple of doors down, would already be there with a cup of coffee ready for Tucker. "I said to myself, Jesus Christ, I've got to beat this guy to work," Tucker remembered. One morning, he arrived at five—only to find Miles's car already in the parking lot *and* he had already made coffee. The day after that, Tucker arrived at four thirty. He didn't see Miles's car and thought he had beaten him. But as he stepped out of his car, he saw a pair of headlights. It was Michael Miles. "He got out of the car and just smiled at me. Both of us knew exactly what was going on."[26]

Miles Davis was going to bed during these predawn hours, not beginning his day. Consider, too, the trademark way he performed—his back turned away from the audience, his attention firmly fixed on his fellow musicians. Davis was concerned with the music itself, not with its reception by audiences or critics. He didn't particularly care if anyone loved what he was playing.[27] His mind-set and self-awareness were in fact the opposite of those of a marketer such as Michael Miles.

Compare Davis and Miles with other superbosses, and you'll find yourself similarly struck by the disparity of their personalities and backgrounds. The food magnate and jazz artist seem miles apart from the New Jersey native who went to France, experienced a "sensual awakening," and devoted her life to the cause of locally grown, sustainably produced food (Alice Waters).[28] Or the Jewish kid from the Bronx who cut his teeth in fashion after a stint in the military, and became, in the words of one journalist, the "American Gatsby-dream designer" (Ralph Lauren).[29] Or the Vietnam War correspondent from North Carolina who, as we've seen, created a newsroom with as many exotic animals roaming around as world-class journalists (Gene Roberts). If you could magically compare the Twitter feeds of any of these superbosses (leaving aside the fact that Twitter didn't exist in those days), you'd find they followed vastly different people. If you monitored their television habits, you'd find that some watched PBS while others favored the most lurid reality television. This is not a group of people who would necessarily hit it off with one another at a dinner party.

To put the diversity of superbosses in perspective, think of the different personalities of executives you've come across in your industry. Superbosses, by comparison, exist in *different* industries, and many aren't even operating in the traditional business world. In addition, they come from different countries and have different social and ethnic backgrounds. Aside from their basic humanity and their uncanny ability to innovate while also developing all-star performers, we might wonder if superbosses have much of anything in common at all.

Iconoclasts, Glorious Bastards, and Nurturers

But superbosses do have certain characteristics in common. After several years studying these talent spawners, I was struck that, despite personal differences, their motivations as bosses fall into three distinct patterns, distributed more or less equally among industries. Some superbosses, such as Miles Davis, don't set out to inspire or teach others, although that is precisely what they end up doing. What they care about is their work, their passion. The single-minded pursuit of this passion naturally contributes to their success as a boss. These *Iconoclasts,* as I call them, are so wholly fixated on their vision that they are able to teach in an intuitive, organic way, as a natural outgrowth of their passion and in service to it, rather than consciously or methodically. These are the artists among the superbosses, the people we would most immediately think of as creative geniuses. Among the superbosses I studied, Alice Waters, George Lucas, Lorne Michaels, Ralph Lauren, Jorma Panula, and Robert Noyce all appear as strong Iconoclasts. Their mission in life is to express what is inside them: to let the rest of us in on what they see, feel, or hear. Younger colleagues flock around these superbosses to learn how to be creative artists, and Iconoclasts welcome their presence because it helps them keep their art fresh and relevant.

Miles Davis was single-mindedly focused on music—*his* music. Nothing gave him more pleasure than those transcendent, almost miraculous nights when he and his musicians were clicking: "The music that we were playing together was just unbelievable," he said of his first great quintet. "It was so bad that it used to send chills through me at night, and it did the same thing to the audiences, too."[30] As his friend Quincy Troupe related, Davis had an almost childlike fascination with his art, what in Buddhism is called beginner's mind. Because he was constantly seeing music with fresh eyes, he was able to remain open to creative possibilities and he directed his energies toward constant growth as a musician.[31] "I have to change," Davis said. "It's like a curse."[32] Talented young musicians crowded around Davis, eager to learn how to develop their own creative vision and capacity for expression. Davis collaborated with them, but not primarily to help them get better; rather he collaborated with them because he hoped they would help *him* get better: "because to be and stay a great musician you've got to always be open to what's new, what's happening at the moment," he said. "You have to be able to absorb it if you're going to continue to grow."[33]

Davis was never especially invested in the success or failure of his younger musicians. He found it "flattering" that he had gained a reputation as a generator of top jazz talent, but noted that it "was also something that I didn't ask for."[34] He certainly didn't feel obligated to play teacher and lead young guns like John Coltrane or Herbie Hancock by the hand. As he saw it, these musicians were professionals with their own technical ability and vision; it was up to them to find their own voice in the context of the group. The saxophonist Bill Evans, who played with Davis when he was just twenty-two, remembered that Davis didn't "tell you anything about what to play. As far as he was concerned, you're supposed to already know how to play . . . he's just there to shape his band, his music, you are just another color on his easel."[35] And if you were smart, you wanted to claim one of those colors for yourself, eyes wide open, learning everything you could.

Then there are the *Glorious Bastards,* superbosses less attuned to developing others than they are to *winning,* no matter what. For a Glorious Bastard, nothing counts except winning—*nothing.* A Glorious Bastard may push his staff to work until three a.m. several days a week. He might be merciless in chastising people when they make mistakes. How could such harsh behavior possibly *help* people? Indeed, Glorious Bastards seem similar to some of the unpleasant and spectacularly unsuccessful bosses I described in my previous book *Why Smart Executives Fail.* They can be every bit as selfish, every bit as unfeeling, every bit as unpleasant.

Yet Glorious Bastards spawn all-star talent, while these other bosses don't.

Glorious Bastards have something about them that makes them "glorious": they understand that in order to win, they need the best people and the best teams. They may be egoists, they may want fame and glory for themselves, but they perceive the success of those around them as the pathway to that glory. As a result, they teach their people how to win, inspire them with examples of what winning feels like, and push them to ever higher levels of performance. Glorious Bastards could not care less about the personal development of their staffs, but, perhaps surprisingly, they don't *need* to care in order to create stellar performers. Self-interested attention to people is enough. As an employee, you might not love a Glorious Bastard—in fact, you might swear at him under your breath—but you will absolutely respect him. And since Glorious Bastards put your career on the fast track, you'll thank your lucky stars you had the chance to work for them. Ambitious young talent will notice your success, and they'll line up to work for him, too.

Larry Ellison, Michael Milken, Roger Corman, Bonnie Fuller, Julian Robertson, and Jay Chiat all had elements of the Glorious Bastard in them. Of these, Oracle founder Larry Ellison is by far the most extreme example. Ellison is known as a huge spawner of talent in the technology field; as Oracle grad and Salesforce.com senior executive Steve Garnett said, "I think half of Silicon Valley is run by former Oracle people."[36] Top executives who once worked for Ellison include Salesforce.com CEO Marc Benioff, Siebel Systems founder and former CEO Tom Siebel, EMC Corporation's executive vice president Harry You, and veteran tech CEO and board member Mike Seashols. Ellison has been named by *BusinessWeek* as one of the most competitive people on the planet.[37] As a former senior executive told me, "He enjoys the losing of the other guy. He enjoys it, and that's kind of sick. . . . It's who he is. It's just who he is."[38] Although Ellison often discussed the importance of chemistry and teamwork, in reality he led more by intimidation. As he himself noted, "I invented my own style of management called MBR. MBR stands for 'management by ridicule.'"[39] One former Oracle executive described the result of this management style: "I think Larry was excellent at motivating people when it came to articulating the company's strategy and where he wanted the company to go. But the rest of his motivation was based upon people's fear and greed."[40] Despite Ellison's hard-driving style, or in some ways perhaps because of it, he had an indisputable knack for boosting people's careers. Gary Bloom, a longtime Oracle employee who has held senior leadership positions at many top technology companies, remembered, "What ends up happening for a large number of people is they end up in positions within Oracle probably years in advance of where they thought they'd be at that level in their career."[41]

Most Glorious Bastards are not quite as outrageous as Ellison, but neither do they seem as nice or empathetic as we might wish our bosses to be. The superboss playbook is not about being nice or empathetic. It's about giving protégés the motivation, guidance, wisdom, creative license, and other elements they need to learn and grow. After all, just because you have a nice boss doesn't necessarily mean you have a good boss, let alone one who will turbocharge your career.

Of course, some superbosses—probably the majority—would never dream of employing MBR. Unlike both Iconoclasts and Glorious Bastards, they truly, deeply care about the success of their protégés and pride themselves on their ability to develop others. These leaders represent a third type of superboss: the benevolent *Nurturer*. In using the word *nurturer*, I mean to sharply distinguish these superbosses from the mentors we usually see in corporate contexts. Most business mentors don't maintain deep, intense relationships with their younger, less experienced mentees. They may meet occasionally, dispense a few helpful tips, or help a mentee make helpful personal contacts, but that's about it. Nurturers are what I'd call "activist bosses." They are consistently present to guide and teach their protégées, and they actively engage with employees to help them reach great heights. Would your typical corporate mentor check in with you at one in the morning to see how your big project is going? A Nurturer would. Would your typical corporate mentor give you the exact feedback you need to hear, when you need to hear it? A Nurturer would. Would your typical mentor sit ten feet away from you, taking time to comment on the nuances of your work so that you literally learned at the feet of a master? A Nurturer would. It is this intense, sustained effort that allows Nurturers to play such a big part in the success of others.

From a talent generation standpoint, Nurturers are not any better than the other two kinds of superbosses on account of their "nice guy" sensibility; all three types of superbosses are extraordinary at spawning talent, and that's ultimately what counts. Among the primary and secondary superbosses we'll discuss in this book, many are Nurturers—including Bill Walsh, Michael Miles, Norman Brinker, Tommy Frist, Mary Kay Ash, Gregg Popovich, David Swensen, Jon Stewart, and Archie Norman. As Brinker once said, "I nurtured people. Over the years, I've employed about 1.4 million people and I've watched these people grow. Some, who worked in the kitchen, became managers, then store managers, and then executives. There are about seventeen or eighteen heads of major restaurant chains now who worked for me. That's really thrilling. I never liked having someone leave. But I was excited to see people take the risk and do something successful."[42]

Memorable Bosses

Finding three superboss "types" was an eye-opener, but as my research proceeded, I was amazed to find even more patterns coming to the fore among individuals who otherwise seemed so eclectic and disparate. All of the superbosses I identified seemed to hold in common a set of basic character traits. Each trait was not equally pronounced in every superboss, but in general they were strikingly, intriguingly evident, and helped define at least the outlines of what might be called a "superboss personality." In mapping out this personality, I felt I had gotten somewhat closer to what I was ultimately after in my investigation: the key behind superbosses' greatness as leaders.

Superbosses all possess *extreme confidence, even fearlessness,* when it comes to furthering their agendas and ideas. They almost universally embrace the axiom that "there are no problems, only solutions." This fearlessness bleeds into their private lives as well. Oracle founder Larry Ellison loves racing sailboats, a dangerous sport that has claimed the lives of multiple competitors.[43] Restaurant magnate Norman Brinker was an Olympian, and even played polo until it almost killed him.[44] Intel cofounder Robert Noyce was even more out there—a pilot, an active heli-skier, and a motorcycle enthusiast known to race through Bali streets in a monsoon. His favorite jacket read, "No guts, no glory."[45]

Another important attribute that all superbosses share is *competitiveness*. When we look at superbosses, we sense competitive blood running through their veins. They thrive on it, they seek it out, and they create it. Financier Michael Milken's competitive streak was obvious to his fraternity brothers in college; as one former roommate remarked, "I don't think I've seen anybody more competitive than Mike. If we were doing the dishes in our apartment, he always liked to time how long it took and said he could do them faster."[46] Robert Noyce made sure to hit the very first pitch at a father-son baseball game out of the park: "My poor father couldn't help himself," recalls his daughter Penny, who was in the stands that day. "He always threw himself entirely into the activity at hand."[47]

A third, vitally important character trait shared by superbosses—and one central to their innovation—is their *imaginative* nature. Superbosses are visionaries. They think intensely about what could be and are fired up to turn their dreams into reality. As one of Alice Waters's protégés said: "I think Alice has been a woman on a mission all of her life. Once she went into food, she wanted the best produce, the healthiest produce. Every bag of little greens that you see in your supermarket, you can send her a thank-you note. She changed the notion of produce and also the notion of raising animals and farming sustainably."[48] Marty Staff, a former marketing and sales executive for Ralph Lauren, had similar memories of his boss: "I remember when I would go to dinner with Ralph we would never talk about business. We would talk about dreams. The dreams were if you were skiing in Aspen what would you wear, what kind of comforter would you have, what kind of car would you drive? You know, would you wear sunglasses? Would they be mirrored? He would construct this world and then he would simply fill in the blanks."[49]

A fourth characteristic that superbosses universally manifest is *integrity*. I use the word not primarily to mean "honesty" in the colloquial sense, but rather strict adherence to a core vision or sense of self. Superbosses don't play games like some leaders do; unlike Bossy Bosses, they're not distracted by the need to satisfy their big egos. They remain consistently true to themselves, their beliefs, and their values. As maestro Charles Prince, music director of Wiener Operettensommer (Vienna's summer operetta festival), told me, his superboss Jorma Panula "is not interested in all the traffic. He's just interested in making music the best that he can; he's not interested in all the nonsense that goes on around a career as a conductor. . . . He only cares about the art, about the work. It's stupendous."[50] Even a leader like Ellison, who was known to do anything to win, always stayed true to his vision for his business, and in this sense showed unusual integrity.

A fifth and final attribute of superbosses, a natural extension of integrity, is *authenticity*. So many bosses cultivate an image for the benefit of their reports. They keep a tight lid on their personalities, saving their "true" selves for when they're away from the office. Not superbosses. In their daily interactions with others, they let their personalities hang out. Tommy Frist, founder of Hospital Corporation of America (HCA), has spawned hundreds of administrators at for-profit hospitals. "If you look around the industry, almost everybody has crossed paths with Tommy at one point or another," said Russell Carson, chairman of Ardent Health Services in Nashville, Tennessee.[51] Notable "offspring" of Frist's include Gene Nelson, founder of Quality Data Management (QDM); Edward Stack, founder, president, and CEO of Behavioral Centers of America; Joe Fisher, a CEO and chief pharmacist at various hospitals; and Sylvester Reeder, founder, former chairman, and CEO of World Healthcare Systems, Inc. As former employees and associates told me, Frist was a family man, and he didn't hide it from colleagues. Victor Campbell, senior vice president at HCA, related how every day during business trips to Europe, Frist would write a short letter to his college-age child and mail it. "He is just so close to his children, his wife, and his family that he prided himself on it and wanted to keep that close contact." Campbell also remembers Frist's constant eagerness to talk about family. "He'll probably be in my office before the day is over asking me how my son's football game went last night."[52]

Other superbosses are also refreshingly authentic and free with themselves—and not just at work. In an interview, Finnish conductor Atso Almila told me about a time when he was with conductor Jorma Panula at a restaurant where music was playing in the background. Panula, no fan of any music without precision and passion, asked the waiter if he could turn the music down. The waiter said no, claiming that some restaurant patrons liked it. Panula was undeterred. "So he stands up immediately and shouts to the whole restaurant, 'Is there anyone who wants to hear?'" When nobody answered, Panula said to the waiter, "'No, there aren't. You can shut it.'"[53]

Thanks to their unrestrained personalities, superbosses typically come across as memorable people—"unique," "one of a kind," even "mysterious." A journalistic insider said of Gene Roberts, "Jim Naughton summed it up best: Gene Roberts, he said, cannot be explained. And unless you were there, it isn't easy to explain the challenge, chutzpah, and camel found in the glory days of the *Philadelphia Inquirer* newsroom in the 1970s and 1980s."[54] Of Miles Davis, bassist Dave Holland said, "There was a tremendous amount of focus coming from him that influenced everybody. We were all drawn in by it; it was almost like a vortex. Once you were in its sphere of influence, there was a certain magic that seemed to be happening."[55] Superbosses possess an energy about them. They are spicy, interesting, and exuberant—all because they make no pretenses. When you're around people like this, you can't help but be energized.

The Superboss Playbook

To the questions I posed at the outset of this chapter—who *are* these superbosses and what makes them tick?—we can now offer some partial answers. No two superbosses are alike. They are ethnically, socially, and geographically diverse and they pursue widely different passions in life. Despite these differences, some common themes become evident. Superbosses are innovative visionaries who compete to win. They are strong-minded, imaginative, authentic people. They aren't all nurturing souls who give others the warm and fuzzies, or fun-loving people who don't blink an eye when camels traipse through their offices. But they are all fully committed to their businesses and to the people who help them succeed. What they say and do sticks with their younger colleagues.

Yet superbosses don't only help others succeed; as a result of their unequaled ability to nurture talent, they achieve tremendous personal and career success. Bill Walsh won three Super Bowls. Ralph Lauren became one of the richest men in the world, with a personal fortune in

2015 estimated at more than $7 billion.[56] At the time of his death at age sixty-five, Miles Davis had won three Grammy Hall of Fame awards and a Grammy Lifetime Achievement Award.[57] By 2015, Larry Ellison had amassed a fortune exceeding $54 billion, making him the fifth-wealthiest person in the world.[58]

Take a moment to reflect on just how extraordinary this track record is. If you're like many people I've met, you're probably looking at your own career and field a little differently now. You might wonder if any of the people you work for are true superbosses. If they aren't, do they show at least some of the stuff that makes superbosses such compelling talent spawners? What other leading lights in your industry have accounted for a disproportionate share of talent? And to what extent are *you* a super-boss? How do you match up? Do you inspire the people around you to raise their sights on what is possible?

You might also be wondering how to *explain* the superboss effect—and what you can learn from superbosses. How exactly do superbosses do it? Is it possible for us to achieve some or all of what they achieve? In my study of superbosses, "how" and "why" questions energized me from the beginning. Despite all the differences visible among superbosses, what truly united them more than anything were their *actions*. Superbosses achieved seemingly impossible results because they didn't hire, motivate, inspire, coach, develop, or fire their employees the way other bosses do. They had their own unique and often counterintuitive behaviors—a clear, powerful "playbook" that allowed them to help others thrive. The great secret of superbosses ultimately wasn't who they were. It was what they did.

Since actions and behaviors were the superbosses' ultimate differentiator, that meant the superboss effect was *teachable*. Though super-bosses usually came to their practices naturally, anyone could learn and adopt these practices to dramatically improve how they develop their people. Many of their behaviors ran counter to what most individuals and organizations did—but this could change. All that was required was an open mind and a willingness to revise conventional practices and what we *think* we know about managing and influencing others.

Developing world-class talent is on everyone's agenda, as it is the only way to survive and prosper. Yet study after study reveals that managers have the most trouble helping others to thrive. It's time to think about this differently, and to start *doing* some things differently. Imagine you had access to the Bill Walsh playbook or the Alice Waters playbook or the Gene Roberts playbook or more than a dozen after that. Wouldn't that be great?

The chapters that follow offer precisely that. They share the common habits and practices of the people who have produced the world's greatest talent. And they begin by tackling a subject that stymies and befuddles so many businesses today: attracting, selecting, and hiring the very best raw talent.

CHAPTER TWO

Getting People Who "Get It"

Y ou show up for a job interview. It's a management position, but not a high-level one. While you're waiting, someone drops down in the chair beside you. "Are you here about a job?" he asks. You look over and are startled to see the legendary head of the company. As you sit there, speechless, barely managing to nod, he asks you about one of the more challenging issues facing the industry. You force yourself to focus and quickly relay some thoughts on the subject. He asks you to elaborate, so you lay out your thinking in detail. He spots the weak points in your argument, and you acknowledge them, but explain why you are taking the position you described anyway.

As the conversation builds, you become so caught up in the subject that you almost forget whom you're talking to. Every so often, the discussion veers off in some unlikely direction as he asks you a question about something barely connected to what you were saying—your personal tastes, your teenage years, your hobbies—but then he steers the conversation back to the subject at hand. You constantly feel off balance, but he seems so interested in everything you're saying that you can't help but enjoy the back-and-forth. Without warning, the living legend gets up. "I've got to run. When the human-resources people call you in, tell them I've just hired you."

Pretty strange, isn't it? The leader in this scenario didn't look at your résumé or other records. He didn't want to know about your most recent position or qualifications. He didn't ask what sort of job you were looking for or your salary requirements. He didn't say what he was hiring you to do. He only seemed interested in your thoughts about an issue that currently concerned him. The few other questions he asked appeared. . . completely random.

How can such a hiring process possibly work? It goes against *everything* corporate recruiters know and do. Senior business leaders aren't supposed to waste their time hiring lower-level personnel. Vetting potential hires is a routine, tedious, and time-consuming process. It doesn't require the unique skills of an industry legend. Besides, human-resources experts have made hiring into something of a science. They have reliable tests and techniques for sorting and testing applicants, analyzing employment histories and work experience, and evaluating personalities and work styles. Everything they do is systematic, and their procedures serve to take the guesswork out of hiring. In modern human-resources management, there is no need for personal, intuitive judgments.

Or is there? Ask a superboss, and you'll get an earful to the contrary. Superbosses might favor people with advanced degrees and other formal credentials. They might employ some of the tests and psychological evaluations popular among human-resources specialists. At the same time, they complement those rote tools with a more creative style of *talent spotting*. The idea of looking for recruits who were already doing exactly the same kind of job and who will be kept indefinitely in that job would probably never occur to a superboss. In fact, if a prospective recruit has any quality that would fit neatly into a traditional hiring criterion, it's almost guaranteed that a superboss will pay little attention to that benchmark. When it comes to hiring, superbosses make their own rules. They forge their own path. They sniff out promising employees in the craziest of places. And the people they get are unlike any other: engaged, brilliant, creative—the raw material that may well be the stuff of future superstars.

Making Lunch for a Legend

It's July 1993. The setting is the brightly lit kitchen of a fine dining establishment in the San Francisco Bay area. The kitchen is largely deserted because the restaurant is closed on Sundays. Standing over an industrial stainless-steel stove, a tall, slender woman with a long brown ponytail is hard at work preparing a meal. Steam rises from a sizzling saucepan; from a corner, the sweet scent of caramelizing fruit starts to waft through the kitchen. Sweat dots the woman's forehead. She's been here since five in the morning, washing ingredients, chopping, slicing, and precooking sauces.

Nearby, a party of older women and men are seated at a table, watching the woman work while savoring their first course, rabbit cappelletti in brodo. Periodically they sip their glasses of perfectly chilled Mâcon-Villages from France. Their table has been set for formal service—cloth napkins, perfectly spaced silverware, freshly cut flowers. These guests are a jovial bunch, enjoying a casual conversation. As the woman finishes the second course, grilled swordfish and summer squashes with salsa verde, she looks up from the stove to describe the ingredients selected and the cooking techniques used. Her customers hang on her words and study every turn of her tongs, every flick of the saucepan. They don't quite know it yet, but after these dishes they will be treated to a dessert of pear galette with Gorgonzola.

You might think this is the ultimate foodie experience, prepared for a group of VIP guests by a celebrity chef. But these aren't just *any* VIP guests. And the objective of the woman cooking isn't to delight them enough so they'll come back. In fact, she isn't even a chef in this kitchen, nor is she even one of the midlevel cooks who work at the restaurant. For weeks now, she's been laboring without pay on a trial basis in an effort to *become* one of those cooks. She did well enough, apparently, because as a final test she has been invited to prepare the most important lunch of her career to date.

Melissa Kelly remembers preparing lunch at the famed Chez Panisse as a "daunting task."[1] The guest of honor was Alice Waters, the restaurant's owner and godmother. Others at the table included Stephen Singer, the wine steward (and father of Alice's daughter, Fanny); Lindsey Shere, the pastry chef; Gilbert Pilgram (now owner of Zuni in San Francisco) and Peggy Smith (subsequently cofounder of Cowgirl Creamery), the upstairs café chefs; and Jean-Pierre Moullé and Catherine Brandel, the chefs of the high-end downstairs kitchen. These were some of the biggest names in the American restaurant scene, and all had taken time out of their busy schedules to taste Melissa's original creations. It was a dream come true for Kelly—and intimidating as hell. If Kelly passed the test, she would receive confirmation that she was good enough to work with the best of the best, as well as the chance to hone her craft at the feet of a legendary food innovator.

Kelly was no newbie. She had graduated from the Culinary Institute of America and had worked in restaurants in West Virginia, New York, and Miami before moving to California.[2] In New York, she had held several senior positions working for acclaimed chef Larry Forgione. Still, as she recalls, she was nervous—*really* nervous. Kelly had been asked to write a menu, shop for ingredients, select the wine, set the table, prepare the meal, and serve it—all by herself. As she cooked and served each course, she was expected to speak intelligently about what she was doing. Upon completion of the meal, she would sit with Waters and her team to receive a frank evaluation. Each guest, one by one, would offer his or her critique of Kelly's efforts. "I had a good amount of culinary experience, although I felt like a little peon in that room compared to those people. It was a great experience. It was very self-revealing for me."[3]

Determined to impress Waters, Kelly had begun working on the lunch days in advance, writing out menu ideas and foraging in the markets for the choicest ingredients. In the end, the effort was worth it. Kelly went on to work at Chez Panisse for six enriching, high-octane months before receiving an attractive offer at a restaurant on the East Coast. Given the success she's known since her time at Chez Panisse, Kelly clearly benefitted from her brush with a superboss (and, yes, even just a brush with a superboss can pay great dividends, thanks to the intensity of the experience). In 1999, she won the James Beard Award for best regional chef in the Northeast. Afterward, she opened highly regarded restaurants of her own in Maine, Florida, and Arizona, all called Primo and all emphasizing fresh, local, farm-to-table cooking. In 2013, she won a second James Beard Award, the first chef ever to win the Best Chef, Northeast Award twice.[4] Today, she looks back at Chez Panisse as a turning point in her career, the experience that allowed her to come into her own as a chef: "I didn't have a style when I got there," she writes on the Primo website. "By the time I left, I did—simplicity, seasonality, freshness."[5] Of her own restaurants she has said, "I feel like I'm passing the torch from Chez Panisse."[6]

That Special Something

It's clear that Kelly had that "special something" every superboss seeks. It's also clear that Waters had a nose (or, perhaps in her case, a palate) for sniffing out that "it" factor. In any industry, superbosses seek out unusual qualities most bosses don't even think about. Superbosses don't want just the candidates whose skills enabled them to score high on some test; they want candidates whose abilities are so special, no one would think to test them. If a candidate seems to have what the superboss is after, he won't hesitate to overrule human-resources specialists. The superboss's quest for superstars will override everything else.

This emphasis on unusual talent is far more extraordinary than it might seem. Nearly all business executives, especially those in human resources, will tell you that they want recruits who are very talented, smart, good at leading, and impressive all around. This is different from what superbosses want. Superbosses don't want recruits who are very talented and smart; they want recruits who are *unusually* talented and *startlingly* smart. They don't want ordinary leaders; they want drivers of change. They don't want most-likely-to-succeed types; they want people who are prepared to transform the very definition of success.

That special something they seek is ultimately quite hard to capture in words. After a technical discussion, Larry Ellison would base his decision to hire someone for a project on his judgment that the person "got it." Gene Roberts based his most important hiring decision—his choice of managing editor—on his intuitive sense that the candidate "had what the job needed."[7] Ralph Lauren made a runway model the head of women's design "for no other reason than she seemed to *get it*—she *got* the clothes."[8] Most superbosses base their choice for key associates on how well they "get" what the superboss is trying to do.

So what does "getting it" mean? One thing that virtually all superbosses look for is unusual intelligence. Norman Brinker believed that the most important part of running a restaurant chain was hiring the smartest people possible. Ralph Lauren looked for a kind of "fashion intelligence." He wanted everyone who worked for him, even in the most menial roles, to have a fashion sense and be able to say interesting things about clothes. Lorne Michaels has a rule that he repeats all the time: "If you look around the room and you're the smartest person in the room, you're in the wrong room. You know, if you look around the room and you think, 'God, these people are amazing,' then you're probably in the right room."[9] Virtually all superbosses place an emphasis on having everyone around them be as smart as possible, and they suss this out through their nonconventional interview techniques and by observing them closely during on-the-job trial periods.

A second component of "getting it" is creativity. Superbosses are *not* looking for employees who think the same way they do. They are looking for employees who, like them, can tackle problems originally and differently. Even more, superbosses are looking for employees who can actually *get* somewhere with an original line of thought, who can creatively apply what they know. When superbosses talk with prospective employees, they want, more than anything else, to hear how they think. This is why superbosses as diverse as Norman Brinker, Larry Ellison, and Roger Corman were known to listen intensely when talking with job candidates, expecting to learn something new themselves.

When former employees describe the hiring practices of superbosses, the emphasis on creativity may take many forms, but it is often overt. Lee Clow, one of advertising mogul Jay Chiat's closest associates, emphasized that Chiat "didn't hire off the conventional portfolio/resume—he looked for people who did things creatively." Clow, the cocreator of the famous "1984" ad that introduced Apple's Macintosh computer during the Super Bowl XVIII telecast, was himself an illustration of this principle. He landed his job with Chiat's firm by carrying out an eccentric yet highly creative ad campaign devoted entirely to the proposition that Chiat should hire him. He created slogans and designs, had bumper stickers and T-shirts made, used mailings and phone calls, and kept bombarding Chiat's firm with his message until they put him on the payroll. It wouldn't have worked if the ad campaign hadn't *also* demonstrated considerable quality. But the real differentiator was the emphasis on creativity.[10]

A third component of "getting it" is extreme flexibility. Although superbosses often hire people with special areas of expertise, they are not usually interested in specialists who can only do one thing. They want a kind of brilliance that can be applied to many sorts of problems. Norman Brinker thought that talented people should be able to handle any position. One of his associates used a sports metaphor to describe his attitude: "Norman wasn't a fan of hiring people to play first base, for example; he just wanted to hire a good baseball player."[11] Although Gene Roberts helped employees build expertise in specific niches, he believed that every reporter and columnist who worked for him should be able to cover any breaking news story, regardless of the subject.

To underscore their appreciation for flexibility, superbosses frequently assign new hires jobs that have little to do with their previous experience and qualifications. Bill Sanders would regularly move people to different jobs in different parts of his company. Gene Roberts was known to take someone who had been processing comic strips and make him a feature writer, or to assign a sportswriter to cover politics. Roger Corman regularly filled the positions needed for film productions with people he had hired for completely different jobs. Jack Nicholson, for example, worked for Corman as a writer and as a director.

The determination of superbosses to recruit the most intelligent, creative, and flexible employees possible may seem startling. Like many superbosses, real estate guru Bill Sanders believed that "if you are going to hire someone, make sure they are great; otherwise don't hire anybody."[12] Ellison had recruiters ask prospective candidates: "Are you the smartest person you know?" If they answered, "Yes," they were likely to be given a further interview. If they answered, "No," they were asked, "Who is?" Then they were dropped from the hiring process and Ellison's recruiters would contact the person who was named as smarter.[13]

Getting People Who "Get It"

It isn't easy for superbosses to recruit the kind of people they are looking for. To pull it off, they frequently must be willing to take a chance on unconventional backgrounds and qualifications. The first chef Waters hired for Chez Panisse was a graduate student in philosophy who had no culinary training at all. Despite the lack of experience, the audition meal she cooked and her conversations with Waters were enough to convince Waters that she "got it." Corman was willing to hire actors with no acting experience, directors with no directing experience, and production designers with no production design experience. Walsh hired someone for his NFL coaching staff who had done little more than coach high school football.

Somewhat surprisingly, superbosses in technology-based industries—where employees must meet exacting standards—are just as fond of recruiting employees with unconventional qualifications as superbosses in more creative industries. Larry Ellison was happy to hire someone who had dropped out of college, as he himself had done; he didn't need someone with multiple advanced degrees. In fact, in at least one case, he *preferred* a candidate who had dropped out of college shortly before graduation because he thought it showed an independence that was commendable.[14] Formal qualifications never mattered as much as other signs of talent. Ellison would pay special attention to anything a candidate had done that seemed genuinely difficult, regardless of what it was. "When we're hiring," Ellison said, "we look for people with a strong aptitude in mathematics and physics and music (which is very highly correlated to mathematics), but who can also make judgments as to where they're going to invest their time."[15] If recruits were gifted enough, Ellison believed, they would rise to the technical challenges.

Many superbosses make a special effort to extend their search for new employees into groups that other companies have overlooked. Bill

Walsh started an internship program in the NFL for minority coaches, allowing participants a fast track into the NFL and himself a chance to tap into a vast new source of talent. Jay Chiat was one of the first in advertising to regularly hire women and minorities to creative positions. This was not because he was trying to achieve greater social justice but because he saw these groups as a new pool of potential all-stars.

Superbosses also tend to be extremely opportunistic in their hiring. Constantly searching for outstanding new blood, they will jump at the chance to scoop it up whenever and in whatever form they find it. There are many stories of superbosses setting out to recruit one sort of employee and returning with a completely different one. Bill Walsh went to Kansas to check out a promising quarterback, but his attention was drawn to the quarterback's roommate, who was catching passes as the quarterback demonstrated his throw. Walsh said no to the quarterback and drafted the roommate instead, even though Walsh's own scouts thought it was a bad idea. That receiver was Dwight Clark, who became a 49ers legend.[16]

To further tease out people with extreme ability, superbosses regularly employ interview methods that other executives would regard as highly eccentric. Ralph Lauren would often decide whether to hire designers without even looking at their portfolios. Gene Roberts and Lorne Michaels would fall silent for long stretches of time during interviews, causing the interviewees to say revealing things in an effort to fill the silence. Corman often relied on interviews for his films when other producers would have auditions. One of the techniques he used in these interviews was to ask the candidate for an opinion about some scene in a film and then start an argument about it.

Some interview techniques were so unorthodox that they bordered on observational research methods employed by ethnographers. When Miles Davis became interested in Herbie Hancock, he invited him over, led him to his basement, introduced him to two other musicians, suggested they try playing together, and then left. He repeated this routine for two or three more days. While Hancock and the others played, Davis listened to their sound over his home intercom. When he felt that he had heard enough, he went down, played a few numbers with them himself, and told Hancock that he was hiring him as his new pianist.[17] Or consider the tradition of "Super Saturdays" developed by real estate mogul Bill Sanders. He would bring thirty finalists for jobs—often MBAs—to Santa Fe, New Mexico, for morning interviews, followed by a long hike at Sanders's ranch in the hills outside the city. Constance Moore, the former managing director at Security Capital Group under Sanders, remembers that Sanders and others in the company would "take these kids to seven thousand feet and talk with them. They were generally exhausted at the end of the day. We learned a whole lot about them on these hikes, so then afterward, we would all sit down and talk about each one of them and figure out which ones we wanted to ask to join."[18]

Superbosses are also interested in how candidates react to unexpected questions they couldn't possibly have prepared for. When candidates would walk into an interview with Jay Chiat, sympathetic managers used to warn them to "expect something weird or out of left field to see if he can shock you."[19] Alice Waters often began job interviews by asking candidates what books they had read recently as a way to get them to talk about subjects they wouldn't have thought relevant to working in a restaurant. Ellison simply asked candidates about whatever he was currently interested in.

Once a superboss thinks he has found someone with that "special something," he takes dramatic steps to follow through. Often, Bill Sanders would personally call candidates who interested him the instant they came to his attention—late at night, on Christmas, whenever he heard about them. Gene Roberts once authorized his chief recruiter to deliver a baby-blue Mustang as a gift to a columnist he wanted to hire. When she nonetheless turned down his job offer, he thought it only fair to let her keep the car.[20] John Tucker, Kraft's head of human resources, recalled that Kraft under Michael Miles wanted to hire Jim Kilts (later CEO of Gillette) so badly that they even took to calling Kilts's wife every few months to try to get her on board.[21] For superbosses, recruiting all-star employees is such a high priority that it justifies almost any amount of time and trouble.

The Power of Feeling Unthreatened

Despite claiming to be interested in hiring the best people, most managers aren't actually comfortable with the very best. They don't feel at ease directing employees who understand the task at hand and what it requires better than they do. They worry that employees who are too gifted will make contributions that outshine theirs. They have no idea what to do with proposals from subordinates that are too original and unexpected. They may even fear being replaced by those whom they have hired and promoted. As a consequence, most managers will unconsciously choose second-tier talent, because it is easier to categorize and deal with. They usually don't admit this to themselves, but they describe second-tier employees as first-class talent and write off first-class prospects as oddballs.

The imperious, ego-driven Bossy Boss types are extreme examples of this tendency. The last thing such bosses are able to tolerate is anyone whose skills or aptitudes might rival their own. Donald Trump, at least as seen on TV, is able to seem big only by surrounding himself with people who seem small. If someone does anything genuinely impressive in his presence, he needs to belittle it. When someone shows sparks of real creativity, he treats them as a misfit. Working on a regular basis with anyone who may upstage him seems to be more than he can bear.

Superbosses (a group that does not include Trump) have none of these problems. They are self-confident enough to feel completely unthreatened by extreme intelligence, mind-bending creativity, and forceful personalities. They are arrogant enough to be completely oblivious to the possibility of being outshone. They have no problem with subordinates who are better than they are, perhaps because they don't entirely believe *anyone* is better than they are. There's a famous joke about Larry Ellison: "What's the difference between God and Larry Ellison? God knows he isn't Larry Ellison." A similar joke could be told about almost any superboss, despite the fact that some of them are deceptively mild-mannered. They all feel supremely effective and completely comfortable in their respective domains. Their status is not founded on any outward trappings. So strong is their personal sense of self that they can never be seriously unsettled by any level of ability, no matter how remarkable. In fact, they *enjoy* being challenged by new employees, especially if the challenge is founded on a genuine insight. If someone working for them can provide them with an opportunity to improve their understanding, do better, or come up with a better solution, they usually find it irresistible.

John Griffin, who was second in command to hedge-fund legend Julian Robertson at Tiger Management before leaving to run his own fund at Blue Ridge Capital, recalls that his superboss was so eager for new ideas that he was like a "Venus flytrap saying 'Feed me!'"[22] Robertson delighted in hiring people who "saw things in often free, new, and different ways," people who "didn't worry about tilting the windmill."[23] Larry Ellison was likewise especially proud of employees he described as "driven by a drummer only they can hear." His reason was that "they will constantly question my wisdom, and won't be the least bit shy about challenging me, and I hope they'll keep me from making mistakes."[24] Despite falling out with some Oracle executives who questioned his judgments, Ellison seemed to relish the sort of interaction that was possible only when people were willing to argue with him. Superbosses appreciate unusual talent, not just because of the benefits that talent can bring to their company but also because they enjoy the energy boost unusual talent can provide.

Most superbosses make sure that their comfort around other supremely skilled people is publicly known. This is partly because they are proud of it, but even more so because they want the most capable people available to *seek them out*. Norman Brinker was constantly and explicitly on the lookout for executives who knew far more about something than he did. Bill Sanders liked to talk about "how many people I have hired that were four times smarter than I was."[25] When superbosses see their employees shine, they feel it reflects positively on them as leaders. If their employees gain a public reputation for brilliance, then it will be easier to recruit more employees like them.

Room *for* Others *to Shine*

The extreme self-confidence of superbosses means that there is always room for other stars around them. They feel that collaborating with outrageously capable individuals is only appropriate for someone of their stature. When people who are working for superbosses emerge as new stars, superbosses are almost always extremely pleased. Glorious Bastards are something of an exception, because they sometimes treat stars who have emerged within their ranks as rivals to be ousted. But even these superbosses manage to keep stars around them whom most executives would find overwhelming. The other superbosses seem to have no limitations when it comes to celebrating the success of their employees. Miles Davis recruited John Coltrane when he was not well known, but soon after, jazz fans and fellow musicians began to revere Coltrane almost as much as they did Davis himself. Davis was quick to acknowledge that Coltrane was becoming as much of a star as he was and, instead of feeling threatened, was energized by it.[26]

Davis was so enamored with Coltrane, in fact, that he kept him in his band between 1955 and 1957, even though the saxophone player was struggling with a long-standing heroin addiction (Davis at this time was clean). Davis fired Coltrane in 1957 but took him back in 1958 and continued to play with him for another two years.[27] Seeking out star protégés like this and relishing their success is pretty typical of superbosses. Moreover, because they expect most people who work for them to become stars, they will often tolerate personal problems, eccentricities, and big egos. Roger Corman would recruit young actors, writers, and directors whom he judged to be the most promising, even if they already had a reputation for arrogance.

If superbosses are eager to nurture soon-to-be or emerging stars, they also have no hesitations about hiring people who are already stars. Gene Roberts offered jobs at the *Philadelphia Inquirer* to journalists who were already famous, who were working for publications that were more prestigious, and who were paid more than he could manage. He simply assumed they would be tempted by the opportunity to work for him and, more often than not, he was right. Alice Waters invited some of the world's most celebrated chefs, such as Jacques Pépin and Thomas Keller, to join her restaurant as guest chefs. She assumed they would welcome the opportunity to interact and learn, and a great many did. Others, such as the star British chef April Bloomfield, spent a summer at Chez Panisse as a way to see how America cooks before opening her first New York City restaurant.[28] Larry Ellison jumped at the chance to hire Mark Hurd immediately after Hurd was let go as CEO of Hewlett-Packard. Although superbosses are notable mostly for making *new* stars, one of their most impressive assets is their ability to collect existing stars.

The confidence of superbosses also enables them to adapt their organizations to utilize their brilliant new hires. To most people in talent management, this is absolute heresy, but to a superboss, each outstanding new recruit offers a new opportunity to create value, and the company isn't really seizing this business opportunity unless it is finding ways to use the new hire to the fullest. One critical way superbosses do that is by adapting the job description to fit the person, rather than make the person fit the job. Ralph Lauren once spotted a beautiful woman, Virginia Witbeck, in a burger restaurant in New York and loved her outfit: a man's jacket, old corduroy pants, and an old fur jacket she had turned into a vest. He approached her table and offered her a job, telling her he wanted people with style. She served as Lauren's muse, working in his design department for four years without a formal job title. To Lauren, she was a presence; he wanted to hear what she had to say . . . but he did it without ever actually defining what her job was supposed to be.[29]

In the case of some superbosses, having new employees define their own jobs is almost standard practice. When it came to working at Waters's restaurant, according to one of her chefs, once you were in, "you just sort of . . . created your job."[30] At Industrial Light and Magic, George Lucas's employees didn't even *have* job descriptions. They were assigned tasks on various projects, according to what was needed and who was available. Lorne Michaels let his ensemble's ideas and abilities constantly shape and reshape their contribution to the show. As this happened, writers sometimes became performers, and performers or assistant directors sometimes became writers. Utilizing people to the greatest extent possible often requires extreme flexibility, as well as a willingness to relinquish a degree of control. It requires boldness, which, as we've seen, is a hallmark of the superboss's personality.

The extent to which superbosses can adapt their organizations to utilize promising employees is often extraordinary. For example, Jay Chiat remade his whole advertising agency to make the most of the capabilities that a British account-planning expert brought on board. Bill Walsh changed the very way his teams played football in order to find the best use for new talent. He let the position be defined by "what the player can do" instead of expecting the players to execute plays they were given. He expected the coaches writing the playbook to familiarize themselves with the team roster and adapt plays to the athletes' special talents. Other superbosses took this approach even further. Miles Davis would let a new addition to his band—a John Coltrane or a Herbie Hancock—take the band off in a whole new artistic direction, bringing in diverse musical traditions, influences, and ideas. The result was something new, something Davis would never have created on his own. But for this jazz great, that was precisely the point.

Churn: Better Than We Think?

Because superbosses see uniquely capable recruits as business opportunities, they are rarely willing to pass up a candidate on the grounds that she "wouldn't fit in." Instead, a superboss will usually give the person a try. If the new recruit isn't producing according to expectations, then the superboss will simply move the person to a different position or let her go. The idea that an employee's placement might need to be rethought is not something that would cause a superboss even a moment's hesitation.

This willingness to try people out often results in higher employee turnover than most businesses find desirable. Ellison acknowledged that his hiring practices resulted in an abnormally high rate of employees being let go or shifted to different jobs, but said this was necessary if he was going to field the best team possible. Roberts advised his editors to accept any resignations immediately, so that people who weren't working out in the organization could be moved out quickly. Corman went even further in defending a high rate of employee turnover. He said that if his people weren't constantly being lured away to high-paying jobs at major studios, it would mean he wasn't doing a good enough job recruiting.

Waters simply accepted it as a feature of her business that many people would only stay at her restaurant for as little as three months and that celebrity chefs might only stay for a week. Lucas assumed that when his employees developed their skills enough, many of them would leave to apply those skills to their own projects.

Their casual acceptance of employee churn is another important way in which superbosses chart their own course. Human-resources specialists consider it a failure if a new hire doesn't stay long in the new job. Indeed, the length of time that new recruits stay is usually a key part of a human-resources specialist's performance evaluation. Superbosses, in contrast, tend to prize talent and creativity over stability of staff. This means that a superboss will usually not hesitate to hire a person who is "intellectually overqualified," who seems like "too much of a high flyer," or who might not "stay around."

The irony is that superbosses often create such an attractive work environment that many of their recruits do stay around—seemingly forever. Roberts's recruits didn't just leave desirable jobs with prestigious publications to come and work for the *Philadelphia Inquirer*; they turned down offers of desirable jobs with prestigious publications to *stay* at the *Inquirer*. People who worked for superbosses like Norman Brinker, Jay Chiat, Alice Waters, or Bill Walsh often didn't *want* to work for anybody else. When they moved on, it was usually because they wanted to run their own operations. In these cases, many superbosses actually encouraged the employee's departure, applauding it as the right move for them—even if the employee happened to be a star protégé.

Magic Reputations

Over time, all of the hiring practices common to superbosses become easier because superbosses become talent magnets. Gifted people are attracted to business leaders who appreciate their exceptional capabilities. The extreme talent that a superboss has already recruited creates an environment to which other great talent is attracted. People also start to notice that those who have worked for the superboss are achieving remarkable levels of success, and soon the superboss becomes someone every rising star wants to work for.

The extent to which people are eager to work for superbosses is often demonstrated by their willingness to accept lower salaries to take the job. Melissa Kelly was hardly the only experienced chef who worked a trial run without pay at Chez Panisse—it was a standard practice. There were no guarantees she would wind up with a job, either; many people who worked weeks for Waters didn't get hired. As one former employee remembers, "When you finished work for the day, they'd say, 'Would you like to come back tomorrow?' You'd always talk at the end of the day to see if it was going to work for you and if it was working for the restaurant and the team."[31]

Chiat's son Marc recalled, "Everybody would give their left arm to work at Chiat/Day" despite the firm's "notoriously low salaries."[32] Roberts noted that people's eagerness to work for him was a major asset when it came to recruiting new hires with a limited budget. "We couldn't attract them with money," he said. Bill Sanders actually made it a policy to pay people *less* than what they were receiving at their previous job. That way, he said, he knew that no one was joining his firm just for the money.[33]

The superboss's status as a talent magnet often comes to be regarded in almost mystical terms. People would describe Larry Ellison as possessing a unique magnetism, or charisma. "There's no one like him," one of his long-term employees said.[34] One of Alice Waters's colleagues commented, "Alice is sort of a magnet. She has this light, this energy that people are attracted to."[35] Steve Sullivan, a busboy who later opened the Acme Bread Company, remembers how the phone at Chez Panisse would ring at four in the morning with calls from college students seeking jobs. "It was some kid saying, 'I've been reading about Chez Panisse and I really want to come to Berkeley and be an apprentice.'"[36] Lorne Michaels's manager, Bernie Brillstein, commented, "He was like the conduit for all the comedy brains at the time. He was just 'The Guy.'"[37] One of George Lucas's associates at Industrial Light and Magic used the exact same words to describe George Lucas. "He was 'The Guy.' He attracted a lot of talented people."[38] Superbosses become the "magic names" in their industries, because in certain respects, they seem to have magic powers. But in fact it wasn't magic at all; instead, as we've seen, it was a radically different way to think about attracting, selecting, and hiring the very best talent.

The beauty of being the talent magnet is that despite losing some stars who are ready to move on to bigger opportunities (and maybe precisely because you are losing them), you are constantly replenishing your bench, regenerating talent in your team and in your organization. And not just any employees, but the best! After all, the people with the highest aspirations, the greatest drive, and the strongest skills and aptitudes to back them up are the ones who most often move toward talent magnets. Superbosses offer a path for personal growth that is simply unrivaled. Who *wouldn't* want to work for them?

Hiring like a Superboss

Most people in business know that unusual performance and innovation rest on the abilities of unusual people. What superbosses appreciate is that you need unconventional hiring practices to get those people. As we've seen, this translates into *personal* hiring, *intuitive* hiring, *bold* hiring, *inventive* hiring, *opportunistic* hiring, and ultimately, *passionate* hiring. This is not to say that superbosses, with their unique personalities and perspectives, do *all* the hiring at their companies. Of course not. Superbosses have HR professionals working for them as well—often whole teams of them. Over time, superbosses can get others around them to hire in their particular way, too. Including HR.

In 1987, Seen Lippert had just graduated from the Culinary Institute of America and was returning to her native California to look for a job. She badly wanted to work at Chez Panisse, and after much effort, finally landed an interview with Paul Bertolli, an executive chef. She showed up assuming she'd experience an ordinary corporate interview. When she sat down with Bertolli, she passed him her résumé—only to watch as he flicked it off the table. "I looked at him, and he said, 'No, don't pick it up.' I was confused . . . He began to ask me questions like, 'Tell me about yourself.' 'Where'd you grow up?' 'Where did you eat yesterday?' 'What did you eat last week?' 'What books do you read? Not necessarily cookbooks . . .' 'What books are you reading now?' 'What do you care about?'" Lippert reports having been "caught off guard"—how could it be otherwise—"but pleasantly." (!)[39] A month later, Lippert got a call. Would she like to come and try out?

By this time, sixteen years after Chez Panisse's founding, Waters's hiring practices had spread to others in her organization. This underlines a key argument in this book: the extraordinary practices that define superbosses and contribute to their success are *teachable*. If you are responsible for hiring in your organization, why not consider incorporating some of the techniques for selecting new hires that I've described here? You don't need to throw everything you learned about human resources out the window. Take small steps and allow the superboss's mentality to seep into your existing hiring process.

For starters, you should resist the urge to automatically eliminate prospective hires solely on the basis of their past credentials and experience—remembering that in doing so, you may be weeding out the very best, most creative candidates. Don't eliminate job descriptions, but at the same time, don't slavishly follow them by hiring only those prospects who allow you to check off every last criterion. Don't throw out the format of the formal interview, but feel free to loosen it up and incorporate new elements, such as holding the interview in an unusual venue.

When you're first beginning to experiment with the superboss approach, don't make every person you hire an unorthodox pick. Start with just one or two hires and work from there. You'll have to follow up by borrowing other practices discussed in this book; you can't just hire an unusual person and expose her to all the ordinary ways you manage people. If you really attracted genuinely unusual talent but did no more, they'd probably head for the hills before they even downloaded your company's iPhone app. Be prepared to behave as a partner and to learn and adapt. And don't forget about the rest of your team; if left to their own devices, they may well drive out the "strange" newcomer. Let them in on your game plan. You might be surprised by how receptive they'll be once they understand and, even more important, experience firsthand what the superboss's world looks like.

Making a superboss-style hire isn't a Hail Mary pass to try when your business is in trouble and you're desperate to show results. It's something to try when you're open to deliberately rethinking what you do in an effort to get better. The risks aren't that great—you won't be stuck for five years if you fail—but when hiring more intuitively and unconventionally, you still have to make an investment of time and effort. You need to accept that you're figuring it out as you go and that there are no guarantees that any particular hire will pan out. But there never is, anyway, so why not try? If it doesn't work out, or even if it does and the new hire eventually moves on to other things, you'll have your first lesson in churn. If you're lucky or if you're even better at this superboss thing than you think, your former employee will make a name for herself elsewhere. When that happens, as it eventually will when the superboss playbook starts to take hold, expect more messages from LinkedIn that people are "looking at your profile," and expect to start hearing from outsiders who are now "curious" about what you're up to and wondering whether you may be hiring. Gaining a reputation as a talent magnet doesn't have to take long; you can begin to develop one after just a few employees successfully spin off. And when people do begin to take notice, you'll experience one of the greatest feelings of accomplishment in your career. Add in the upside that comes when the greatest talent starts seeking you out, and you'll really have something.

Discovering the "diamond in the rough," that one person who doesn't fit the narrow constraints we place on so many things in life—well, that does take courage. It's hard to give up the sense of control that conventional ways of choosing give us. For hiring managers, the superboss methods of spotting desirable employees may feel risky and dangerous, especially if you've never done it before. But remember: the track record that superbosses bring to the challenge is so overwhelmingly positive that we'd be crazy not to try.

Spotting and hiring the right "raw material" are vital for anyone who seeks to generate exceptional talent, but it is only a first step. Once you have unusually talented people, you've got to motivate them to excel. You have to get them to push as hard as they humanly can to achieve extraordinary results, both for the organization's sake and to promote their own growth. What's the secret to such extreme motivation? Superbosses crack the whip as well as anyone, constantly raising their demands for performance. But they also do something else that exceedingly few bosses do, even good ones. As we'll see in the next chapter, it's this ingredient that creates such die-hard emotional commitment, propelling even the most talented people to do more than they ever thought possible.

CHAPTER THREE

Motivating Exceptional People to Do the Impossible

If you had walked into the Bloomingdale's on the corner of Fifty-Ninth and Lexington in New York City during the early 1970s and proceeded past racks of suits, slacks, and ties to the center of the men's store, you might have noticed an attractive man in his early thirties inspecting displays of clothing. Another man might have been dutifully assisting him, rearranging shirts on a shelf, moving a display of ties from one place to the next. At this time, menswear was usually sold according to classification, with individual departments for ties, shirts, and suits. That's how JCPenney did it. That's how Filene's did it. That's how every local department store did it. And that's how Bloomingdale's did it—until now.

This area of Bloomingdale's was visually set off from the rest of the men's section, like an individual boutique inside the larger department store. It brought together a whole line of clothing items and was designated for one brand: Polo Ralph Lauren. Featured prominently was a new product: a casual sporting shirt similar to the old Lacoste shirts people used to wear, the ones with the crocodile insignia. This new shirt was of a higher quality than those Lacoste shirts. It sported a tiny polo player instead of a crocodile and came in twenty-four dazzling colors. The polo player and the quality of the material marked this shirt as "high end." In fact, the entire boutique embodied what many lower- and middle-class Americans aspired to: wealth and distinction.

The young, good-looking guy checking his wares was none other than Ralph Lauren. Since the early 1970s, he's become a fashion icon and billionaire several times over. Before Lauren, designers made either formal wear or sportswear; Lauren combined the two into a cohesive collection that reflected a new, aspirational American lifestyle. He believed that his customers (like him) wanted different outfits for work, home, and travel, so he brought them together for the first time. He created a mythical world of class and prestige that middle-class customers could buy into simply by wearing the proper clothing—*his* clothing. A writer for the *New York Times* once proclaimed Lauren "the ultimate producer of a completely packaged, perfect life."[1] But it may have been designer Joseph Abboud who best captured Lauren's contribution not only to fashion but to American culture: "No one has done a greater job of inventing the myth of Ralph Lauren than Ralph Lauren."[2]

Who was that man assisting Lauren at Bloomingdale's back in the early 1970s? It wasn't Abboud or fellow designers Vera Wang, Jeffrey Banks, or John Varvatos, although all of them worked for Lauren at some point. It was a young designer and merchandising specialist named Sal Cesarani. Cesarani would go on to win multiple awards for his own designs, have *New York Times* articles written about him, and become known to some as "New York's Dean of Good Taste."[3] Between 1970 and 1972, though, he served as Lauren's right-hand design assistant, involved in "literally all aspects" of the design process—from fabric selection to showroom display to sketching Lauren's design ideas.[4] It was an exciting job, a wonderful learning experience—and indescribably intense.

As Cesarani remembers, he and Lauren would work late into the night and walk home together, discussing designs. Lauren was "always so soft spoken" yet managed to exert an incredible amount of pressure to perform—he was "demanding but in a non-demanding way."[5] If Lauren asked you to do something, you did it because you wanted to please him, and above all, not disappoint him. "You felt the need to do it simply to receive his recognition or because you knew it was the right thing to do. . . . He made you feel you were so much a part of the business."[6] Some bosses inspire so much affection that employees are willing to do anything for them—even take the metaphorical bullet for him or her. Lauren was *that* kind of boss. "If you were to talk to [any other former employees of Ralph Lauren]," Cesarani says, "they would tell you the same thing: they would have given him their lives."[7]

Much as you might have loved Lauren and feared disappointing him, sometimes you had to; the 100 percent commitment he demanded was too onerous for most people to sustain. Cesarani left Lauren because he had a wife and children at home, and the "ungodly" hours were exacting a heavy toll. He remembers it as an excruciating decision: "Lauren never jumped up and down but he would shake his head in disbelief that I would have betrayed him, because he always felt that I was there for him. And I really took enormous amounts of stress to decide what I wanted to do."[8] Even years later, the very memory of leaving Lauren seems to arouse sadness and regret in Cesarani; his voice hung heavily during our interview.

The kind of attachment Cesarani felt—a loyalty so strong that it lingers decades later—is common among protégés of superbosses. Numerous times, I came upon what is akin to a Stockholm syndrome of leadership: employees push themselves to their limits for their superbosses, but rather than resent the superboss for it, they feel even greater loyalty. They'll do anything to keep from disappointing this larger-than-life figure and they yearn to please him, not only because they've completely bought into the boss's vision but also because they want to feel that their boss was correct in selecting them for the job.

Ron Marston, who worked with Tommy Frist for years before becoming CEO of Health Care Corporation of America (HCCA), told me, "You never wanted to let Tommy down. If you did, you were harder on yourself not because of anything he did or said but because you knew you failed to live up to his standards."[9] Joseph Abboud recalls that working for Lauren was "very much like a cult. You wanted to be part of it. Ralph was our hero. We believed the myth; we dressed the myth. We were the legions. It was all-consuming, and you were sucked into it."[10]

Think for a moment how powerful this kind of motivation is. Many companies today measure how engaged or emotionally connected members of their workforce are. In all too many companies, engagement is disappointingly low. For superbosses, engagement is the least of it. They know that to succeed they need the world's best team, which doesn't mean engaged talent; it means energized, supercharged talent. One reason Lauren was able to build his great fortune was because for decades he had people like Cesarani working their hearts out to do the impossible. His people *wanted* to excel and, as a result, they were able to blow past preconceived constraints of what they could do.

If you manage others, imagine what you might accomplish if all or even just a few of your team members felt this internal drive to succeed. And if you're just starting out in your career, think of how satisfying it might be to feel that kind of commitment to your work. Most millennial employees you talk to get this. Survey after survey[11] indicates that they want to feel part of something meaningful. They're not interested in a "job"; they're looking for passion. Regardless of how the over-forty crowd might perceive it, the millennial train has already left the station, so if you want to tap into the most highly educated, mobile-enabled generation ever (and secure the future of your organization), you'd better start thinking about how to bring some of that superboss motivation and inspiration to your own people.

Perfect Is Good Enough

So how do superbosses do it? The first thing to know is that all super-bosses, even the more supportive Nurturers, drive their people exceptionally hard. "Everybody knew that Bill demanded results," said Ronald Blankenship, president and CEO of the Verde Group and longtime associate of Bill Sanders, "and if you were going to work with him, you needed to be prepared to make that the primary focus in your life."[12] Victor Campbell, senior vice president at Hospital Corporation of America, remarked of Tommy Frist: "You were expected to get done what needed to get done and get it done in a timely fashion."[13] Comedian Andy Samberg remembers that after working for Lorne Michaels at *Saturday Night Live*, acting in movies was a "cakewalk." "The pressure doesn't really seem that high. You've dealt with this thing that's *SNL*, which is just this crazy, intense, beautiful pressure cooker."[14]

Superbosses don't want merely strong performance; they expect world-class performance. As one protégé remarked of Larry Ellison, his great strength was "to make exceptional people do the impossible,"[15] accomplished in part by setting the impossible as a clear goal. As Carmen Policy, former president and CEO of the San Francisco 49ers and Cleveland Browns, remembered, "Bill Walsh came to the 49ers with a hunger, a vision, and a strong desire to do more than just 'coach' the team. He wanted to create a dynasty."[16] Bill Sanders wanted his real estate investment company to have the national footprint and reputation of Goldman Sachs, so anything less than extraordinary effort from his staff just wouldn't cut it. "One of the things Sanders taught me," said Don Suter, former managing director at Sanders's Security Capital Group (SCG), who went on to become CEO of M3 Capital Partners, a multibillion-dollar real estate investment and advisory company, "was if you are going to be in the service business, if you are going to have clients or investors, good is not good enough. . . . Perfect is good enough."[17]

What does "perfect" mean, exactly? Suter told me about a time when he had to persuade the CEO of a public company to buy into an important financing deal involving SCG. He had prepared "for three days for this forty-five-minute meeting." He wound up doing a great job—such a great job, in fact, that the CEO agreed right then and there to what Suter was proposing. But Sanders still wasn't happy. After the CEO left, Sanders came into Suter's office and shut the door. "I thought he was going to give me one of those pats on the back." He had nailed the presentation, hadn't he? Instead he got an earful because he had spoken too informally at one point, using the term "you guys" to describe the CEO's company. "Sanders said, 'If you ever use the term "you guys" again in a meeting, I'm sending you back to Kokomo [where Suter is from].' That is Bill's obsession with making sure whatever you do is perfect."[18]

Insisting on perfectionism wasn't a onetime thing for Sanders; it was a constant practice. Constance Moore, a former managing director at SCG, told me that before SCG's 1993 annual meeting, Sanders made it clear he wanted each member of his leadership team to make a presentation before shareholders and the board. Many of these presentations were to be short—as brief as thirty to ninety seconds. Sanders insisted they practice the day before in the same venue at which the meeting would be held. During practice, each executive gave his or her presentation and received a "grade" from Sanders as well as recommendations for improvement. Later that day, each executive presented again. "For a lot of us," Moore said, "it was an 'oh my gosh' moment. We all knew we were proven executives, and here we were back in school, getting a grade for our individual performance. But [Sanders] wanted to make sure that when we got up in front of his board and shareholders, we did a great job. The only way he could do that was to make sure he provided feedback through lots of practice. That is the way it was for years."[19]

For *years*? Didn't Moore and her colleagues ever get to relax and bask in the glory of their accomplishments? In a typical company, people who perform well do get to relax, and they often come to feel a sense of entitlement. They think of themselves as "heroes," and sometimes even believe that their bosses and team are beholden to them. In a superboss-run company, such entitlement doesn't fly. You can never rest on your laurels, because as high as a superboss's expectations are, they're always increasing. Andy Samberg explained that when his *SNL* digital shorts became a success, his first thought wasn't that he was established and could take a breath; it was, "Okay, I might not get fired next year."[20] Chase Coleman, a protégé of hedge-fund billionaire Julian Robertson who eventually built a $9 billion fund of his own, described a time in his career when he had an idea that a particular company's stock would go down, and he made a lot of money for Robertson by persuading him to bet on that outcome. Shortly afterward, Coleman was sitting in his cubicle when Robertson walked by. "I was expecting a big 'high five,' and he just gave me a wink. That was it."[21] That wink was Robertson's way of saying, "Yeah, you did good, but I've already come to expect that of you. Let's see what else you've got."

In setting ever higher expectations, superbosses aren't bound by last year's figures or by a sense of what "normal" performance would be for an employee in a given position. They're certainly not bound by what *employees* conceive as their natural limitations. Superbosses want to see how far people can go. They treat staff like Olympic athletes, pushing them to the limit and beyond. Jay Chiat was "always demanding of everyone to do something better than they very often knew or thought they could or were capable of," Lee Clow, now chairman of TBWA/Media Arts Lab, told me.[22] As Kenny Thomas, former Polo employee and senior vice president for Lucky Brand Dungarees, related, young designers flocked to work with Ralph Lauren because "Ralph was fantastic at giving opportunities to people who didn't even know themselves what they were capable of."[23] Junk bond king Michael Milken summed up well the superboss's general attitude about performance: "Maybe we set our ob-

jectives too low, in school, in our daily lives. We are all capable of performing at a far higher level than we have. Faced with a challenge, we
can do it. Maybe we're not challenging ourselves enough."[24]

Note Milken's use of the inclusive "we." Superbosses credibly push
others into their discomfort zones because they *model* high performance
themselves. As Ronald Blankenship said of Sanders, "He is sort of a
twelve- to fifteen-hour-day kind of guy, and if you are not, you probably
won't end up in senior management."[25] Lorne Michaels typically held
office hours on Wednesday nights—and he held them *all* night. Buffy
Birrittella, one of Ralph Lauren's most long-standing employees, noted
that her boss was "always hungry in the best sense of the word. Ralph
challenges everyone around him to keep sharp and improve things because someone out there is looking to top you—and you have to top
yourself."[26]

You might wonder if superbosses push themselves and others too far.
Although some employees might nod in agreement, superbosses would
strongly disagree. "I don't think I should be criticized for working hard,"
Michael Milken once said. "Some people like to play basketball. Some
like to play golf. I like to work hard."[27] Bonnie Fuller, former editor in
chief at *Marie Claire, Cosmopolitan, Glamour, Us Weekly,* and other
magazines, is well known in the magazine business for her sparkling record of success. Recognized twice by *Advertising Age* magazine as "editor of the year," she doubled *Us Weekly*'s newsstand sales in less than a
year,[28] and then went on to double the subscription base of *Star* magazine.[29] Meanwhile, her protégés have gone on to big jobs of their own,
playing leadership roles at such magazines as *Glamour, Us Weekly, Real
Simple, Seventeen, Maxim,* and *Cargo.* Yet some former employees have
chastised Fuller for her perfectionism and overall intensity, perceiving it
as "rudeness" and "imperiousness."[30] Some of her ex-employees have
been so angry that they went public with their complaints, joining a
now-defunct website called isurvivedbonnie.com. The site, founded in

2003, was for "former and current employees of American Media editor Bonnie Fuller to discuss how they coped and survived her reign of tyranny."[31]

Superbosses don't fear criticism like this, as evidenced by their utter refusal to moderate their standards. If you can't meet a superboss's expectations, he will simply invest less of his energy into pushing you forward. Or he might drop you. As John Griffin told me, Julian Robertson would "cut his losses very quickly if he had hired someone and that person wasn't the person he thought they would be."[32] According to Scot Sellers, chairman and CEO of Archstone, Bill Sanders could "be very tough on people he perceives to not be pulling their weight. . . . You either survive that and move up, or you get washed out."[33] Such "up or out" accountability is surprisingly unusual in many traditional businesses. Bosses tend to let performance slide for extended periods, "getting tough" only when serious problems arise. Superbosses, by contrast, are performance mavens. They eat, breathe, and sleep high performance. There's never a time when they're not driving hard. As a result, it's when they *aren't* challenging you that you need to worry.

The Ladder of Confidence

Isn't all this hard-charging, whip-cracking perfectionism ultimately counterproductive? Doesn't it lead to employee burnout and disenchantment?[34] In many traditional "high-performance" cultures, that is exactly what happens. Investors and boards apply pressure at the top of the organization to boost productivity, and this pressure cascades downward as bosses at each level tighten the screws on their reports. Managers are told they have a number they need to hit. They hit that number, and as a reward, the target goes up the following year. When they hit *that* number, the target goes up even more. The demands just never seem to end, leaving employees feeling as if they were on an endless treadmill. You're punished if you succeed, but you're punished even more if you don't. Add in the pressure to be "always on," thanks to mobile technology, and it's easy to understand why large percentages of employees report that they dislike their jobs—and eventually leave them.[35]

Some employees at superboss-led companies do drop out, but those that remain respond to the constant and continually expanding pressure by developing an even deeper emotional bond with the superboss. That's because even though superbosses keep the pressure up, they also inspire performance, emboldening employees to push themselves up. Superbosses "get" that individuals—even the most driven and talented— accomplish so much more when high expectations come with a message of *possibility*. They understand that people will work their hardest to become bigger, better, tougher, more resourceful, and more creative when they first see themselves as these things. And they sense that it is their paramount job as leaders to inject a strong and unforgettable sense of possibility in their workforce.

One important way superbosses inspire is by instilling self-confidence in their protégés. Again and again, protégés told me that the greatest strength of their superboss was to make staff members believe in themselves. As I unraveled how superbosses did this, I found that they actively modeled self-confidence. The gumption of a Lorne Michaels, who "seemed to have no doubt that *Saturday Night Live* would be a television landmark,"[36] or of a George Lucas, who stuck with *Star Wars* even when people predicted it would fail—this rubs off on people. Protégés notice and feel elevated by it, more aware of their own greatness by virtue of their proximity to the superboss.

Lucas protégé Howard Roffman remembered that when he first took the position of head of licensing at Lucasfilm, *Star Wars* had already lost traction in the market. Roffman's job was to sell people on the film again and get them excited about it. When he met with retailers, licensees, and other industry players, however, he found that they weren't buying it. "Every one of them looked at me like I was crazy," telling him that "*Star Wars* was dead." Roffman feared having to go back to George Lucas with this message in hand—"I thought the 'wrath of God' will come down on me." But Lucas just laughed it off. "[*Star Wars* isn't] dead," he said, "it's just sleeping. Just give it some time. . . . Someday all those people who saw it are going to have their own kids and are going to want to introduce them. We can try to make a comeback then." That ability to sustain confidence in the face of deep industry disbelief made such a profound impression on Roffman that it jumped to mind decades later during our interview.[37]

Coach Bill Walsh's confidence made a similarly powerful impression on former San Francisco 49ers wide receiver Dwight Clark. "There was just an attitude. He walked with a strut almost. He was very confident in what he could do—not cocky, just very confident. When you were around him, you started feeling it, too. . . . He made us confident despite ourselves. He made us believe just by being that way."[38]

Sign Me Up!

Imagine you're relatively new to a company and you attend a planning meeting with your work group. The group leader outlines a problem that the team has been wrestling with. It's not hopeless, but the best solution anyone has come up with so far is mediocre at best.

Then someone leaning on the wall just inside the door asks a question. You turn and recognize the company's founder and CEO. You met him when you were being interviewed, but haven't seen him in several weeks. When no one seems able to answer his question, the company's founder starts talking about the vision he had that led him to start the company. At first, what he's saying hardly seems relevant. It's as if he's reminiscing about an earlier time. But gradually you realize there is a connection. The founder is talking about what the company delivers to its customers. He is describing things the company does that distinguishes it from its competitors. He is explaining how the company has regularly been able to provide new features without large increases in cost. It sounds simple and clear.

You realize the founder has just redefined the problem the group was wrestling with and expanded the options available for dealing with it. All of these new options are going to require more changes than the group had been considering, but what had looked like a problem is now beginning to look like an opportunity for delivering more value. "Wow," the group leader says, articulating the feeling of everyone in the room. "If we can put this together, it's really going to pay off, isn't it?" You can't help smiling and shaking your head in wonder. You are now participating in the kind of pioneering effort that has made the company special since its inception. And you can't wait to get started.

We've heard a lot of talk in recent years about the importance of vision for organizations. Yet vision still tends to get lost at most organizations. At best, people see it as something that managers transmit from the very top of the corporate pyramid, a notion that can be so far removed from everyday work that it seems meaningless. When I work with management teams, even relatively high-performing ones, I ask them about vision, and more often than not they aren't even able to articulate what their organization's vision is. They need to look it up on the company website. Vision becomes mere window dressing rather than what it should be: motivational, compelling, energizing. The idea that every competent boss needs to craft a unique vision for her own team is also nonexistent. And if vision plays such an unimportant role for managers, imagine how employees see it. I have to think that much of the time it barely even enters their consciousness.

Superbosses become talent magnets not only because of their track record as bosses but also because they envision future possibilities in a way that is utterly compelling. Take Lorne Michaels. As longtime NBC executive Dick Ebersol remembered, when *Saturday Night Live* was in the planning stages, "Lorne just took my breath away in the way he talked about things, how he wanted to have the first television show to speak the language of the time."[39] Bill Sanders likewise struck colleagues as someone who could "see around corners." Scot Sellers related that Sanders "would lay out his vision and he would say, 'I would like you to be a part of it.' You were so honored to be asked to be part of this great vision that you just wanted to jump in and say, 'Sign me up!'"[40]

Superbosses' visions are without exception unique, authentic, and consistent. As one of his protégés excitedly related to me, George Lucas "changed the way movies were made with *Star Wars*."[41] Another emphasized that Lucas "was the guy who pioneered digital sound and digital imaging. It was all analog. He started Pixar. . . . He is not afraid to think of the way things might be and how different they will be from the way they are today."[42] Still another, Michael Rubin, the author of *Droidmaker* and a young member of Lucasfilm's Graphics Group in the 1980s, recalled that hearing George Lucas talk about his vision of technology was transformational. "I heard him explain what the future could be like and I was infected with that at age twenty-two. I believed him. And it changed my career."[43]

Superbosses aren't just trying to make money or become famous. They want to have an *impact*; they want to change their industry and even the world. Miles Davis wanted to "reach as many people as I could through my music."[44] Alice Waters wanted to "educate ourselves and the public" about food.[45] Gene Roberts wanted to publish high-quality, hard-hitting stories that would improve society. Such visions make everything on the job more meaningful. It gets employees fired up to think harder, reach higher, and go further.

It helps that superbosses are masters at communicating their visions.

Journalists, protégés, and other observers routinely describe superbosses as outstanding salespeople. As Emmy Award winner and *SNL* writer Tom Schiller said of Lorne Michaels, "He has the power to galvanize people around him who can help him realize his dream."[46] As I discovered, even just *listening* to former superboss employees describe their boss's vision is inspiring. Linda Lewis, former executive at Bill Sanders's Security Capital Group, recalled, "Seeing Bill speak, you wish you could have joined the company last year. You didn't want to wait, there was a train moving and you wanted to be part of it."[47] Remembering his initial encounters with George Lucas, film director and special-effects producer Phil Tippett said, "It wasn't a calculation on any level [for Lucas]. It was like, 'I'm going to do this stuff until somebody shoots me.'"[48] For one of winemaker Robert Mondavi's many disciples, working for his superboss seemed akin to what employees of a company like Google might say today: "You felt you were on the zeitgeist of a new era in which an exciting, groundbreaking business was being born. . . . Robert Mondavi was truly the fuel behind that fire."[49]

Superbosses take for granted that employees buy into their visions. As a result, they don't need to constantly monitor their employees to make sure they're putting out their best—alignment with the vision does that naturally. Many employees I spoke with reported being utterly riveted to their work, so much so that almost nothing could tear them away. Joyce Goldstein, the James Beard Award–winning chef at Chez Panisse in the early 1980s, remembers that she was "there from five in the morning till six at night. I worked six days a week. I inventoried on Sunday and I did the ordering for both restaurants [the formal dining room and the café]. But I was in love with food. I discovered that I loved the business and I never watched the clock."[50] Employees of superbosses never watch the clock, and they're not in it for the fame, the glory, or the money. They're in it because they see what the superboss sees. And it's irresistible.

It's Hard to Go Back to Being Ordinary

Superbosses are geniuses at motivation. Unlike some bosses, they don't want 80 percent of the attention and dedication of their people. They want 100 percent. And they *get* 100 percent. But not by waving big bonuses in front of their people. As we saw in chapter 2, many protégés eagerly accept jobs with superbosses even though they often pay less. Don Suter remembers that when a member of Security Capital Group achieved something great, Bill Sanders would come by his or her cubicle to offer congratulations. He'd tell them how important their contribution was to the firm and how grateful he was to know that they were doing a good job. That, Suter said, meant more to the people he hired than an extra $10,000 in bonus at the end of the year, because being singled out by Sanders said it all: you were making a difference.

In a capitalist society, money is a perfectly fine thing to strive for, and many superbosses and their protégés do become very, very wealthy. In Robertson's case, almost all of his people have become multimillionaires, some even billionaires.[51] But money doesn't fully motivate most people. By contrast, people know when they're working for a special boss—someone who is changing the rules, is unafraid to take risks, deeply cares about achieving a higher objective, and invites employees to be a part of it. When a boss like *that* is giving orders or, as is more often the case, pushing and inspiring you in a powerful way, you don't perceive the pressure to perform as tedious or unwelcome. You perceive it as part of a gigantic, unbelievably important and exciting mission.[52] You thrive on this pressure. And, just like your boss, you lose yourself in the mission.

It is the superboss's combination of big-time expectations and aspirations, then, that enables the exceptional people under their wings to do impossible things. An upward spiral of performance takes root among protégés of superbosses: as they become accustomed to surviving and thriving in an intense environment, their ambitions only increase. They become so addicted to success that they seek out ever more challenging assignments. And they feel so great upon meeting or exceeding the superboss's expectations that they want to do it again and again. They yearn to be *even closer* to the superboss, his inspiration, his energy, and they will do whatever it takes to stay in his orbit. It's a cyclone of pressure, success, acknowledgment, rising confidence, and even more success that makes the protégé, the superboss, and the superboss's organization utterly unstoppable. An employee of Jay Chiat summed it up well: "He left something in people that makes it hard for you to go back to being ordinary. Once you feel it, you can't change it."[53]

Inspiring People like a Superboss

Understanding how superbosses motivate and inspire people can give you a framework for understanding your own boss a little better. Perhaps you have an extremely demanding boss—one who is working all hours of the day or night or who assigns you gargantuan tasks—and yet you find, strangely, that you don't mind all that much. Your boss might just be a superboss or share some superboss characteristics. Or maybe you've just started a new job and your boss suddenly piles on an incredible amount of work and sets crushing performance goals. Is he a superboss who will change your life or just another drill-sergeant boss who will burn you out? You can find out by asking yourself a few quick questions: Does your boss articulate a vision for why you, your team, and your organization are doing what you're doing? Is that vision energizing, exciting, and important? Is it clear how you fit in? If the answer to these questions is yes, then you just might be in for a life-changing experience. If it's no, then you might find yourself on a soul-deadening performance treadmill.

If you're a boss focused on getting superior performance from your team and you're struggling, maybe it's time to stop doing what doesn't work and start doing something new. Cracking the whip does not a leadership philosophy make. At some point, if you don't instill a sense of possibility in your people, the engine will grind to a halt. Regardless of your position in an organization, you've got to craft a vision to energize your team and spend lots of time effectively communicating it. Vision is not just for CEOs. As an exercise, try performing a quick audit of how you're spending each day. If your schedule is filled with meetings, how much time do you actually spend doing what superbosses do—asking opinions, affirming abilities, establishing employees' status as members of an A team, alerting them to the underlying purpose behind shorter-term priorities and objectives, and so on? If you're already pushing people to their limits and you can't push any harder, you might find that spending more time on the "softer stuff" of meaning, purpose, vision, and identity will result in even greater performance. Inspiring others is not an incidental activity for superbosses. Rather, it's at the core of what they do.

In many organizations, the "why" of work gets lost as teams focus on hard, financial performance metrics. Employees forget why they need to sell a thousand more service contracts, for instance, or extract $486 per customer interaction as opposed to $483. Getting those extra contracts or dollars might be a big deal—if it's linked to the fundamental purpose of the team and organization. If you find yourself thinking less and less about the fundamental purpose, chances are your employees are, too. Ask yourself these crazy questions: Why does your organization exist? Why does your team exist? Can you communicate it succinctly and in a way that really hits home? Can you connect it to specific items on your agenda for this year, this quarter, this month?

Any company can get energized around a purpose. Any department within a company, too. An internally focused, process-oriented department like accounting may seem especially far removed from lofty ambitions. Can managers really frame an inspiring vision for this department?

Of course! A business needs to get its numbers right. Financial filings must be accurate and professionals doing the work must follow appropriate procedures. If an accounting team isn't doing its job and mistakes happen, the whole company might be at risk, and with it, the larger purpose it serves. The accounting team *is* linked to the organization's calling. It contributes vitally to work that affects people's lives. If you are a superboss-style manager or leader, your role is to explain this to your accountants, underscoring how each of their specific jobs factors in and how they might innovate to do their job even better. Maybe there's an early-warning system that could be deployed to catch mistakes. Or new procedures for interacting with others during audits. Whatever the case, the time to get your people fired up about what they do is *now*.

If you want to slack off and bide your time, then a job with a superboss is not for you. But if you're willing to attack your job as if nothing else matters, then you'll find having a superboss as a boss is truly invigorating. I know, because as a graduate student at Columbia University, I worked for a superboss myself. My supervising professor, Don Hambrick, gave rise to a generation of scholars in my field and he lived almost all of the behaviors described in this book. Nobody worked harder than Don— and that's probably still true today, thirty years later. He had a quiet confidence that was infectious. He also had a vision for our research that transcended any other project or study I might have been doing. He wasn't afraid to boost my confidence and tell me he believed in me. And you know what? I internalized his words of support because I could tell he was speaking from the heart—that what he said was genuine and not just lip service to get me to work harder.

This suggests one additional lesson about performance we can learn from superbosses. Don't just evoke possibilities for your people because you think it might result in an extra market-share point or an extra percentage increase in revenue. Do it because you really feel passionate about your people and your mission. In everything superbosses say and do around their protégés, they are authentic. They're not reading from a script or playacting. They're not framing a vision because they think they should, "checking the box" and moving on to something else. Super-bosses know such machinations only backfire, as most people are smart enough to recognize a fake when they meet one.

Remember Sal Cesarani, Ralph Lauren's right-hand man during the early 1970s? Thirty years later, he remains utterly taken with his boss, seeing him as head and shoulders above any other fashion icon. Other former protégés agree. A former Polo executive has remarked, "The thing that set Ralph apart was his single-mindedness of purpose. Everybody else moved from place to place, from trend to trend. He wasn't trendy. . . . It's the single most important thing about him."[54] That single-minded purpose came from deep inside Lauren, as it does with every superboss. His people sensed this. They knew what he said and did counted. They knew he had a special mission to fulfill, and he'd chosen them from among many qualified candidates to help him. And they rose to the oc-casion.

Lauren didn't merely inspire his people to perform exceptionally well. He also got them to break new ground in fashion, to do things that no-body else in the business was doing. He got them to work *creatively,* to take risks, to inject their own talents and insights into their work. Most organizations today are looking for ways to foster creativity, and many, sadly, are coming up short. Without exception, the superbosses I studied had cracked the code. And as we'll see in the next chapter, it all comes down to their masterful and, at first glance, puzzling way of giving up control over their employees' work, and at the same time asserting it more uncompromisingly than anyone.

CHAPTER FOUR

Uncompromisingly Open

If you're a movie buff of a certain age, you may remember the historic 1956 film *Forbidden Planet*. An early big-budget science-fiction production, *Forbidden Planet* was the first film that took place entirely away from planet Earth, the first to feature a robot as a humanlike character, the first to depict travel via starship, and the first to feature a musical score composed entirely of electronic instruments.[1]

Audiences today would laugh at the movie's primitive production values. However, in 1956, one eight-year-old boy was so gripped by *Forbidden Planet* that he felt as if he really had been transported to an alien world: "I can remember being in the theater, wishing that it would be over so I could get back to Earth. At the end of the movie, when they finally do start the voyage home, I was greatly relieved, because I was kind of terrified to be on this planet the whole time."[2] The electronic soundtrack in particular blew him away, sounding like both special effects and music at the same time.

That boy was Ben Burtt, who in 1977 was offered a chance to work on another pathbreaking science-fiction film called *Star Wars*. A graduate of the University of Southern California's film production program, Burtt jumped at the opportunity; "I realized, here's a film I've sort of wanted to do all my life."[3] Yet the film's creator, George Lucas, gave him a difficult assignment. In Lucas's vision of filmmaking, sound figured prominently; it had to be fresh and original, customized to the demands of the film. You couldn't just borrow sounds from a studio library and hope they would suffice. Up until this time, science-fiction movies had featured electronic sounds, like the ones in *Forbidden Planet*. By the 1970s, filmgoers had come to perceive those sounds as dated and corny. Lucas asked Burtt to take a new approach: rather than start with tones produced by synthesizers, could he collect recordings from the real world as raw material and then modify them in the studio?[4]

Burtt did exactly that. He recorded kitchen appliances, freeway traffic, wild bears, and the sound of breathing in scuba equipment.[5] As he soon realized, different actions and characters in *Star Wars* posed different challenges. The greatest challenge of all was developing sounds for the charismatic robot R2D2: "R2D2 is a character and he beeps and moves and he doesn't speak English," Burtt told me. "But you have to understand what he is meaning. Yet the script said R2 didn't say anything; he just made electronic noises."[6] Burtt had to figure out what those noises were, and he had to get George Lucas to say yes to his ideas.

As Burtt knew, Lucas had a general sense of what he wanted for the R2D2 character. The sounds had to be "organic," not too robotic, and they had to express a humanlike personality. Beyond that, Lucas didn't specify what he wanted for R2D2; Burtt would have to come to him with different possibilities and Lucas would see if they worked. Burtt began by experimenting with different types of sound, seeing which ones seemed promising and which didn't. When he came up with noises he thought might work as part of R2D2's "language," he invited Lucas to hear them. Lucas rejected many of Burtt's early sounds on the grounds that they weren't "organic" enough.[7] Eventually it became clear that the best noises were ones they initially vocalized themselves and then mixed with synthesized sound. "And you end up with two boys making sound effects together. Something like you would get thrown out of third grade if you did it."[8]

In other ways, though, the imagination behind R2D2 was quite different from casual third-grade antics. As fun as Burtt's work ultimately was, there was never any question about who was in charge. Whether it was for R2D2 or any other part of *Star Wars*, George Lucas knew what he wanted and never hesitated to say no. Burtt remembers that Lucas never spent much time explaining himself: "He would just tell you what he thought. He might not give you a lot of details, but he would say, 'I don't like this—is there something else?' You got used to that." At the same time—and this is a key point—unlike other top producers, Lucas expected his people to put forward well-crafted, "semi-complete" ideas of their own. "I just had the freedom and I could just put an idea together and present it to him. Then he could pick through it and take out what he doesn't like, and be inspired and add his own ideas to it. . . . I had a chance to crystallize my own ideas about something and then see if they would work."[9]

Apparently, they did. Burtt's pioneering work in modern sound design led to four Academy Awards, including two for the Indiana Jones films with George Lucas.[10] He also created the voice for *E.T. the Extra Terrestrial* (allegedly pirating a recording of his wife sleeping in bed with a cold for the lead character)[11] and the leading man—robot—in Pixar's *Wall-E*.[12]

In every industry I investigated, I found superboss protégés every bit as innovative and accomplished as Burtt. These talented people were helping re-create how a restaurant chain can serve its customers, reinvent how universities invested their endowments, reimagine what a comic book could be, and, yes, revolutionize the science-fiction film. This was no surprise; as we've seen, superbosses make a point of seeking out the most unusual and creative talent available. But I wondered, once superbosses had talent like Burtt on board, how did they not only motivate them to perform but also unleash their potential for innovation to the fullest?

The answer lay in a wonderful paradox all superbosses possess—one illustrated by Lucas's distinct way of working. On one hand, superbosses have a clear, uncompromising vision of what a project, a company, or even an entire industry could be, and they drive their people hard to help realize these dreams. At the same time, superbosses encourage their people to *rethink virtually everything else* about their jobs. In fact, they expect such rethinking and view it as a core job responsibility. Burtt wasn't asked to mindlessly follow Lucas's vision in coming up with R2D2's voice; he had wide latitude to generate his own, original solution, as long as he remained within the broader confines of Lucas's vision. Superbosses want to be surprised and delighted by what their protégés do. They push people to seek out new opportunities and, if necessary, to change direction at a moment's notice. It is this strange, seemingly impossible blend of unshakable vision and openness to change that allows superbosses to unleash a torrent of new ideas among their people, and in the process, drive their own extraordinary business success.

Protect the "Why" (and Only the "Why")

How can superbosses move in such a seemingly contradictory way? In a few (exceedingly rare) workplaces, you may find laissez-faire bosses who are open to anything their employees may care to try. In most workplaces, though, you'll find the exact opposite: bosses who are not at all amenable to new ideas. They may talk about innovation and the necessity of adaptation, but they really only want employees to do their jobs the way they were told to do them—with clear rules, instructions, boundaries, goals, and no excuses. At best, most bosses implicitly relegate innovation to second place behind the imperative to just get the work done. Rather than weaving innovation into the fabric of daily work, they contain and limit it by setting up special task forces, committees, and project teams devoted to adaptation and change. They "carve out" time for innovation rather than living and breathing it every minute. It is particularly difficult to find bosses who are uncompromising in what they do *and* open to almost constant change.

Superbosses are able to operate in this way because, as we've seen, they themselves are innovators to the core. Their visions aren't recipes for inertia or minor amplifications of the status quo. They break with industry norms, in some cases so fundamentally that they wind up defining entirely new industries. When superbosses hire employees, they implicitly invite them to buy into their vision and become part of the revolution. But they also invite them to buy into the mind-set of openness and innovation that made their vision possible in the first place. Superbosses expect everyone else to be visionaries like they are. For them, innovation and uncompromising vision aren't necessarily incompatible choices. On the contrary, they're inextricably linked.

The combination of clarity of vision and constant innovation enables superboss-run businesses to sustain innovation over extended periods. Employees cannot innovate in meaningful ways unless they have a frame within which to work—and the superboss's fundamental vision provides precisely that grounding. Consequently, employees are liberated to move around and innovate the specific mechanisms, processes, methods, and policies they use in their own positions. Superbosses are astoundingly successful because they willingly and eagerly change anything and everything, so long as it doesn't contradict or dilute their inherently innovative vision.

In many companies, you see a sharp divide between senior managers who focus on "strategy," and mid- or low-level managers who are supposed to focus on "execution." The strategists (the thinkers) are expected to be inventive, while the much larger mass of executors (the doers) are supposed to follow orders. Superbosses will have none of this. Everyone at every level is expected to think, whether they're crafting a three-year corporate plan or coordinating logistics for next week's sales operations. To a talent spawner, even the smallest executional tasks can be opportunities for doing something a little bit better, or even a *lot* better. Everybody in the organization experiences the fulfillment and responsibility of moving the company toward a more profitable, vibrant future. And as we'll see in chapter 6, superbosses likewise will not hesitate at times to get their hands dirty and immerse themselves in the details of daily work. They keep their vision current and vital by bringing it in touch with on-the-job realities.

Alice Waters's restaurant Chez Panisse perfectly illustrates the superboss's merging of strategy with execution. When Alice Waters opened Chez Panisse in 1971, she was determined to replicate the respect for fresh, local food that had so impressed her during a stay in France. Having grown up on a typical American diet, she was transformed by what she had experienced—her eyes were opened by farmers' markets where growers could describe the provenance of every last lettuce, leek, and aubergine; where chefs from small neighborhood bistros arrived early to snap up the best peas and cauliflower that would adorn their dishes that night; and where housewives lined up to buy the entrecôte from Limousin, the fish from Brittany, and the Cantal from Auvergne that they would serve for dinner, perhaps with a nice glass of Sancerre or Burgundy. Waters also wanted to spread the distinctly French habit of making time to sit with others and enjoy a good meal. This clear vision led her to do many things that were unheard of in restaurants at the time. Whereas most restaurant owners purchased from wholesalers, Waters and her staff did the painstaking work of seeking out the best small farmers and purchasing directly from them. Rather than adopt a fixed menu, she created a new menu each day to reflect the local ingredients she was able to procure at their peak of freshness. "Although it would seem to be one of the most natural ways to cook and plan menus," her protégée Seen Lippert told me, "it was (and still is) unknown to many people."[13]

An ordinary chef will create a menu with an eye toward the cost of raw ingredients, but not Waters. "If she wanted a certain ingredient— truffles, say—she declined to notice the price," one observer has written. "Shaver in hand, she would stroll through the dining room snowing truffles left and right, no charge, 'just to see the delight on their faces.'"[14] In an interview, Waters confessed that she always thought of herself as unrelenting in her standards, at the expense of business concerns. "I always think of myself as uncompromising. . . . I guess really better to say idealistic . . . but I just am completely focused on the quality of the food."[15]

You would think a boss like Waters who took food *so* seriously would leave little room for employees to innovate, but that was not the case. Star Chez Panisse pastry chef Lindsey Shere observed that Waters "always listened to a lot of people, and she brought a lot of people in who gave her ideas . . . but she was the person who was able to synthesize it all and turn it into something that everyone could understand and appreciate."[16] Joanne Weir referred to her as "the conceptualist of the restaurant."[17] Waters operated in a way similar to how George Lucas worked with Ben Burtt; she would leave her team more or less on their own but would pop in to inspect and adjust their work, collaborating on solutions as necessary. Seen Lippert related that Waters was not someone who liked to boss people around: "What she does very well is . . . she can 'edit.' She would always be walking through the kitchen just when you were struggling. Sure enough, she'd look down at the worktable and zero in on exactly what was troubling or just 'off.' She would describe how she wants it to feel or something a bit more esoteric. But it pushed you in the right direction"[18]

Lippert further related that in meetings, Waters was never the only one talking; she almost always solicited employees' opinions and wasn't upset when they ran contrary to hers. As a result, ideas were free to develop quickly. Waters herself stresses openness, flexibility, and collaboration as central to her philosophy. People who didn't want to collaborate with her or others "shouldn't be working at Chez Panisse" she told me. "I think of myself as needing and wanting that kind of collaboration and that we're trying to make something really greater than the sum of its parts."[19] In Waters's mind, her restaurant contained all the complex teamwork (and beauty) of a symphony orchestra. "You have to have great musicians, and you have to inspire them, but they are the ones that make that music."[20]

For managers running organizations of any size, the superboss's practice of being uncompromisingly open casts light on the classic problem of how far or intensely to pursue innovation. Most bosses understand the need to innovate, but they fear that too much innovation will bring an organization too far from its roots and main competencies. What should you change and what should you keep the same? Where do you draw the line? Superbosses suggest a very clear solution to this problem: protect the "why" of your business, but be prepared to constantly improve everything about the "how" of your business as if your life depended on it. Because, as superbosses will tell you, it does.

Nothing Is Sacred

Innovation is in the DNA of superbosses. But when you look closer at what these master innovators actually do, a clear pattern emerges from which every leader, every manager, and every employee can learn. There are three distinct kinds of action superbosses take to nurture openness and innovation in their people. First, superbosses encourage constant risk taking and rule breaking. Kyle Craig, former chairman and CEO of

Steak and Ale, remembered that his superboss Norman Brinker "would challenge you. He would say: 'What do you think you could do there? What is working? Go try something. . . .' It was very empowering because it gave you a license to say, 'We *can* do some things differently!'"[21]

Even more powerful than their words are the examples superbosses set. The superbosses I studied are celebrated among their protégés for their willingness to overturn established practices and challenge their own assumptions. Bill Walsh's West Coast offense, for instance, arose as a midseason response to a losing streak. In 1970, Walsh was working as an assistant coach for the Cincinnati Bengals under Paul Brown. The Bengals' offense had been struggling without star quarterback Greg Cook, whose career had abruptly ended the previous season due to injury. In Walsh's estimation, Cook was "probably the greatest prospect the game had ever seen"[22]—a bigger, taller version of Hall of Famers Joe Montana and Steve Young combined. Walsh's offense with Cook was a deep passing game, which set an NFL record that still stands today for yards per completion for a rookie.[23] However, without Cook's talents, the vertical passing game Walsh favored was ineffective, and the Bengals had lost six straight games before turning to backup quarterback Virgil Carter.

While Carter was not blessed with Cook's arm, he possessed mobility, accuracy, and intelligence—three traits that would come to define the typical Walsh (and West Coast) quarterback. To take advantage of these traits, Walsh replaced his vertical offense with a timing-based horizontal offense, which focused on making accurate throws within ten yards of the line of scrimmage. Most of all, the offense was designed to highlight Carter's strengths and hide his weaknesses.[24]

Walsh's new offense not only changed football history, it changed the Bengals' fortune midseason. Cincinnati went on to win seven games in a row and capture the team's first division title. However, despite the success, the offense was nowhere near as dangerous as it needed to be in order to dominate, forcing Walsh to further refine his scheme. Walsh recalled that Brown came in one day asking for more "swish and sway"— meaning more motion in the offense, more creativity. Walsh explained, "Despite having some talented players, at the time our offense ranked somewhere in the middle of the league and wasn't scaring many teams. So I put more man-in-motion plays in our playbook."[25] It was this efficient passing game (often run with man-in-motion offense) that would bring Walsh acclaim as a head coach, first at Stanford and later in the NFL. With swish and sway, the other teams *were* scared—and Walsh's teams became virtually unbeatable.

In some cases, intuitive, spur-of-the-moment adjustments wind up defining the look and feel of superbosses' businesses. Norman Brinker's first restaurant venture, a Dallas coffee shop called Brink's, sought to offer high quality at a low cost, but the average check size was too low to make the business profitable. During the summer of 1965, a few years after opening Brink's, Brinker and his business partners put together a plan for what was then a new kind of restaurant: a casual dining establishment somewhere between fast food and fine dining. Because check sizes were usually higher at dinnertime, this new restaurant would be in a position to outperform Brink's.[26] As part of this concept, Brinker inadvertently came up with two features that would soon take root across the country. The first was the now much-lampooned phrase: "Hi, my name is . . . and I'll be your waiter tonight," an idea that sprang from Brinker's view that a casual restaurant should offer a friendly atmosphere. The second was the salad bar, which until then was only featured in low-end cafeterias.

Brinker initially intended this restaurant to be a Mediterranean-style eatery. But one night after construction had already begun, he happened to see the 1963 British adventure-comedy *Tom Jones*. In one of the movie's funniest and most famous scenes,[27] Tom Jones sits down with Mrs. Waters (no, we're not talking about Alice Waters here) in an eighteenth-century English tavern as the two wordlessly consume a voluptuous dinner, expressing sexual desire through the biting of fowl off the bone, the slurping of oysters, and the indulgent munching of juicy pears. Brinker awoke the next morning buzzing with an epiphany: He would scrap the Mediterranean idea and transform the restaurant into an Old English concept.[28] Steak and Ale, as the restaurant would be called, would have the kind of bold and funny atmosphere Brinker had loved in the movie— complete with a young and attractive waitstaff that could pull off the frilly bodices and knee breeches of the costumes he had in mind.

To find this staff, Brinker improvised, turning to a source of talent that had barely been tapped by the restaurant industry: college students. It seems obvious in retrospect—college students would be friendly, not too expensive, and the epitome of "casual." Brinker drove to the campus of Southern Methodist University looking to hire. Brinker knocked on the door of a fraternity house to announce he was hiring students—for tips only, but they could set their own work hours to accommodate their class schedules. Brinker: "The next day, forty or fifty students showed up for interviews. It was wonderful."[29]

Steak and Ale launched in 1966, and was a rousing success. The chain expanded rapidly and went public in 1971. In 1976, when Steak and Ale was acquired by the Pillsbury Company, it boasted more than a hundred locations. Brinker's constant risk taking and rule breaking would continue later as he led Brinker International, a multibillion-dollar company with chains like Romano's Macaroni Grill, On the Border Mexican Grill & Cantina, Maggiano's Little Italy, Corner Bakery Cafe, Big Bowl Asian Kitchen, and Rockfish Seafood Grill. As his protégés remember, Brinker drove success by constantly adapting to shifting consumer trends. "Norman would always say to you that the trick is to be riding the wave." Former Steak and Ale COO and Burger King CEO Lou Neeb explains, "Not in front of the wave to be crushed or in back of it, where you get left behind. The thing you always believed with Norman was that he understood the way the industry was and where it was going."[30]

Brinker was also known to say, "Nothing is sacred, other than that the guest returns."[31] Of course, one thing *was* sacred: his vision, the casual restaurant concept itself. But within that context, agility and reasonable risk reigned. As one protégé recalled, you were expected to take risks and "as a matter of fact, you got yourself into more trouble with Norman if you weren't doing anything differently."[32] For most superbosses, risk taking alone isn't enough: employees are expected to take risks *proactively*. Have you ever heard an executive say that he wishes his team would just take initiative when someone has an idea? "Why are they always asking for permission?" he wonders. Often, people know just what the answer is to that question: they're better off checking in first because the executive probably isn't as open-minded as he thinks. Superbosses blow right through this dance. Adelaide Horton, a protégée of Jay Chiat and former chief operating officer at Chiat/Day, remembers that at the agency "doers were rewarded and anything was possible. If you came to Jay with an idea for how things could be done better, he would say, 'Go ahead and do it.'"[33]

Safe Spaces

The second way superbosses nurture openness is by removing anxieties that get in the way of people doing new things. If you analyze why individuals in your workplace just don't seem to come up with anything new, I bet you'll find that fear of failure plays an outsize role. This isn't such an irrational fear, either; in many companies, failure is a dirty word. Mess up and you get labeled as unreliable, incompetent, or worse. Superbosses, of course, don't think about failure the way most people do. Rather, they are masters at reframing failure as an opportunity in disguise. By implication, they don't *fear* failure but instead view it as just a step you sometimes end up taking on the way to success.

Scott Ross, a digital media executive who worked with both George Lucas and Miles Davis, told me, "These guys had no fear. Maybe in the middle of the night, they'd be afraid, but when I would see them they acted like they were twenty years old. They were constantly prepared to walk into battle and get shot at."[34] Kyle Craig, who worked with Norman Brinker at Burger King in the 1980s, remembered the superboss openly acknowledging his failure with Brink's coffee shop. "He was never unwilling to admit his failures and mistakes, which puts people around him very much at ease."[35]

Superbosses also blast away at fear by creating work environments where creativity and innovation can thrive. According to Steve Alburty, Jay Chiat's ad shop was "the most unique work experience of our lives because there was such a sense of creativity and personal freedom."[36] Legendary film producer Roger Corman was known for letting his actors do their own thing when they were in front of the camera. Recalling Corman's logic, one actor mused, "I don't recall him ever telling me how a line should be read or telling actors I was working with what our motivation was."[37] Without a boss breathing down their necks at every turn, employees felt as if they had implicit permission to take chances and express themselves in their work. Their superboss *trusted* them—and that's precisely why he hired them. Compare that to many offices today, where employees send emails to colleagues at all hours of the day and night because they "don't feel confident to make a decision on their own."[38]

Another way superbosses help protégés overcome any reluctance to innovate is by creating new opportunities for them to contribute. Hedge-fund impresario Julian Robertson would sit in the middle of his company's large workroom and loudly debate ideas his analysts presented. Not every analyst who volunteered an idea got a pat on the back; when

Robertson thought an idea was dumb, he would say so. Sometimes he grew angry and confrontational, but not unproductively so. "People didn't take it personally, because they saw everyone going through the process. . . . [He would say things like:] 'You say this company has got some great product, and I just called so-and-so and he said the product is just terrible.'"[39] Employees understood that unfettered debate was simply Robertson's style, that he deeply appreciated new ideas, and that they didn't need to fear pushback from him. Robertson's office became what so many offices today aren't: a safe space for fresh thinking and experimentation.

The Show Must Change

A third way superbosses nurture openness and innovation is by encouraging their employees or associates to never, ever rest on their laurels. "To be and stay a great musician," Miles Davis used to teach, "you've got to always be open to what's new, what's happening at the moment. You have to be able to absorb it if you're going to continue to grow and communicate your music."[40] Time and again I found that superbosses were consummate cool hunters—always on the prowl for the next great product idea, the next great trend, the next great person to hire. Speaking of *Saturday Night Live,* comedian and *SNL* alum Conan O'Brien once said: "You always get the sense that the show is almost like a shark that's constantly on a mission to find what's new, what's hot, what are people into now? And chomp its teeth into it."[41] Lorne Michaels affirmed this observation in an interview, noting that constant change and a future-oriented outlook were perpetual features of running the show: "The show must change. I know it's supposed to be 'must go on,' but 'must change' is important also."[42]

The image of a shark always on the hunt is apt for every superboss I studied. They all had an inexhaustible drive to improve, in part a reflection of competitive pressures. As Waters told me, she perceives the constant need to change as "just kind of a compulsion, an obsession, and I don't know where it comes from. It's just pushing me."[43] David Murphy, who worked for Jay Chiat from 1975 to 1980, noted, "Jay's middle name was innovation. He had a singular vision that it was totally acceptable to risk; playing it safe was just not acceptable."[44]

If superbosses fear anything, it isn't that they'll go off the deep end with their innovations, but that they'll *stop* innovating and get old and complacent. As confidant Sal Cesarani remarked of Ralph Lauren, "I will tell you that Ralph doesn't ever want to be the older guy. . . . Cary Grant was great but when Cary Grant got older, what kind of parts do we put Cary Grant in? Do we put him in as a grandfather? It's not going to work. . . . Ralph is not going to do film but what Ralph could do next, no one knows. He will think of the next thing."[45]

Take any superboss, and you'll find that he is responsible for numerous innovations that belie a restless curiosity and passion for novelty and growth. The renowned television producer Roone Arledge revolutionized sports broadcasting during the first few years of his career by introducing experiments like instant replay, field-level sound (traditionally, sports broadcasts didn't include the down-and-dirty sounds of the game), game-time interviews, slow motion, graphics showing statistics, cameras mounted in race cars, and more. A closer look at the development of instant replay offers a glimpse of the shark mentality at work. As Arledge described in an interview with *Playboy* magazine, he and ABC engineer Bob Trachinger went to have a few beers one day, and Arledge took the opportunity to ask Trachinger "if it would be possible to replay something in slow motion so you could tell if a guy was safe or stepped out of bounds."[46] Trachinger jotted down on napkins how slow motion might work. "We talked and sketched and drank beer that whole afternoon and when we were finished, we had the plans for the first instant-replay device."[47] For a superboss, having a few beers with a colleague isn't just a nice social encounter—it's a chance to map out the next industry-shaping innovation.

A superboss's cool hunting can take any number of forms. Norman Brinker was so good at anticipating emerging restaurant industry trends because he was constantly probing the minds of consumers. Not content to peruse the usual market research reports, Brinker would spend hours in his restaurants, talking to customers and staff, developing a reputation in the industry for his approachability and willingness to learn.[48] He often posed as a confused tourist outside his restaurants and asked departing customers about their dining experience. He also did competitive research by pretending to be a manager in competitors' restaurants, asking customers what they thought of the food and service.[49] Even into his twilight years, when he was riddled with health issues, Brinker continued to ask unsuspecting guests what they *really* thought of their dining experience, all so that he could stay one step ahead. "You've really got to stay tuned in," he once said, "because the customer is changing all the time."[50]

I had a chance to see such sharklike behavior with my own eyes when J. Crew CEO Mickey Drexler came to speak to MBA students at Dartmouth College's Tuck School of Business. Some executives content themselves with politely answering questions, but Drexler used the occasion to run an informal focus group. He actively worked the room, squeezing any piece of potentially usable insight out of students (who, after all, were in J. Crew's target demographic). "How do you like your Ludlow jacket?" he inquired of a student wearing J. Crew merchandise. "Where did you buy it? Do you find it matches well with our chinos? How many of your friends have Ludlows?" Then he turned to the entire group. "Okay, class, how many of the guys here have Ludlow coats? Come on, how many?" This continued throughout the day Drexler spent with us. When students weren't sure how to answer a question, he handed them his business card and asked them to email him with an answer. Every minute was a chance to learn something new that would help him push his business forward.

As you might expect, leaders like Drexler are so concerned with what's next that they have little nostalgia for what already exists. Eivind Aadland, chief conductor and artistic leader of the Trondheim Symphony Orchestra, told me that his superboss, Jorma Panula, was "very, very free from tradition and from history. If he finds a simple, good solution to a problem, he will not be interested in what the traditional way of doing it is."[51] In Aadland's view, it was this attitude, sustained over time, that enabled Panula to teach his students that the conductor's role must change from "the dictator of the old days" to "a fellow musician with the orchestra."[52] This refusal to bind oneself to the past applies just as strongly to the superboss's own accomplishments. When one of Roger Corman's assistants happened upon a historic review of one of his films, Corman read it and then promptly found a suitable place for it—the trash.[53] As film director Joe Dante put it, "I don't think Corman thinks backward at all. I think he thinks forward."[54]

Superbosses' nonstop cool hunting doesn't just inspire protégés to become more open-minded; it infuses them with sizzling energy that they find exhausting, exhilarating, and impossible to resist. Of his time working with Brinker, former Burger King chairman and CEO Lou Neeb reflects, "It is hard to put in words the feeling and emotion and intensity that you sense . . . but when you are there at the time, it just makes absolute sense."[55] Sid Ganis, a Lucasfilm alum, told me that the environment there "buzzed from the day I started until the day I left six and a half years later. It never stopped buzzing. It was great every single, solitary day."[56]

Employees of superbosses get swept up in a whirlwind of constant innovation, and in many cases their internalization of the superboss's omnipresent drive to grow leads them to ultimately leave the superboss and pursue their own visions. For what they teach—most powerfully by doing—is less a perspective on business than a perspective on life. They teach protégés to take what exists and bravely go not one, not two, but many steps beyond. And they teach them to do this obsessively. They energize people around them to inject creativity into their work each and every day. The result is not merely great wealth and influence for the superboss; it's a lifetime of career success for those lucky enough to become his protégés.

Fostering Creativity like a Superboss

Superbosses begin by hiring unusual talent, people who are often more intellectually gifted than their peers and also simply *different*. They unleash this talent by inspiring them with a vision, fueling their motivation, pushing them to the limit while giving them the confidence to excel. But if that weren't enough, superbosses go one crucial step further. They tell their people, "Okay, now you're expected to rethink everything. Go change the world!" And guess what? Their people *do* change the world.

What superbosses have to offer us, then, is nothing less than a formula for creating dynamic organizations—companies that never stop changing, that adapt constantly to new circumstances, that plunge headlong into the future. Managers and business academics alike have long pondered how leaders can help create such organizations. In his seminal book *Leading Change,* Harvard Business School's John Kotter argued that leaders who seek to change their organizations need to create a sense of urgency among their people. Change is hard, so you need to create what Kotter called a "burning platform" on which to build change initiatives. The implication of this entire model is that change can happen only when an organization is in a really bad place—when a market or an industry has already evolved and a company is so woefully out of touch that immediate change has become necessary.[57]

Kotter's model has much to recommend it. But superbosses, with their practice of remaining uncompromisingly open, present us with an alternative that opens an entirely new way of thinking about change. The organizations superbosses create are so continually adaptive and inventive that they are in effect "built to change" (a phrase adapted from business researcher Jim Collins's bestselling book *Built to Last*). Superbosses never get to the crisis point envisioned by Kotter because they are constantly growing and evolving in an organic way. They *lead* the change in their industry, leaving it to executives in other companies to follow and feel a sense of crisis when they lag too far behind. Isn't such a proactive stance better? Why would a person want to wait until he is on his deathbed before starting to eat right and exercise?

Kotter's model goes on to argue that once leaders convince others of the need to change, they should mobilize a coalition of allies in the organization to bring that change about. In the case of a superboss organization, this step (and others Kotter suggests) isn't necessary. The superboss's very way of being has assured that such a "coalition of the willing" is already firmly in place. The superboss has hired people attuned to change, has inspired them to change, and has given them confidence to change at every turn.

Few leaders have mastered how to make change happen consistently over an extended period. Superbosses, operating in plain sight, have figured it out. Ultimately, a superboss doesn't construct his organization around a specific framework or formula, as Collins's book and many others suggest. Instead, superbosses embrace a mind-set of change, within the framework of their unyielding vision. That mind-set leads in turn to the welcoming of creative people into the company, to shared experiences that reinforce openness, to an ingrained culture of openness, and ultimately to a track record of sustained innovation and growth.

If you're a boss and you're clear about your nonnegotiable vision, then why not commit yourself to declaring open season on changing all that *is* negotiable? Sit down with your team and have everyone write down three major assumptions behind a strategy, initiative, or project you're currently working on. Don't be surprised if you and your team members write down different assumptions. What you're really signaling is that it's okay to examine, compare, and challenge how you go about doing what it is you do. You and your colleagues will find there may well be multiple ways of approaching a problem that are equally valid. The implicit message here is that no singular rationale for *how* something is done is sacred. And anything can be changed if something better comes along.

So many organizations have "elephants in the room," or specific practices or rules that never change because nobody has the courage to question them. With time, more and more of these "undiscussables"[58] emerge, restricting the flow of ideas and impeding a healthy process of questioning. To "open up" the organization to change, explicitly invite conversation around the undiscussables, rewarding employees for raising tough issues. You could also perform an audit of your own communications and attitudes. Do you secretly regard some practices as sacred and unchangeable? Which ones? You can't expect your reports to suggest ideas for reforming or improving established practices if you're sending messages that discourage such efforts. Finally, you could assess whether your KPIs (key performance indicators) support innovation around execution. If they don't, then it's time to change how you evaluate what employees do.

Don't fear what is new. Open yourself up, secure in the knowledge that you're also staying true to what you really value. Of course, it's much easier to open up yourself and to encourage employees to open up when you've already built trust via an intimate working relationship with them. Superbosses I studied developed exactly such relationships, invested as they were in constantly teaching young employees personally and by example. Learning retreats and training modules are great, but superbosses intuitively know that whether you're teaching creativity or anything else, experiential, on-the-job learning at the foot of a master works best. One of the most successful and cutting-edge ways of imparting anything might also be one of the oldest models for organizing a workplace: the ancient bond between masters and apprentices.

CHAPTER FIVE

Masters and Apprentices

I f you aspired to become a successful artist during the fifteenth-century Italian Renaissance, there was one skill you needed to master above all others: the ability to draw. But where could you go to learn this? Master's of fine arts programs didn't exist back then, and you couldn't very well just hop online and watch instructional videos. What you *could* do was go to a master artist and work for him as an apprentice. If you were just a beginner, you would receive training from the ground up; if you were already fairly accomplished, you would hone your craft by assisting with the master's commissioned artworks.

Budding artists tended to flock to one master in particular in Renaissance Italy, a man named Andrea del Verrocchio. Beginning in 1460, Verrocchio operated a workshop that produced a variety of media for wealthy patrons, including painted, sculpted, and cast-bronze works. But Verrocchio was especially famous for his drawings, most of all for his ability to render the intricacies of the draperies commonly found in Renaissance paintings.[1]

Scholar Gigetta Dalli Regoli noted that Verrocchio was able to "recognize among the youths of his time the gifted and the imaginative, and [was] quick to obtain their collaboration."[2] Projects like the Medici Tomb in the Basilica of San Lorenzo, Florence (circa 1473) were complicated to execute, but thanks to Verrocchio's expertise in assembling a talented group of apprentices, he and his team could complete them with ease, and on a tight schedule.[3] In Verrocchio's hands, the master-apprentice relationship also served as an immensely powerful structure for imparting skills and knowledge. Researcher Liletta Fornasari has characterized Verrocchio's workshop as a veritable "school of design," with Verrocchio teaching his pupils the rules of perspective and encouraging them to practice drawing from life.[4] Experiments with drapery formed "a special branch" of his teachings, and Verrocchio also made plaster casts of figures and body parts, such as hands and feet, for his assistants to study and sketch.[5]

Verrocchio's workshop must have been an exciting place for young protégés to work and learn: it was in the forefront of artistic technologies, such as the chemical preparation of pigments, new ways to handle tools, and innovative metal-casting processes. Verrocchio's efforts also allowed him to become a superboss of his day. The artists who passed through his workshop were some of the most recognized of Renaissance Italy, including Pietro Perugino, Sandro Botticelli, Domenico Ghirlandaio, and Francesco Botticini.[6] Verrocchio even spawned one of the greatest artistic talents in the history of Western art: Leonardo da Vinci.

With all of Leonardo's genius, it's easy to forget that he was, at one time, just another young artist learning his craft. As Leonardo expert Jill Dunkerton noted, "Behind all of Leonardo's innovations as a painter lies an approach to the first steps of making an under drawing on the panel surface that has its origins in his training in the Verrocchio workshop."[7] Leonardo began his apprenticeship with Verroccio at the age of fourteen. After some time, however, it became clear that his skill had eclipsed that of his master, and that his talent was, in fact, extraordinary. Secure in his own capabilities and stature, Verroccio continued to rely on Leonardo's genius in his shop, all the while taking the opportunity to also learn from him and further his own skills.[8] Leonardo eventually became a master himself and secured his own commissions, going on to become one of the most famous protégés any superboss has ever had.[9]

Given how successful apprenticeships such as Leonardo's have been over centuries, you'd think they'd still be *everywhere* in developed economies. In some countries, such as Germany, apprenticeships are relatively common (although less so for managerial jobs).[10] Elsewhere, though, on-the-job training has largely disappeared, replaced by formal education at universities and specialty schools. Young people just starting out learn through internships, while older employees receive ongoing training from their employers, usually via formalized and highly structured programs and online courses.

So much of how people learn in the workplace today, from 360-degree performance evaluations to mentoring to coaching, has become bureaucratized and impersonal—a far cry from the personal relationship of learning that existed between Verrocchio and a protégé such as Leonardo. In 2003, there were fewer than a half million structured apprenticeships in the United States; by 2013, cost cutting in organizations had brought that number to below three hundred thousand.[11] Moreover, the best, most competent bosses today generally don't prioritize engaging reports informally in an immersive learning experience. Aiming for more certainty and clarity in their organizations, they promulgate rules and establish bureaucracies that distance them from employees. They also choreograph their days to assure that work gets done, leaving very little unstructured time for instructing or coaching. They certainly don't use the word *apprentice* very much. The very concept seems quaint, the product of a bygone age.

Close, direct, on-the-job training worked wonders for a genius like Leonardo—imagine what it would be like for mere mortals, with such modern jobs as marketing manager, attorney, and sales rep? In the absence of such a personal master-apprentice relationship, employees may learn technical basics, but they don't necessarily learn the subtleties and nuances of their professions, nor do they learn critically important "softer" skills that matter in any industry, such as networking, giving and receiving feedback, negotiating, or leading. Up-and-coming managers might be able to come up with the "right" answer to a business problem on their own, but they'll often need personal coaching to learn how to communicate that answer, convince bosses of its viability, and inspire colleagues and subordinates to help implement it. They may even need help understanding that having the right answer isn't worth very much if you can't bring other people with you. When highly educated managers start a job these days, their bosses almost always assume they already have everything they need to excel. Quite often they don't.

Unlike many of their contemporaries, but very much like Verrocchio, superbosses embrace the apprenticeship model wholeheartedly as a way of doing business. When they hire, they *know* they are giving an employee a chance to learn a craft at their feet. Staying in the trenches with protégés and serving as something akin to a player-coach, superbosses use this informal manner of instruction not only to convey knowledge but also to exert a powerful, almost parental influence on their protégés.

Today, most good bosses spend time teaching and mentoring the employees who work for them. They keep lines of communications open, ask questions designed to impart wisdom, accompany employees on sales calls, visit them on the front lines, and offer valuable advice. Superbosses, however, take such laudable practices much further than even the typical "good" boss does, effectively raising the bar. By apprenticeship-style management, I'm talking about workplace relationships that are more sustained, all-encompassing, intense, and intimate than the best traditional corporate "mentorships." Although the boundaries of these relationships may be unspoken or undefined, superbosses take much deeper personal responsibility for the growth and development of employees than conventionally good bosses do, and apprentices in turn expect far more in the way of attention and instruction than their counterparts at other organizations. And they *receive* this attention and instruction, often by working with superbosses on a daily basis. Of course, they don't work only with superbosses; again, it's not that rigid or formal. Leonardo da Vinci would hardly have been able to accomplish what he did if all his time was spent with Verrocchio. Like any apprentice, protégés of superbosses need time to interact with colleagues and to acquire know-how, but they also need time to be alone, practice what they've learned, and invent their own ways of doing things.

It's worth noting that some superbosses don't necessarily take pride in the role of "master." Glorious Bastards like Larry Ellison, Jay Chiat, Michael Milken, or Bonnie Fuller tend to shoulder the responsibilities of the master opportunistically; they're not touchy-feely types who care much about how apprentices "feel" along their career journeys. What they care about are *results*. But as it turns out, results are precisely what the apprenticeship approach delivers. You don't have to be attuned to employees' feelings to be a superboss and to embrace the apprenticeship model. Operating as masters, all three varieties of superbosses forge remarkable connections between themselves and the people who work for them. Staff members often come away learning far more than they may have from formal training alone. They perform far better, pushing the superboss's business to new heights and furthering their own careers. Like Leonardo da Vinci, some even go on to produce dazzling "masterpieces" and to become recognized masters in their own right.

Managing in the Moment

It's eight thirty in the morning and you're sitting in your cube, starting the workday. You're sipping coffee, checking emails, maybe taking a quick peek at what's happening with friends and relatives on Facebook. Just as you open an unfinished presentation you're slated to give tomorrow, you sense a presence hovering over you. Looking up, you're shocked to find your company's legendary CEO smiling at you and saying hello. Hundreds of people work at your company's corporate headquarters; you're just a midlevel manager. Yet here he is. He introduces himself and asks what you're working on. When you tell him, he says, "I'd like to hear more. Are you busy now? Can you come up to my office for a chat?"

If you were starting your career at Kraft during the 1980s, you might have had an encounter such as this with Michael Miles, the company's then president and COO, and later CEO. In his varying leadership roles, Miles brought Kraft into the modern era of food marketing, transforming the company's image from an unhealthy, fatty foods purveyor into one focused on healthier offerings. Kraft introduced line extensions such as "light" Philadelphia Brand cream cheese and low-fat and fat-free salad dressings, cheese, and ice cream. Between 1986 and 1988 alone, Miles oversaw the introduction of some 350 new products.[12] Growth on several of Kraft's brands increased from 1 percent annually to about 4 percent.[13] Miles also formed a venture group to look into acquisitions that would complement Kraft's existing product line, eventually buying consumer favorites such as Lender's Bagels and Tombstone Pizza. Miles didn't do all of this alone, of course; he had an uncanny knack for nurturing top-flight marketing talent. His list of protégés reads like a who's who of American consumer marketing, including the future CEOs of Mattel, Young & Rubicam, Gillette, Sears, Heinz, Hershey Foods, and Quaker Oats. Want more? Add Marks & Spencer, 3M, CVS, and Campbell Soup to the list.

When I interviewed Miles's protégés, I discovered that one of his trade secrets was making himself unusually accessible to employees. As longtime Kraft employee John Tucker told me, Miles was a "walk-around manager"[14] who took time to get to know people throughout the company. He made a point of having lunch with employees two or three rungs lower than him, and he did so in the cafeteria, where other employees could see. He kept his office door open so that anyone could just drop by to ask questions or talk strategy. And there were also those impromptu morning conversations with younger staff. When Miles first arrived at the company, he picked someone at random every morning, brought him up to his office, and spoke with him for about an hour. Don't be mistaken, though, these were not casual chats about sports or the weather. "His questions were very direct, very pointed," Tucker said. "It was like taking a final exam."[15]

Tucker speaks from experience. He was serving as head of human resources for Kraft's global manufacturing group when Miles asked him in for a morning talk. Tucker apparently did well, because three months later Miles called him up again, this time to offer a huge promotion, to senior vice president of human resources for all of Kraft, reporting directly to Miles. "My first meeting with Mike . . . was the basis on which he offered me the job," Tucker recalled.[16] It's not every CEO who will spend an hour chatting with a low- or midlevel manager. But Tucker's promotion was just the beginning of his contact with Miles. For years thereafter, the two would talk on a practically daily basis, and a full apprenticeship under Miles would blossom.

The most basic and critical set of practices underlying the apprenticeship model concerns simply being there with employees, getting to know them, and letting them in. You can't develop a personal approach to training staff if you aren't there in person (or, if necessary, via communications technology), day in and day out. Yet most bosses don't do this—in fact, they don't even come close. The CEOs appearing on the hit television show *Undercover Boss* are, sadly, not all that unusual. Imagine resorting to impersonating low-level employees to find out what's really going on in your own company. These clueless, distanced bosses are the complete antithesis of the superboss. Whereas many businesses today focus on getting closer to the customer, superbosses are very much focused on getting closer to their employees or team members. In deploying an apprenticeship mind-set, superbosses like Michael Miles let their employees know that they're *always* available to be consulted.

As Dr. Paul Batalden, a former VP at HCA and professor emeritus at the Geisel School of Medicine at Dartmouth College, told me, his superboss, Tommy Frist, was "such an unusual CEO of a Fortune 100 or whatever the size of the company was at that time. You could always get to see him. He always had time."[17] On some occasions, Frist, who was also a pilot, would even fly his protégés to events in other cities, letting them sit in the copilot's seat and talking business with them. The world-renowned conducting teacher Jorma Panula would spend all day with his students, and then he would invite them to a restaurant to talk even more.[18] "There's one very important thing that Mr. Panula has," protégé Juhani Poutanen related. "He has time." The *Philadelphia Inquirer*'s Gene Roberts was known to stay up until two in the morning talking to staffers—at his home. John Carroll, who went on to run the *Baltimore Sun* and *Los Angeles Times,* recalled that when Roberts wanted him to take on a new project, "he couldn't just call me into his office and say, 'John, I'd like you to do this.' No, you'd end up spending the whole damn evening with him."[19]

In the corporate world, employees who seek to speak with their bosses normally attempt to "book time." They might send an email to an assistant, and the resulting "meeting" occurs outside of the "actual work" being done. Such practices seem to bring bosses and employees closer together, but in reality they distance and control the degree of contact bosses have with staff. While today's hyper-scheduled executives obviously need to control their time, we often forget about what we lose when we run from event to event—the casual, ongoing contact *in the moment* that is essential for learning, serendipity, and building meaningful relationships.

More than just making themselves available for meetings, superbosses are often in the thick of it with employees—not just for a half hour once a week, but regularly and informally. Superbosses often work side by side with protégés, coaching them in unmediated ways. Remember how George Lucas collaborated with Ben Burtt to invent the characteristic bleeps of R2D2's language? He gave him space and he gave him freedom, but he also stepped in for direct and often unannounced intense one-on-one discussions.

When I interviewed hedge-fund mogul Julian Robertson, he took a quick call and decisively instructed one of his young protégés on how to handle a business situation. As I heard from Samuel Howard, chairman of Phoenix Holdings and Xantus Corporation, Tommy Frist also "worked as hard as anybody else. When you asked him to do something, he would roll up his sleeves."[20] Michael Milken got up bright and early at four thirty and wrote notes to every member of his team, probing decisions they'd made and asking for opinions on pending business matters.[21] Norman Brinker's former CFO reported that she'd see him in restaurants picking up a dishrag and bussing tables.[22]

Traditional managers often talk about the importance of coaching subordinates, but they don't *actually* spend their time that way. That's because managers today tend to view work relationships as strictly transactional to them: "I'm giving you a paycheck, and in exchange it's your job to get your work done, not mine." If there is coaching, it tends to come from specialists brought in for limited purposes, such as helping members of a team get along better or preparing a young executive for a senior role. What you likely won't have is a boss who coaches you day in and day out, and views coaching as a fundamental part of her job.

Superbosses, on the other hand, invert the classic boss-subordinate relationship—not entirely, but significantly. Superbosses think about strategy and vision, as we've seen, but they also think about doing. To a surprising degree, they join employees in getting their hands dirty with actual work, modeling behavior and guiding employees in the process. They can do this, in the first instance, because they are extraordinary subject-matter experts with deep reservoirs of lessons to impart. It's an important precondition for the apprenticeship model: You can't be a master to an apprentice unless you truly have mastered your craft. Protégés, for their part, walk away impressed by and appreciative of this mastery. Jorma Panula had "X-ray vision for the technical side of conducting," remarked Eivind Aadland, chief conductor and artistic leader of Trondheim Symphony Orchestra. "His knowledge is extremely, extremely big."[23] Sid Ganis related how after Steven Spielberg and George Lucas screened the first Indiana Jones movie, *Raiders of the Lost Ark,* Lucas gave Spielberg "three hours of notes on the movie." To Ganis, "that describes who he was and how he was."[24] Walsh, Brinker, Lauren—all were revered by the protégés I interviewed for their knowledge of craft, not just leadership.

Ultimately, though, many superbosses make it a priority to work side by side with junior staff because they're convinced it's critical to the successful operation of their businesses. Thomas Keller, a successful superboss-chef whose restaurants include the renowned French Laundry and Per Se, spends time with sous-chefs because "that's our next generation," the people who will one day be running his kitchens. Keller feels this way, even though he knows that staff members might eventually work for someone else. As Keller noted, you never know if talented staff members will leave and then return years later. It's worth the risk to take the time to work with them now.[25]

"West Coast" Companies

Look around your workplace. Do leaders enjoy special parking spots, cafeterias, bathrooms, offices, and the like? Why do many bosses think of executive perks as the reward leaders enjoy for "making it to the top"? To most superbosses, the usual perks, distinctions, and hierarchies are just not that meaningful. In fact, they're counterproductive. Superbosses are so focused on engaging with their people that they disdain anything that might create physical or even emotional distance. They want person-to-person involvement that enables everyone to make stuff happen. If all it takes to connect with a superboss is a quick phone call or knock on the door, that's because a disregard of hierarchy is not merely tolerated—it's explicitly encouraged.

Robert Noyce, creator of the integrated circuit[26] and a founder of Intel, influenced so many tech entrepreneurs that he became known as the Mayor of Silicon Valley.[27] The company he helped found before Intel, Fairchild Semiconductor, spawned a family tree of hundreds of companies, including Raytheon Semiconductor; Kleiner, Perkins, Caufield & Byers; Advanced Micro Devices; and Intel itself. Charlie Sporck, Fairchild's manufacturing guru who later became CEO of National Semiconductor, said it well: "It is no overstatement to say that Bob Noyce made what Silicon Valley is today."[28]

At Fairchild, Noyce became known for his "West Coast" management style (not to be confused with Bill Walsh's "West Coast offense"), which was much freer and more egalitarian than the formal, hierarchical, "East Coast" way of running a company. The West Coast style has since become associated with any number of hugely successful Silicon Valley companies, suggesting that although superbosses influence their industry by unleashing cohorts of superstar individuals, their impact is often far greater.

Noyce dispensed with hierarchy because it just didn't make sense for an entrepreneurial business. Just over thirty years old at the time, Noyce was one of the oldest people at Fairchild. He hired engineers fresh out of college and graduate school because "experienced" people didn't exist (sound familiar in today's Silicon Valley?)—the transistor was too recent a technology. Noyce got new employees acquainted with Fairchild by thrusting them headlong into the heart of research and development, expecting them to learn on the job, side by side with him. Intensity, not privilege or seniority, defined the culture. Writer Tom Wolfe described in *Esquire* how "a young engineer would go to work at eight in the morning, work right through lunch, leave the plant at six thirty or seven, drive home, play with the baby for half an hour, have dinner with his wife, get in bed with her, give her a quick toss, then get up and leave her there in the dark and work at his desk for two or three hours on 'a coupla things I had to bring home with me.'"[29]

On a more basic level, the trappings of titles and distinctions eluded Noyce; it just wasn't what he was about. As Gordon Moore, cofounder of Fairchild and Intel, and a legend in his own right, told me, Noyce was "a very down-to-earth guy" with "a beat-up old car. One of his technicians hung a sign on it saying, 'Please park this in the back. It's giving us a bad reputation.' . . . No pretensions at all."[30] In one illustrative story Moore told me, the CEO of Fairchild's parent company came out to California to check on Fairchild Semiconductor. He arrived in a limousine driven by a uniformed chauffeur. Noyce was shocked at what appeared to him to be an unconscionable indulgence. How could the CEO enjoy himself all day long while the driver sat in the car the entire time doing nothing? It just didn't make any sense. "Bob just could not imagine somebody sitting around all day doing nothing," Moore said.[31]

When starting Intel with Moore, Noyce made a point to again create a "flat" structure, banishing bureaucracy. There were no executive suites or special parking spaces; stock options were standard for most office workers and all of the engineers. Intel's workspace consisted of one large room divided into individual "offices" by low partitions, and everyone, including Noyce and Moore, worked under these conditions.[32] Noyce and Moore didn't want any employee to feel that anything stood in his or her way of advancing. At least while Intel was still small, every employee had access to Noyce and to Moore. Under this model, all questions could be asked and all ideas voiced. Staff meetings were not the domain of a few select managers—all employees could attend and share their thoughts.[33]

The rules of the game were similar at so many other superboss-run organizations I studied. At Kraft, Michael Miles shook up hierarchy by declaring one day that all parking would be on a first-come, first-served basis, with no special treatment for executives. John Griffin, one of Julian Robertson's "tiger cubs," described Robertson's office as follows: "Imagine a room. . . . Julian was plop in the center. No door, no [individual offices], no private conversation . . . mostly everything was open."[34] Jay Chiat instituted an open office as well, with everyone sharing desks separated by low dividers.[35] According to Stevan Alburty, a manager at Chiat/Day, Chiat "felt that ideas should come from everywhere . . . that ultimately people will not change until you change their physical space and force them to change. It was a radical idea and people felt threatened and terrified by losing the trappings of power."[36]

Any resistance some managers and employees might put up doesn't dissuade superbosses. Archie Norman is a superboss in the British supermarket industry whose many protégés have gone on to lead companies such as Boots, HBOS, Vendex, Levi Europe, Royal Mail, Halfords, Cable & Wireless, and Sainsbury's. In 1991, Norman became CEO of the British supermarket chain Asda, where a stultifying bureaucracy had taken hold. Norman's turnaround strategy combined cost cutting with a series of moves to eliminate all formality. Cubicles were torn down in favor of open offices, meetings were held standing up, name badges with titles were removed, letters to the CEO from the rank and file were encouraged (Norman received forty thousand letters in the first three and a half years), and store visits from executives that used to be about ceremony (think ribbon cutting and entourages) were recast as learning opportunities. Meanwhile, Norman cast a wide net for young talent to take on leadership jobs.[37,38]

Some superbosses I studied took the abolition of hierarchy and bureaucracy even further than Norman did; they seemed to harbor an almost visceral hatred for *any* bureaucratic elements that might obstruct, impede, or diminish casual interactions at work. Can you imagine life without the ubiquitous memo? Former employees of Chiat/Day can: Jay Chiat banned memos for an entire year, calling them a "corporate disease that people hid behind."[39] Gene Roberts banned staff meetings and formal speeches.

Although they might complain about bureaucracy, many bosses still retain formalized practices such as standard memos, endless meetings, and formal titles because they fear that without them, uncertainty and chaos will reign inside an organization. You need organized processes and people who are clearly in charge, don't you? Superbosses' collective response appears to be "Maybe not." To be precise, superboss businesses are not *perfectly* flat; the superboss ultimately does retain control at the top. But to superbosses, sacrificing a bit of order is well worth it if, in the process, you obtain the innovation, creativity, and dynamism that accompany informal relationships.

A relatively flat organization and unpretentious culture enable superbosses to enjoy close, unmediated, in-the-trenches contact with *all* employees, regardless of age or experience. In Verrocchio's workshop, master and apprentice worked simply and side by side, with knowledge and expertise flowing back and forth between them. Though modern-day superbosses may run larger, more complex organizations and grapple with Kafkaesque regulations unheard of in the time of the Medicis, they, too, sense that bureaucratic processes and fancy titles are distancing almost by definition. They treat them as necessary evils to be used sparingly. To a superboss, the ultimate goal is never to be simply a manager to an employee. It's to be a perceptive, responsive, authentic master to an apprentice.

"How Do You Do That?"

At middle age, conducting master Jorma Panula would seem fairly ordinary on first glance—short, a little heavyset, steel-gray hair, a long, rectangular face. But such an unassuming appearance belied his arresting personality. David Curtis, artistic director of the Orchestra of the Swan, a British chamber orchestra, told me of a teaching session with Panula in which about a dozen student conductors took turns leading an orchestra through a Brahms symphony while the other students looked on from the back of the hall.[40] Unfortunately, one student was having trouble. He was not making the correct motions, and as a result, the orchestra was not accenting properly. Panula got upset, growling and grumbling. He tried to correct the student, but to no avail. Finally, he got up and stormed out, slamming the door.

Sometime later, he came back in, and the orchestra tried again with the student. The notes still weren't being played with the proper accents, so Panula came up to the podium, stood behind the student, and growled some more. Once again, the orchestra played the offending section of the piece. At the precise moment where he wanted accents played, Panula "just sort of shrugged or put a fist down—not a big movement, nothing flashy. It was just a sort of bear gesture. You can imagine a grizzly bear just sort of looking at you and *grrrr*."[41]

Somehow, that did it. "A huge sound came from the orchestra. Well, we all just looked at each other," Curtis said. "How do you do that? The orchestra didn't know he was going to do anything. The students didn't know, nobody knew. He just made the typical Panula gesture and the orchestra . . . exploded. We just stood there looking at each other thinking, 'Oh, shit.'"[42]

Curtis offered this story to illustrate just how intense Panula's in-person presence was as a teacher. He related that Panula was effective because he not only conveyed specific points of craft (for instance, how to have musicians accent certain notes in an appropriate way) but also initiated a deeper developmental process in the minds of students. Panula's idiosyncratic interactions seemed to help students improve by triggering a powerful process of self-examination. That student who wasn't hitting the accents needed to become more aware of what he was doing as well as of the deeper assumptions or motivations behind his conducting actions. Behaving on stage without rigor or focus just wouldn't cut it, and Panula's feedback helped root out these often unconscious actions.

The ultimate lesson Panula had to teach was one of integrity as a musician. The intention of the conductor was everything, and Panula would suffer no bullshit of any kind. Panula would also explicitly coach his students to remove any trace of ego from their performances. The conductor's ultimate objective was to offer a natural experience of the composer, not of the conductor: "It is about the music . . . about honesty and integrity . . . and if you're going to stand up on the podium and show off, [Panula] is really not interested. He will just say, 'Oh, yes, marvelous, marvelous . . . next.'"[43]

Protégés of all superbosses related similar powerful, career-shaping lessons they learned during the course of informal, apprentice-style interactions. How, precisely, do superbosses teach so efficiently? Panula's methods were no doubt unique to him. But the other superbosses were equally idiosyncratic. No matter how many times I reviewed the thousands of pages of interview notes from my research, I could not discern a single teaching style or method employed by all superbosses. Sometimes they carved out specific times for group teaching, as Bill Walsh did during end-of-day sessions at training camp; other times, they worked one-on-one with protégés, as in the walks through department stores Ralph Lauren used to take with individual protégés. Sometimes they told stories, such as the one Gene Roberts would tell about a blind editor he once worked for who clutched his arm and said, "Make me see!" in an effort to get journalists to write in a vivid way that would evoke images in readers' minds;[44] other times, it was a phrase they coined that conveyed *precisely* the wisdom a protégé needed (Luc Vandevelde, former chairman at Marks & Spencer and Carrefour, told me that Michael Miles advised him to bring out the best in people by using "eliciting skills" and avoid "limiting skills." "I'll never forget those two words," said Vandevelde. "It profoundly changed my management approach, creating an environment where people can be at their best").[45] Still other times—in fact, much of the time—superbosses asked questions of their protégés, forcing them to articulate a fresh idea in the moment, thus giving the superboss a new window into their way of thinking.

One reason superboss teachings are so memorable is because they are frequently delivered in intimate settings and in unusual ways. Over dinner, Gene Roberts would offer John Carroll "little hints" about how to handle certain situations; as Carroll remembered, these dinners were "the best seminar you could ever have."[46] Pianist Herbie Hancock once told a story (recounted to me by sound engineer Scott Ross, who worked with Davis) about how he and Miles Davis were recording, and Miles told Hancock to sit on his left hand and only play with his right: "For a piano player," Ross observed, "that's like having your hand amputated." But it was Miles's way of teaching Hancock how to control sound in a more deliberate way than he ever had before.[47]

Superbosses may convey ideas as "nuggets" of wisdom, but they just as often seem to teach by simply being themselves and letting employees observe. As saxophonist Bill Evans said of Miles Davis, "I learned the most from just watching and seeing how he did it."[48] Mary Sue Milliken, co-owner and chef of Border Grill in Santa Monica and Las Vegas, re-called looking to Alice Waters as an "inspiration" for how to have a ca-reer and be a mom at the same time. "When Alice had her daughter, Fanny, it really perked up my interest. I thought, I gotta watch and see if she was going to keep working and how does it all fit in?"[49] Edward Stack, a former executive of HCA who left to become the founder of the Behav-ioral Centers of America (by spinning out HCA's psychiatric hospitals),[50] recalled that long before exercise became fashionable, Tommy Frist would jog to and from work, sending a message to the whole organization that staying healthy was important. Many executives subsequently got in the habit of running or lifting weights as part of their daily routine, but Frist "never said to anyone, 'You ought to do this.' He never made anyone that I was aware of feel uncomfortable if they didn't do what he did. He would set an example, do the things, and allow other people the opportu-nity to do it."[51]

Superbosses deliver multiple layers of lessons at once. First, they teach technical nuances about their business—insights employees can't get anywhere else, as well as memorable reminders of the fundamentals that protégés are already expected to know. If you want to learn the finer points of running a newspaper, who better to teach you than Gene Rob-erts? If you want to learn the secrets of starting a successful restaurant chain, who better than Norman Brinker? Director Roger Corman was known to teach an array of useful filmmaking precepts, including "prior-itize your shots; rehearse while the crew is lighting the set; chase the sun; use foreground objects to enliven a dialogue scene; bring in move-ment to stimulate the eye; and above all, wear comfortable shoes and sit down a lot."[52] Actor Jack Nicholson remarked of his old boss that "with Roger, you learn the basics, good basics and tough basics; you never re-ally forget it."[53]

Just as valuable is a second layer of lessons, the make-or-break advice superbosses impart on how to run businesses and lead organizations.

Billionaire entrepreneur and designer Tory Burch credits Ralph Lauren with teaching her "the importance of having a complete vision for a company, from product to marketing to store visuals."[54] Alice Waters taught Gayle Ortiz, now chef and owner of Gayle's Bakery in San Francisco, how to "pay attention to detail and demand perfection" in all aspects of a restaurant's operation, a lesson that became "my main focus of the way that I looked at business."[55] Michael Miles taught his protégé Richard Lenny, former CEO of Hershey Foods, how to develop strategic initiatives that would deliver superior shareholder value."[56]

One business lesson we would expect all superbosses to impart is the importance of talent. And they do. Superbosses don't simply urge their protégés to "hire well," they emphasize the importance of hiring genuinely unusual talent as well as the importance of helping that talent fulfil all their potential, and then some. Doug Conant worked for about six years under Michael Miles before becoming the CEO of Campbell Soup. As he told me, "It's hard to have extraordinary performance if you don't have extraordinary talent. . . . The importance of this is what I really learned at Kraft. When I went on . . . I was much more aggressive on talent management than I would have been had I not had that Kraft experience."[57]

Some of the most valuable and enduring lessons employees glean from superbosses fall into a third category, what we might call "life lessons." A recurring lesson superbosses teach, for instance, is discipline—the importance of working hard to perfect your craft and to stay true to your values, beliefs, and vision. A hedge-fund manager learned a thing or two about discipline one day while watching Julian Robertson consider whether to buy a stock. Robertson had spent a lot of time researching before deciding to invest $100 million in the company's shares. He placed the order, but in the meantime, he still wanted to consult a few people to learn about the company and its industry. He made his calls, and the information he obtained suggested that perhaps the stock was not as attractive as it had first seemed. Another manager might have rationalized a way to stay in the deal, especially since pulling out would have cost 10 percent of the transaction ($10 million!). Robertson didn't care about taking the loss—he pulled out anyway. As the protégé recalled, "He never looked back. I am not sure if it worked out or didn't—it didn't matter. Because what that told me is when the story changes, get out, you can always reevaluate."[58]

Such intellectually honest behavior leads us to another core lesson superbosses impress on their people: the importance of cutting away the nonessential and prioritizing what is real, even if this requires that protégés behave independently and flout social conventions. "I think the main message we got from him," conductor Esa-Pekka Salonen said of Jorma Panula, "was to question all the basic axioms of culture and society and just try to develop integrity."[59] There is, at bottom, a simplicity to what superbosses do, whether it's Ralph Lauren tailoring the image of his brand, Norman Brinker staying true to his concept of a casual restaurant, or Roger Corman pursuing his model of how best to produce a low-budget film. In their daily contact with superbosses, protégés feel the burden that such simplicity entails but also experience and are inspired by the richness of its results. It's a lesson they never forget.

The life lessons superbosses share often stick with protégés, informing forever the way they conduct themselves. As David Curtis told me, "Every time I get on the podium, I'm thinking that if Panula were sitting there at the back of orchestra watching, what would he be thinking?"[60] One well-known hedge-fund manager who worked for Julian Robertson for years confided that, on occasion, he considered an investment that just didn't feel exactly right. "I will just hear Julian's voice: 'Big guy, don't do that, think about it, wait a week and see how you feel in a week.' And I think, 'That's right.' And I will wait a week and say, 'Stupid, why did I think I wanted to do that?'"[61] Accounts such as these testify to the extraordinary impact superbosses have as teachers. Some bosses have trouble getting employees to do anything unless they're standing over them; the minute they leave, employees revert to old habits. Protégés of super-bosses internalize their teachings and make them their own. They mobilize these lessons again and again during their careers. As David Murphy said of Chiat, "It wasn't until Jay died that I realized what a significant impact he'd had on me as a young executive. That it was okay to risk, it was okay to ask questions, that it was about the result of the work you were doing and to take it seriously."[62] What greater tribute could Murphy have paid to his boss than that?

Teaching like a Superboss

Apprenticeship might sound like a crazy idea for organizations and bosses to adopt. In our fast-moving, twenty-first-century economy, it may not seem helpful or even realistic to go back to the fifteenth century when dealing with something as vital as talent. Yet the track records of superbosses speak for themselves; theirs is a *proven* playbook. In work-places where organizations or individual bosses adopt superboss-style approaches (remember, superbosses exist in even larger numbers in the middle of many companies and nonprofits), we find that employees really do benefit. In schools, for instance, the best principals are typically those who spend time in classrooms with their teachers, as opposed to playing the "CEO role."[63] In Teach for America, an internship program that offers young, inexperienced teachers an opportunity to cut their teeth at tough, low-performing schools, research shows that participants whose principal is actively involved in coaching them are more success-ful.[64]

Most good bosses today understand the importance of face-to-face contact. Management experts have coined a term for this: management by "walking around." Yet management by "walking around" as it has long been practiced doesn't begin to encompass the constant, deep collaboration that exists between superbosses and protégés. Despite most managers' best intentions, apprenticeship-style management doesn't actually happen. Calendars get filled up so quickly. Executives feel pressured to perfect the strategy and leave the execution to their subordinates. Hierarchies and bureaucracy remain firmly entrenched. Under these conditions, it's the rare manager who would accompany protégés and lower-level employees, coaching them as they actually do what they do.

If you're a manager, you cannot and should not just toss out formal training programs. You can't spend all of your time interacting one-on-one with people—keeping some sense of control and order is important. But coaching in the moment is important, too, and deserves higher priority. The good news is that you don't need to do away entirely with personal assistants, Outlook calendars, meetings, or other elements of bureaucracy. Remaking processes and structures incrementally so they're closer to those of superbosses can yield significant results. See if room exists to dial back formality or to spend more unstructured time with your people. The point is not to allow hierarchy and bureaucracy to dominate. Let structure influence how you organize workplace relationships, but don't let it constrain them unduly.

The apprenticeship model doesn't need to be a substitute for what you're already doing, but rather it can be an enhancement, part of a rebalancing that might occur in how your workplace operates. Training programs can and do teach the kind of basic instructional knowledge that superbosses expect their protégés to possess. So keep training programs, but don't make the mistake of thinking such programs are *all* you need.

A good place to start is to revisit some of the assumptions you bring to the workplace. We get in the habit of not interacting closely and personally with subordinates; we see management as "just a job." Likewise, we look upon the idea of "pitching in" as a negative, a sign that our subordinates may not be up to the task. Superbosses don't want to do their subordinates' work for them, but they do want to remain deeply engaged. Try to think about your relationships with reports in a less transactional way. They're not only there to "get the job done," nor are you only there to oversee them. You're *both* there to get the job done *and* come up with bigger-picture ideas that will help drive the business forward.

As you modify your thinking, take stock of what you currently do and how you might improve. How much time do you actually spend with your team members? If that time turns out to be considerable, does an imbalance exist, with too much time spent on formal interactions, such as meetings or filling out performance evaluations, and not enough time on informal, one-on-one interactions? Think of the specific things super-bosses do: Are you performing any of these actions already? Are there ways to perform more? Try experimenting at first with having more direct contact with one person or a couple of people in your organization, and encourage your reports to do the same. Do you see any positive results? Galvanize people in your organization to reorganize processes and eliminate red tape. Are there ways to streamline decision making? Are there ways to make communication easier throughout the hierarchy?

Don't forget technology in all this. I've compared modern business practices to Verrocchio's fifteenth-century practices, but in some ways, we're better equipped today to incorporate the apprenticeship model into our organizations. We're so good at communicating with strangers on Facebook, Twitter, and LinkedIn; why can't we get better using these tools *inside* organizations? Bosses and employees in today's global corporations are often separated by multiple time zones, but technology easily effaces that distance. It could allow for far more regular and consequential contact—if we're willing to prioritize it.

We all need to perform well and make our numbers; to that end, what superbosses do is critical to observe. But there's a higher benefit. Think of how meaningful it is to personally impress upon someone lessons they may carry with them throughout their lives. Think of how satisfying it is to share your passions with someone. Think of how incredible it is to help someone along, the way *you* were probably helped along. We all remember our best bosses . . . and our worst. It turns out we have a choice about what kind of boss we'll be. When you teach and coach people the way superbosses do, your people will come away feeling fulfilled, fortunate, and grateful. Chances are, so will you.

CHAPTER SIX

The Hands-On Delegator

In October 2012, I sat down with billionaire hedge-fund manager Chase Coleman for an interview in his office at 101 Park Avenue in Manhattan. The waiting room was graciously appointed with white couches and chairs, and an assistant offered me a coffee while I waited. I wasn't the only visitor that day; Coleman shared his office with several other immensely successful hedge-fund managers, and one of them was receiving a guest whom I knew, the dean of a well-known business school.

He and I chatted, and after a short wait, I was ushered into a glass-enclosed conference room. I interviewed a couple of Coleman's colleagues first. About an hour later, Coleman himself strolled in wearing a beautifully tailored suit, and I was glad I'd worn my own new Hugo Boss suit that day. He sat down and we began our conversation. As he spoke, what struck me most was his intensity. With a baby face and a shock of sandy brown hair swept across his forehead, Coleman might have passed for a man a decade younger than his thirty-seven years. Yet throughout the forty minutes we spent together, he spoke earnestly, chose his words carefully, and did not once crack a smile. He was polite, for sure, although I suspected he didn't agree to many interviews, and perhaps was curious about my motives. He answered my questions directly and seriously, without undue elaboration. He kept us on topic—strictly business. Chase Coleman was clearly a formidable professional, and he owed a not insignificant part of his runaway success to the sharp eye of one of the most successful investors in hedge-fund history.

If you didn't know Coleman, you'd take him for just another successful Wall Street trader. He grew up affluent and went to elite schools—Deerfield Academy, followed by Williams College. He also has an impressive family tree, with a lineage stretching all the way back to Peter Stuyvesant, the seventeenth-century Dutch governor of what became New York.[1] In some ways, though, Coleman's career trajectory is actually quite unexpected. He got his start working for investor Julian Robertson, who just a few years earlier had suffered one of the most high-profile investing flameouts in recent memory. Long one of Wall Street's most successful hedge-fund titans, Robertson's Tiger Management lost 4 percent in 1998 and 19 percent the following year.[2] By 2000, headlines in financial media were speaking of "Never-Been-Right Robertson," "Cat Defanged," and "A Tiger Slaughtered." Not exactly the most promising place, it would seem, to start a Wall Street career.

In fact, it was. You see, Robertson was not an ordinary hedge-fund manager—he was a superboss whose initial success had grown out of a strict fidelity to his unique vision. Robertson built Tiger Management by embracing the approach of a "value investor"; performing exhaustive research to understand the intrinsic value of a company, buying stocks that were undervalued, and then selling at a profit once their prices had risen. Robertson's great innovation was to apply this approach to stocks that seemed *overvalued* as well. He would perform the same research to locate companies that were *less* valuable than believed, placing bets that they would decline in value (a practice known as "short selling"). This dual approach had been enormously successful, allowing Tiger Management to provide average annual yields of 31 percent from 1980 to 2000.[3] But it was also what landed Robertson in serious trouble.

During the late 1990s, as prices of Internet stocks soared to seemingly impossible heights, driven in part by fad and a get-rich-quick mentality, Robertson refused to abandon the tenets of value investing. He would stick with his core vision even if it wasn't popular. By 1999, it wasn't—investors were yanking their money from Tiger, shrinking the size of Robertson's formerly $22 billion fund by nearly 75 percent.[4] Still, Robertson refused to budge. Instead of shifting strategy, he shut Tiger down and returned funds to his investors.[5] Explaining this decision, he wrote that "the key to Tiger's success over the years has been a steady commitment to buying the best stocks and shorting the worst. In a rational environment, this strategy functions well. But in an irrational market, where earnings and price considerations take a backseat to mouse clicks and momentum, such logic, as we have learned, does not count for much."[6]

The uncompromising visions of superbosses may sometimes cause them to stumble, but it's a mistake to count them out too quickly. In Robertson's case, a brilliant second act was in the making, one rooted in his ability to nurture Wall Street's best talent. Robertson singled out some of the most promising young analysts who lost their jobs when he closed his fund and provided them with seed money to start their own funds. Afterward, he also gave seed money to other young analysts who hadn't worked for him before but whom he saw as "high potential." These "tiger seeds," as they were dubbed (not to be confused with "tiger cubs," an existing group of former Robertson employees who benefitted from his wisdom and went on to run their own hedge funds, but not necessarily with Robertson seed money), could call on him if they wanted advice, and they could also have access to his Rolodex. In exchange, Robertson got a piece of the action—20 percent of the tiger seeds' incoming fees. "I was practically seventy years old," Robertson told me, "and I decided that

I could stand being seventy, but I didn't want to be Methuselah, and I thought I would be if I didn't have some of these young people around."[7]

Robertson was betting heavily on his ability to impart wisdom to his young analysts, as well as on his ability to determine which of his analysts were ready to step forward in their careers and which ones were not. Coleman seemed confident and competent enough, so in 2000, at the tender age of twenty-five, he was handed a $25 million check and told to go build something. "I viewed it as a huge opportunity," Coleman told me. "I was highly anxious on what I was setting out to do, given my lack of experience, but I felt confident in my authority to execute because I have a lot of expertise in a lot of things. I was also very appreciative of someone having that level of confidence in me."[8]

Coleman has gone on to reward Robertson's confidence many times over. From its inception in 2001 to 2007, his Tiger Global Fund yielded average annual returns to investors of over 35 percent.[9] In 2011, Tiger Global was the best-performing hedge fund of its size, returning 46 percent and beating out a number of funds managed by veteran investors.[10] And Coleman (who as of 2015 was worth $2.1 billion[11]) was only one of a number of successful tiger seeds. By 2015, about *thirty* tiger seeds were managing $32 billion in assets,[12] many of them operating out of Robertson's own offices in midtown Manhattan.[13] Their record was so strong that budding hedge-fund managers were willing to agree to tougher-than-usual terms in exchange for an investment and mentorship from Robertson. "It's a very good system," Robertson says, "particularly for me, at my time in life. I've gotten reenergized. It's wonderfully fun."[14] It's also lucrative. Robertson, who was worth $3.4 billion in 2015, realized a 400 percent return on his own personal capital over several years during the 2000s.[15] Not bad for the cat the Internet bubble supposedly defanged.

Traders in Opportunity

How did Julian Robertson *know* that Coleman was ready for the enormous responsibility of running his own fund? For that matter, how did Roger Corman know when his young directors were ready to take a $1 million investment and come back with their first movies—on budget and on time? How did Tommy Frist know that a young associate administrator in his early thirties was ready to build and run an entire hospital? How did Jay Chiat know that an unproven young writer was ready to oversee the creative work for a major advertising client?

Superboss organizations are widely regarded in their industries as launching pads—places where employees can, in the words of protégés, "find themselves" and become "capable of doing what we were ultimately meant to do." "To go from a guy building spaceship models to art director to second-unit director in those three steps, that doesn't happen anywhere else,"[16] a confidant of director and Academy Award winner James Cameron, a Corman protégé, marveled. One of Larry Ellison's acolytes said that "the primary kind of skill you pick up at Oracle is opportunity . . . the one thing Oracle was incredibly good at was on a continual basis throwing new responsibility at people."[17] Protégés often attribute such rapid advancement to intuition on the part of superbosses; these leaders simply have a "knack" for promoting people into the right jobs and, more generally, for providing experiences people need in order to grow. "It was instinctive, in his gut," one protégé said of Jay Chiat. "He knew how to make people better."[18]

There's more to it than just instinct. First, superbosses practice a keen brand of opportunity spotting. Just as they're always on the lookout for "diamonds in the rough" to hire and for the next great business opportunity, they're also consciously prowling for people inside their organizations who are ready and willing to tackle the next great challenge. Rick Pitino put it this way: "I only look for [assistant coaches] who want to be heads. Other than watching your children grow and your players develop, nothing is more thrilling than seeing your assistants move on and do well. But eventually they realize the hard part: They've got to come back and try to beat me."[19]

Hayden Fry, longtime head coach of college football's Iowa Hawkeyes, developed a practice of selecting certain players to be "player-coaches" in their positions. Many of these player-coaches have gone on to become assistant coaches and eventually head coaches of other teams, making Fry one of the most successful progenitors of college football coaches in the country. As Fry tells it, this practice originated in his childhood, growing up on his father's two-thousand-acre ranch in Odessa, Texas. Told to feed the cows, Fry happened on a solution: He'd find the "bell cow," the member of the herd who led the others. Find the bell cow, you find the herd.[20]

Like Fry, superbosses are always on the lookout for the "bell cows" among their protégés, and many of them have formal or informal systems for doing so. Jon Stewart, for instance, has worked the identification and showcasing of talent into the very structure of *The Daily Show* under his watch. Whereas his predecessor Craig Kilborn had other comedians serve as "correspondents" who reported humorously from the field, Stewart broadened these roles when he took over in 1999, bringing the correspondents in for frequent, in-studio exchanges. The upshot: performers work more closely with Stewart and the show's writers, enabling Stewart to gauge their progress and help them grow organically as on-screen talent.[21]

Underlying superbosses' constant opportunity spotting is an expansive view of what people can accomplish. Many bosses place arbitrary limits on the potential of their employees: you have to be a certain age or of a certain background before you can take on more responsibility.[22] You're typecast, relegated to a niche—despite your broader aspirations. Superbosses will have none of this. Their core belief is that the people they hire can and should do *anything,* and, further, that their protégés should continue to develop rapidly and in new directions throughout their careers. With this mind-set, they're more than willing to promote deserving people into jobs that may seem crazy to other bosses—jobs that even protégés themselves aren't sure they can handle.

Many of us can well remember those moments when someone important saw something in us, a potential that even we may not have been aware of. Superbosses are the kind of people who are always on the lookout for that possibility. As a protégé said of Coach Hayden Fry, "He knew more about what we could do than we knew. You can't imagine the kind of confidence and motivation that gives you. It makes you feel like you can't let him down."[23] Working for superbosses is almost like getting a chance to perform on *America's Got Talent*—anyone can be plucked out and groomed for greatness. At HCA under Tommy Frist, physical therapists would sometimes become senior executives, simply because Frist saw something that others didn't. Employee number twelve at Oracle, Anneke Selcy, started as a receptionist, but after Larry Ellison personally taught her the SQL programming language, she went on to occupy management positions in customer relations and later started Oracle's inside sales department—a multibillion-dollar operation now.[24]

What superbosses give protégés, then, is something quite rare in professional life, an opportunity to rebrand themselves. The career of actor Ron Howard is a great example. Beloved by many TV watchers as Opie in *The Andy Griffith Show* and later as Richie Cunningham in the sitcom *Happy Days,* Howard wanted to move away from acting and instead direct films. Enter Roger Corman, who struck a deal whereby Howard would star in one movie (*Eat My Dust!*) in return for directing another (*Grand Theft Auto*). Corman would get the Ron Howard name on two properties; Ron Howard would get the opportunity to direct his first movie. It worked. Later, Howard went on to win an Academy Award for Best Director (for *A Beautiful Mind,* in 2001), as well as direct several other well-known movies, including the Academy Award–winning *Apollo 13*.

On a day-to-day basis, superbosses also customize their general teaching style to fit the individual. "He didn't react the same way to everyone," saxophonist Bill Evans said of Miles Davis. "Everyone was different and personal to him, and that is one of the things that he was able to do . . . get to know each person and what each person needed. Some people he would be harder on than others. He was interesting in that way." Of Julian Robertson, Chase Coleman said, "He was very good at understanding some combination of what motivated people and how to extract maximum performance out of people. . . . For some people, that was encouraging them, and for other people, it was making them feel less comfortable. He would adjust his feedback."[25]

While other bosses will certainly go the extra mile for their reports on occasion, superbosses' clear commitment to personal and informal career development is far from the norm. Many large companies conceptualize careers in terms of "ladders" that define a standardized upward path for employees and managers. To get to a certain point on the ladder, you have to go through the intermediary rungs one by one. Sophisticated companies go even further, deploying rigid "competency models" to help groom executives for advancement; they figure out the key skills required for a given position, evaluate whether employees have these competencies, and provide training or coaching to "fill in the gaps." On one level, ladders and competency models make a good deal of sense, as it's obviously helpful to advance people in a graduated, orderly way. The superboss approach is a bit messier and more chaotic, yet as we've seen, it can give worthy employees opportunities to advance rapidly, in line with their true capabilities.

That's the key point: superbosses deploy an approach to development that is closely tailored to the individual needs of each protégé. It's the difference between buying a car off the dealer's lot and customizing your

Mini Cooper online. The customized car fits your life better because it's made for you—it has exactly the features you want, and nothing you don't want. Customized development of talent requires a lot more effort. As one former player noted of Bill Walsh, he "put in the extra work to figure out each of [his player's] personalities and what drove each."[26] Customized development also requires fearlessness, a willingness to depart from the fixed "road map" and make an unorthodox decision that might just be perfect for *this* particular employee.

The Mini Cooper comparison is apt. Superbosses regard protégés not as generic employees but as individual customers whose needs must be served. Imagine an organization where leaders take it upon themselves to identify *exactly* what customers need and then create appropriate ways of delivering it. Imagine an organization where the CEO stays close to the customer and feels connected. Replace "customer" with "employee," and that's just what superbosses do to help people advance in their careers. To a much greater extent than other bosses, superbosses create suitable opportunities for employees that fit their developmental needs, rather than slotting employees mindlessly into an existing, bureaucratic system. The employee as customer—what a strange idea!

Hire People and Get Out of the Way

As a young writer, comic book legend Stan Lee once worked on a comic strip that used the phrase *pogo stick* in the punch line. His editor told him that the phrase wouldn't resonate with rural audiences, and instructed Lee to change the gag so that the punch line had the phrase *roller skates* instead. In Lee's opinion, this was a big mistake; *roller skates* deflated the entire joke. Lee changed it anyway, though, to please his boss.

Lee wasn't happy to have made the change, in the end, and it taught him a valuable lesson: the importance of effective, fearless delegation. As a boss, you need to give subordinates real responsibility, and you can't stand over them, second-guessing and editing. "When you hire an artist to do a job, you let him do the job," Lee said.[27] At Marvel Comics, Lee would take a largely hands-off approach; like other superbosses, he would be quick to hand real responsibility to enterprising young people. One writer, Jim Shooter, was made editor in chief of Marvel comics at the age of twenty-seven.[28]

Superbosses are able to constantly and rapidly propel their protégés to new heights because they are the consummate delegators, relinquishing a degree of authority and oversight that would make many ordinary bosses cringe. Gene Roberts allowed writers and editors absolute freedom to follow stories as long as they adhered to certain quality standards. On one occasion during the mid-1980s, reporter Don Drake hatched a plan to cover the rising risk of AIDS in a story called "AIDS: A Day with a Global Killer." Drake's idea was to send reporters all around the world—to Thailand, an African village, a pharmaceutical company, a factory manufacturing prophylactics—to show what was going on with the disease of AIDS at a particular moment in time. Roberts's response? Go for it! He authorized a dozen reporters and half a dozen photographers to travel around the world for the story. On the appointed day, the stories rolled in, and Drake and a fellow reporter found themselves unexpectedly overwhelmed. Without direction from Roberts, the entire newsroom stopped what it was doing and spontaneously pitched in, enabling the story to make deadline with seconds to spare. When an entire team pitches in to solve a pressing problem, and when the response is unprovoked by an edict from up top, you know you've got an incredible culture coursing through the business, shaped by a superboss.[29]

Superbosses possess the deep, underlying trust that is essential to effective delegation. "Norman Brinker gave us incredible autonomy," one former senior manager told me. "We definitely had the ability to fail."[30]

Ron Gilbert, who worked in the games division of Lucasfilm during the late 1980s and 1990s, agreed: "One of the best things George Lucas did for us was to leave us alone. He just kind of gave us the resources to go off and create and come up with things."[31] As a group, superbosses believe that their people are fully capable of arriving at solutions themselves and that the experience of doing so supports their development. "Every conductor has his own solution and must look for it," Jorma Panula once said. "It's a longer way to go, but worth it. You have to have the courage to jump into the water before you learn to swim. I don't throw in the life belt until someone is really drowning."[32]

Scot Sellers, the chairman and CEO of Archstone, told me of a special assignment Bill Sanders gave him early in his career. Major investors were coming to town, and they were considering whether to pour hundreds of millions of dollars into a brand-new residential property development Sanders was envisioning. With only two days' notice, Sanders asked Sellers to create a compelling strategy and vision for the development. Sellers and his colleagues had only just begun thinking about the concept, but that didn't seem to matter. Sanders "believed that if he gave me those marching orders, I would come back with something that was close enough to what he envisioned, that we would be able to sell it together."[33] Sanders was right. Sellers buried himself in research and by the next afternoon, he had a draft presentation on Sanders's desk. Sanders made only a few adjustments, and when Sellers made the pitch, it was a home run. Imagine how great Sellers felt to secure this win—and to have even been given a shot in the first place.

What superbosses also do to support the learning experience is to hold protégés strictly accountable for their performance. In superboss organizations, the rule is clear: Sink or swim. "You just knew when you were around Brinker expectations and accountability were givens because of the way he conducted himself," one member of his inner circle recalled.[34] That said, superbosses aren't unfeeling tyrants; they will let you fail once—but you better learn from that mistake. "The only people that don't make mistakes are people who don't do anything," Michael Miles told me, "so in saying that we wanted action, we also said that we have to be tolerant of mistakes."[35] Superbosses will also tolerate it when you admit you don't know something, as long as you make it your business to find out the answer—and quickly.

With so much responsibility on their shoulders and a clear sense of accountability, not to mention the trust of their superboss, protégés come away feeling a sense of their *own* power and worth, as if they are more like partners than subordinates. Ralph Lauren "made you feel you were so much a part of it," Sal Cesarani related.[36] Bill Walsh made a point of emphasizing to each player how he contributed to the team's overall success. He would tell players that "at some point, [you] will be in a position to win or lose a game," and that each player had "to be prepared both mentally and physically to play that role."[37]

Enhancing protégés' sense of partnership also comes from superbosses who really *listen*. Many superbosses I studied were known not merely as founts of knowledge but as great listeners—bosses who took seriously what employees had to say, even if they didn't wind up agreeing. Bob Noyce had a distinctive way of listening that involved staring and never blinking or swallowing. "He absorbed everything you said and then answered very levelly in a soft baritone voice, and often with a smile."[38] Gene Roberts zoned out when others were talking, entering what his managing editor Jim Naughton termed his "fugue state."[39] At least he seemed to be zoning out; every now and then, he'd chime in with an incisive question and they realized he'd been listening all along.

Superbosses don't merely listen; they relentlessly *ask* employees their opinions as well. When facing decisions big and small, Ralph Lauren would ask even the receptionist's and cleaning staff's opinions. Robert Green, former fashion editor at *Playboy*, remembered that Lauren "would ask your opinion as though he couldn't make a move without it."[40] According to Raleigh Glassberg, a former buyer at Bloomingdale's, you would "sit in [Lauren's] office, you'd go through things together, he'd listen to ideas. It was very much a partnership. You didn't influence his style, but you'd talk about what would be commercial and what wasn't, in terms of timing and certain shapes. . . . You'd go for the afternoon to look at preliminaries and work on the line, and it was as much a family relationship as you can have in business."[41]

Even better, basketball coach Rick Pitino is known for calling upon his assistants to give scouting reports without notes. Courtside fans have heard him turning to his assistants at key moments in games and shouting, "I need a play! Gimme something!"[42] The mere fact that he would solicit their advice suggests to all those within earshot just how much he values their abilities.

We're back to a point we saw earlier—the relatively egalitarian nature of superboss organizations. Most employees would find it refreshing to work in an organization where what they do really counts, where people are paying attention. Under these circumstances, employees' career goals cease to be abstractions that may or may not materialize at some undetermined future date. Like their boss's own aspirations, they're in play *right now.* They either rise to the challenge or they don't. It's easy to see why protégés of superbosses progress so much more quickly than their peers at more traditional organizations—their bosses have the guts to let them see what they're *really* made of.

The Big Personality Paradox

How could superbosses be such strong delegators at the same time that they are deeply involved in the substance of the work, to an extent that verges on that famous evil of leadership, micromanaging? Working in the trenches with their apprentices, immersed in the action, superbosses will not hesitate to make their opinions known about relatively small matters. As journalist Stanley Gellers told me, Ralph Lauren was "the original micromanager. Nothing leaves that office without passing his eye. He is the one to put clothes on a mannequin if a major retailer is about to look at the line. He is the one who personally inspects his own stores. He is the ultimate detail man."[43] George Lucas, Alice Waters, Lorne Michaels, Jorma Panula—all were described by their protégés as, if not micromanagers, at least deeply engrossed with tiny, seemingly random details.

How can this be? How can a boss be *both* an extreme delegator and a micromanager? Life would be simple (and not in a good way) if not for the endless capacity of people—well, at least some people—to internalize two seemingly incompatible behaviors. And that is the case here. Superbosses have found a third path between micromanagers, who are afraid to delegate because they don't trust their subordinates, and free riders, who delegate without control because they are lazy or incompetent. Let's just call them Hands-On Delegators. It's *because* superbosses exert such command over details that they are able to delegate effectively and create opportunities for their protégés. They know exactly what's going on in their businesses. They know who is performing well and who isn't. They know the strengths and weaknesses of their reports. They know the latest trends impacting the marketplace. All this know-how gives them the confidence to delegate, as does a practical grasp of when, how, and to whom to delegate. Meanwhile, the clarity of their vision and its dissemination throughout their organizations further assure them that team members will get the basics right without needing constant supervision.

According to protégés, superbosses skillfully oversee and exert control without stepping on toes. They articulate their absolute vision to others, set specific work goals, and then step back to see what happens. When all goes well, they let it ride, while still paying close attention to what's happening under their watch. If they don't like what's going on, they don't hesitate to step in and change it. As comedian Andy Samberg told me, Lorne Michaels chooses to be more involved on some days and less involved on others, depending on his assessment of what's needed. "There will be weeks where you have a scene where you don't really hear from him at all about it—it just goes as it's going to go. And then there are some weeks where he'll take a very strong interest and have a lot of thoughts."[44]

One thing superbosses are definitely willing to do—and that a pure delegator might not—is jump in to help protégés with unforeseen crises. Chef Michael Sullivan recalls spending an afternoon cooking an important meal with several Chez Panisse alumni. The roasted pigs didn't come out right; they were raw inside. Although Waters was working the front room and was nicely dressed, she came to the kitchen to help the team figure out what to do. "We were all looking at each other and watching Alice kind of orchestrate the whole emergency recovery situation. She was able to do that better than anybody; her attention to detail in a crisis was something to behold."[45] We're so used to thinking of delegation as an either-or proposition. It doesn't have to be—it can be both-and.

Running parallel to the "hands-on delegation" paradox is what I like to call the Big Personality paradox. It's easy to find big bosses who hog the limelight, leaving everyone else in the shadows. Some other bosses seem content to shrink into the background, sometimes more passive than anything else. Superbosses are neither of these. They can have enormous, larger-than-life personalities. They're opinionated, zealous about their beliefs, aggressive, and competitive. They're often type-A people who love to win. They're the *last* people we would expect to step aside so that younger talent can claim the spotlight—yet that's exactly what they do. Miles Davis believed that each band member deserved his "moment in the sun," even if he was the concert's headline attraction.

Norman Brinker operated on a similar principle: "Norman has accomplished, and is as successful as he is, but he never has to be the only guy in the room," former Burger King CEO Jeff Campbell told me.[46] Some superbosses would make a practice of moving on quickly to the next project or business issue, leaving team members clearly in charge of doing what they do. Multiple protégés shared stories of how their superbosses purposely left room for others to take on leadership roles.

Unlike many other bosses, superbosses are so confident, they don't *need* to constantly dominate others. This frees them up to enjoy other big personalities and to even take responsibility for helping younger colleagues rise up and become big personalities themselves. As longtime coach and athletic director Ted Leland recalled, his superboss Bill Walsh "used to say, 'Part of your job as manager is to make sure that the people under you are successful.'"[47] Larry Ellison was no different; he once commented that Oracle had a great succession plan, as it has always been full of employees who have gone on to become CEOs.[48] At Kraft, Michael Miles created an annual development process in which senior managers from all divisions would discuss every person in the organization and what they needed next in their career. "It was very rigorous and it was something that everyone paid attention to . . . something you put a lot of time and effort into because it was important that you demonstrate you were good at developing people."[49] We tend to think that people with authority and a commanding presence can't also behave in ways that nurture others. As tough as superbosses can be, isn't it refreshing to know that some of the biggest personalities of all will also purposely build people up?

The Protégé's Responsibility

Dr. Karl VanDevender, personal physician to Tommy Frist and his family, told me of a time when Frist was piloting his plane and VanDevender was serving as copilot.[50] The skies were clear and beautiful. Van-Devender turned to Frist and asked him an (interesting) question: "Tommy, you're not a brilliant guy in the sense of being a National Merit Scholar or something like that, but you have accomplished so much with your life. How did you do it?"

Fumbling in his left shirt pocket, Frist pulled out a 3x5-inch note card with phrases penciled on it. "Karl, do you see this?"

"Yes," VanDevender replied.

"Every day, I look at my near-term goals, my intermediate-term goals, and my long-term goals. I do it from a health point of view, a moral point of view, and a financial point of view. I polish these goals every day. I've been surprised to see that most people don't write down their goals. May I see yours?"

Frist's note card brings up a major theme of this book: What happens to people in their careers, and in their lives, is seldom random. Frist's question—"May I see yours?"—suggests the deeper challenge that superbosses level at all protégés. Yes, superbosses are willing to advance people, even when protégés don't think they're ready. Yes, they will purposefully step back so their protégés can shine. Yes, they will organize their entire enterprise so that informal, apprenticeship-style learning can take place. But they will ultimately push protégés to step up and take responsibility for their *own* development by cultivating an everyday focus on learning and growth.

Superbosses aren't about to sit there spewing wisdom for their protégés to collect and marvel at passively; they expect their people to ask questions, seek out knowledge, try to get better, and actively jump toward the next stages of their careers. Many bosses have an unspoken rule: Be compliant, don't rock the boat, do what I do, and you'll move up. Compliant employees are the *last* thing superbosses want. On the contrary, they like to take protégés to task, and they value those who don't cave and especially those who have the guts to push back. Jay Chiat's writers and artists had to withstand his frank critiques without crumbling—remembering that it was about the work, not them. Robert Noyce "could be a very, very tough taskmaster," Gordon Moore remembered. "It's not personal, it's all business, so if you were up for the challenge, you could be very successful."[51]

More broadly, superbosses expect protégés to fully step up, to confidently go after responsibility rather than wait for it to be dangled in front of them. Superbosses are 100 percent committed and always pushing forward—protégés have to be, too. If you waited to ask Larry Ellison what to do when facing a particular decision, you waited too long; those who asked permission were like grapes that "kind of died on the vine," as former Oracle senior executive Gary Bloom put it to me in an interview.[52] The metaphor went further: some employees had the attitude that "if you don't spray water on me, I'm not going to grow," and there were others who would "suck whatever water they can out of the vine and continue to grow."[53] The latter were the ones who did well at Oracle; Ellison frequently lost interest in people who were timid or hesitant or who didn't have a firm viewpoint.

Superbosses have a selfish motivation for expecting protégés to step up: they want protégés to teach *them* a thing or two. Recall that Julian Robertson funded his "tiger seeds" because he reveled in being surrounded by youthful energy and insight (not to mention that he also wanted to make lots of money!). Reminiscing about his Second Great Quintet, Miles Davis said, "Those were all young guys and although they were learning from me, I was learning from them, too."[54] A former colleague of Ralph Lauren put it this way: "Ralph is great but he also feeds off greatness as well."[55] Since superbosses are always learning and growing themselves, they see interactions with their people as an irreplaceable opportunity to freshen their perspectives and continue to innovate. The apprentice relationship we introduced in the last chapter thus turns out to be very much a two-way street: protégés get an unforgettable, career-making experience, while superbosses, who realize they can't achieve their visions alone, get to move their life's work just a bit further. Pretty good deal all around, if you ask me.

The Crazy, Intense, Beautiful Pressure Cooker

Looking back on his career, Chase Coleman reflected that Robertson "was good at making people feel that sense of ownership and opportunity . . . and then providing a path, sort of a steep learning curve for people who excelled at their first task."[56] This learning curve in turn translated into an extremely intense work environment. Think of how ferociously Coleman must have worked for Robertson right after college, not to mention during those early years of his fund—and how much he learned.

All superbosses compress learning and growth, which is why some protégés don't need to work for them very long to get that potentially career-altering impact. Gayle Ortiz worked at Chez Panisse for only two months during the summer of 1976, on her way to a long career as a pastry chef. When I asked her what she possibly could have picked up from such a short sojourn with Alice Waters, she said, "It shaped the whole way I run my business, really." In particular, Ortiz learned the principle of never compromising on her vision or on the quality of her food. "I learned to pay attention to detail and demand perfection in the way that things were not only made, but also how they were served, the way the dining room looks, the way the front of the house looks. It was my main focus, the way that I looked at business."[57]

Malcolm Gladwell's book *Outliers* presented an intriguing notion that successful people become successful because they train for a cumulative total of ten thousand hours. But plenty of people get their ten thousand hours and don't become successful. It is the *quality* of those ten thousand hours that surely matters. At most companies, you're able to settle in and relax after spending a period of time on the job. In a superboss organization, there's no settling in—success in one position leads to even more responsibility. One well-known Oracle alumnus recalled that colleagues used to count their time at the company in "dog years"—one year working at Oracle was like seven years working anywhere else.[58]

Shaping Career Growth like a Superboss

How does your work experience compare? Are you constantly being pushed to your limits? Is your boss looking for opportunities for you to stretch your wings—and does she have a sixth sense for what you need? Is she giving you that blend of guidance and freedom to make the most of the responsibility already delegated to you? How fast are your most promising colleagues *really* moving up? Are some people pigeonholed into certain tracks and not others? Many top organizations today tout themselves as "career destinations," emphasizing the great opportunities they offer for advancement, but those opportunities may not be as attractive as they seem if they're not tailored to *you* and your true capabilities. If you're talented, ambitious, and energized to succeed, don't settle for ordinary. Look for a superboss of your own to work for. When you find one (because, remember, they're out there, in greater numbers than you might think), be prepared to take risks and be placed on the hot seat.

If you're a boss who has always operated within a traditional "career ladder"–type system, making "safe" promotions based on indicated employee skill sets and past experiences, don't assume there's nothing you can do. Give a younger person a try—someone who shows great promise and has a growth mind-set. Or consider, as an experiment, promoting an incredibly talented person of any age who can bring an unusual background to the position. Think about your direct reports and what each of them needs, and then consider possible ways within your organization to help them to the next level. Perform this analysis regularly—on an annual basis, at least, and perhaps more often. If applicable, ask your reports to do this for *their* reports. We all know about the challenge of managing up, getting your boss to see things your way, at least some of the time, and we also understand that this is often a key element in moving forward in a company. Well, how about also "managing down," embracing the notion that your success as a manager in large part hinges on your ability to make your own people successful.

Watch, too, how you delegate responsibility. I regularly coach senior executives on how they can best deal with critical leadership challenges. As they describe their problems, it's amazing how often it boils down to a failure to delegate effectively. It's hard to get people in line behind a big idea if they had no part in generating it. When you can't find the "right people" for the team, it may be more about you than it is about them. After all, the right people don't stick around when their boss has all the answers. Whatever you do, you don't want to fall into the vicious cycle some managers find themselves in, where they don't trust their employees to get the job done, so they do it themselves. The more they take on team members' work, the less capable team members become. You're working 24/7 and you don't understand why. Ask yourself whether you meddle too often and in the wrong ways. How would your reports answer these questions? Learn to trust your team members, and if you don't, ask yourself: Why not? You hired them!

You might also work institutionally to make your organization an unparalleled place to grow careers. Some companies are especially strong at setting up succession plans for employees—General Electric and Google being great old world and new world examples. At pharmaceutical company Baxter, longtime legendary CEO Bill Graham created a talent machine by quickly and consistently moving young managers to greater and greater responsibilities. The result was the deepest bench in the industry in his day, and employees who went on to become CEOs at numerous biotech companies, including Covidien, Genzyme, and others.[59] If your organization extends across business units or geographies, you can also exploit this structure to help generate growth experiences for employees.

Jeff Campbell recalled for me a fourteen-month period during the early 1980s when he worked closely with Norman Brinker and was promoted twice. First, he was made president of Burger King's worldwide operations. Then, perhaps six months later, Brinker came in and "dropped the bomb" that, thanks to some business developments, Campbell was being named Burger King's new chairman and CEO. "I exploded into a thousand pieces. . . . It was a little bit of a stretch going from region manager to CEO—and this was in, like, fourteen months. It was pretty scary."[60] Think of how it may have felt—the nervous knot in your stomach at knowing you're being called to do something big, something you've never done before, something perhaps you've wanted all your life. Do you have it in you? Can you pull it off? But this is what superbosses give you: the chance to succeed. They open the door to opportunity. And who wouldn't want that shot?

CHAPTER SEVEN

The Cohort Effect

Many of us never get the chance to realize childhood dreams, but actress and comedian Rachel Dratch is one of the lucky ones. Growing up in Lexington, Massachusetts, during the late 1970s and early 1980s, she stayed up past her bedtime once a week to watch *Saturday Night Live* on television. She discovered *SNL* while sleeping over at her friend Jill's house; Jill's older brother was watching, so Dratch sat down in front of the TV as well. "I remember being immediately fascinated," Dratch recalled in her 2012 memoir, *Girl Walks into a Bar* . . . "What was this secret world I had just stumbled upon? It had a feeling like nothing I'd ever seen on TV."[1]

SNL was one of the small screen's hottest programs, and its unique blend of comedy, variety entertainment, and live performances would go on to garner dozens of Emmy awards[2] and become a cultural phenomenon. Executive producer Lorne Michaels was credited for launching the careers of early cast members such as Bill Murray, Gilda Radner, and John Belushi as well as a who's who of comedy superstars, including Dana Carvey, Mike Myers, Chris Rock, Amy Poehler, Tina Fey, Seth

Meyers, and Jimmy Fallon—a record of talent spawning that continued virtually unmatched in the entertainment industry through the 1990s and into the 2000s. Dratch would become another name on that list, famous for characters such as the perpetually depressed Debby Downer and the junior high school student Sheldon.[3]

Dratch started at *SNL* in 1999. Like other cast members I spoke with, she found the show incredibly demanding. Back then (as now), the cast and crew had only six days to create a show from scratch that would air before a live television audience of millions. On Mondays, there was a brainstorming session in Michaels's office. On Tuesdays, cast members and writers crafted sketches together, often pulling all-nighters to get the job done. On Wednesdays, the cast read through the sketches and made revisions while the production team began work on the sets, costumes, and sound. On Thursdays and Fridays, the cast and crew rehearsed, revised, tied up loose ends, and wrote the "Weekend Update" segment, which commented on items in the news. A cast rehearsal took place Saturday afternoon, followed by a dress rehearsal at eight p.m. before a studio audience. For an hour afterward, Michaels would make last-minute cuts and edits, since the show's material was usually overtime by twenty minutes. The staff scrambled to make these changes, up until and even after the moment at eleven thirty p.m., when those famous words echoed from television sets across America: "Live from New York, it's *Saturday Night!*"

Dratch found that *SNL*'s high-octane atmosphere spurred her to work at her very best. Michaels and the other producers didn't coddle her; they threw her into the same proverbial pool that Jorma Panula also talked about, and let her fend for herself. The experience helped Dratch improve her writing skills. It was simple: either write good sketches with funny characters, or sit on the sidelines watching each week's show. She also learned a lot from her colleagues. Dratch had heard that "competition could be really rough"[4] on the show, but as Michaels told me in an interview, "There's something special about an environment in which nobody is more important than the show. On Monday, we face a blank page. Then, in six days, we're on the air. It's a task so difficult that it brings out the best in people."[5]

To get the job done, cast members and writers collaborate closely. Many do so selflessly as well, in some cases helping to refine skits that others wrote and would take credit for.[6] Amid all the chaos of production, deep emotional bonds form: "We were sort of trapped there," writer David Mandel has said. "There was a bunker mentality. You know, there was the siege of putting the show up each week. And that ultimately meant you were sort of eating and drinking, and in some cases, sleeping with these people, the same group of people, and going to the bathroom with them and, you know, seeing them at their best and their worst."[7] Veteran cast members remember that one of their favorite parts of working on *SNL* was the camaraderie that emerged. "I will miss most the moments you'll never see," Will Ferrell has said, "the goofing around during the blocking of sketches on Thursday and Friday. Those were the parts of the week that were the most fun for me. That seventeenth floor has the same feeling of living in a dorm—except that everybody is doing comedy—and I liked that feeling."[8]

Although the contexts and stakes are radically different, we often see similarly transcendent displays of teamwork among other groups of highly competitive individuals—athletes, entrepreneurs running start-up companies, kitchen staff at restaurants, flight crews, first responders, military personnel, and emergency-room teams. These people find themselves in intense situations where every second counts, peak performance matters, and everyone has to work together to achieve a common goal. In corporate environments, sadly, you don't always see such deep camaraderie among team members. The most progressive organizations spend considerable time and money focusing on team building, giving rise to an entire cottage industry of consultants and coaches. Still, many workplaces are lucky if they experience heightened, near-seamless team-work only every now and then. In many organizations, poor teamwork is endemic.

At superboss companies, colleagues compete with one another to perform at their best, but also work together *every day* as seamlessly and effectively as the cast of *Saturday Night Live*. Of course, superbosses are great at building "vertical" bonds between themselves and their protégés, but much more than traditional bosses, they also know how to create winning teams. Protégés typically have a deep respect and affection for their colleagues (similar to what they feel for their superboss), enabling everyone to work together, learn, and perform far better than they would on their own.

To some extent, collaboration and team spirit at superboss-run orga-nizations emerge indirectly as a consequence of other steps superbosses take to spur motivation, creativity, and learning in their individual protégés. However, superbosses understand that teams win more than individuals do—that the potential of a group of immensely talented indi-viduals is greater than the sum of its parts. They explicitly encourage collegiality among colleagues to take root, even as they instill a strong competitive spirit within their teams. For superbosses, extreme collabo-ration and meaningful competition aren't opposites; they go hand in hand. The presence of one enhances the other, resulting in a seemingly magical outcome: a high-performance environment that feels nurturing, welcoming—and fulfilling.

Crafting the Cult

At a glance, it may seem hard to appreciate how special superboss work-places are. Many workplaces have at least some degree of team spirit, right? Colleagues celebrate one another's birthdays. They throw holiday parties. They participate in fantasy football leagues. They connect on social media. And when challenges arise, they help one another out to get the job done. Most of us don't work on the sets of television shows; we work in professional offices or retail environments or production facilities or schools. In these contexts, the teamwork and camaraderie that exist often seem pretty good.

Here's the difference: the teams that superbosses assemble aren't just pretty good—they are *exceptional*. Even at the best workplaces, employees might refer to their team as a surrogate "family," but it's rare for employees to go so far as to describe their teams as "cults." When I talked to protégés of superbosses, however, that term came up over and over. Recall from chapter 3, for instance, how designer Joseph Abboud described working for Ralph Lauren: "It was very much like a cult. You wanted to be part of it. Ralph was our hero. We believed the myth; we dressed the myth. We were the legions."[9]

You might think creating a profound "cult" experience would be hard for superbosses, requiring some sort of special energy, devotion, and commitment, not to mention resources. How else would you overcome all the petty politics, resentments, and miscommunications that normally hamstring teams? Doesn't it take millions of dollars spent on team-building retreats and intensive coaching? In reality, crafting a cult experience isn't that hard for superbosses. As Abboud's language suggests, strong bonds between teammates arise as a happy side effect of key elements of the superboss playbook. First and foremost, Abboud identifies the distinctive *vision* of his superboss (i.e., Lauren's "myth") as the cornerstone of the cultish identity. In agreeing to go all in behind a unique vision, protégés naturally feel *different* from others who don't get the vision, or are unlucky enough to work for a leader *without* a vision.

Superbosses establish a kind of insider sensibility for protégés, constantly affirming to them that they are a uniquely talented bunch unlike any other. Ralph Lauren inspired his staff by saying they weren't ordinary designers or merchandisers, but an elite of "chosen people." "We were on this incredible ride," one employee recalled, "and he'd say that this beautiful stuff wasn't him, it was us—the most talented people in the world were in this room."[10] For superbosses, what most defined membership in the "chosen people" was the ability to set standards for the rest of the industry. Protégés were leaders, not followers. They had what it took to control, change, and dominate the marketplace, not merely keep pace with it, and this is what established them as a breed apart. "Ralph was always telling us that we're the standard," one employee related, "that everybody is always imitating everything we do, that everybody wants to be like us."[11]

Superbosses reinforce their protégés' sense of themselves as a "chosen people" by constantly reminding them that they can accomplish anything if they set their minds to it. Others submitted easily to adversity, superbosses proclaim, but protégés were made of much tougher stuff. Obstacles and challenges weren't evidence of the team's fallibility but rather occasions when teams could rise up together and reaffirm their inherent greatness. Bill Walsh explicitly worked with his team to turn disadvantages into advantages. In his hands, an extended road trip (which usually is a huge disadvantage for a football team) became an opportunity to thrive on the challenge and ride strong emotions to victory. As he explained in an interview with *Harvard Business Review*, "I would condition the 49ers to adversity. We would talk about how it feels to fly into enemy territory. . . . When I talked with the team, I would use examples from the early days of WWII as illustrations of the desperate and heroic fights we could emulate."[12] Standing strong and emerging victorious against the odds, members of superboss-led teams could think of themselves as uniquely talented and heroic, head and shoulders above teams at other organizations.

For most people working at companies today, such a disciplined reframing of adversity would seem unusual, to say the least. How many times have you seen colleagues sit at a meeting and do little but cast doubt on solutions others offer? "We don't have the resources to get this done," these naysayers claim. "We're already overworked and under-staffed." "We've never tried anything like this before." To superbosses, such sentiments are tantamount to treason, even if there might be some truth to them. Superbosses understand that focusing primarily on what might get in the way of change prevents a team or company from ever trying anything new. It also prevents employees from identifying whole-heartedly with the team and giving themselves over to it.

As I delved deeper into the lives of my superbosses, I found them doing everything and anything to inculcate a cultish sense of difference in their protégés. In public, they served as evangelists for their protégés, even to the point of minimizing their own contributions. Alice Waters was quoted as saying, "I don't do anything really. I'm not a chef. I just let them do what they do so well. They are the best, you know."[13] Super-bosses also find creative ways to publicize the unique skills and qualities of their protégés. For decades, artists who drew comic books were anon-ymous. Marvel comics impresario and writer Stan Lee introduced a credits page to his comic books, giving his artists "brands" for the first time. The credits might read something like: "Written with Passion by Stan Lee, Drawn with Pride by Jack Kirby. Inked with Perfection by Joe Sinnott. And lettered with a Scratchy Pen by Artie Simek."[14] Lee also talked up his staff in his monthly newsletter called *The Bullpen Bulletin*. These shout-outs often shaped the careers of people in his department. For instance, Stan Lee proclaimed Jack Kirby, a midcareer artist at the time, the "King of Comics," a moniker that has stuck to this day.[15] Of course, many would argue that Kirby *was* the "king of comics" regardless of what Lee thought. But certainly Lee's coronation of Kirby helped se-cure that stature for Kirby in the public eye.

As if all of these techniques for establishing their protégés unique-ness weren't enough, there's another factor to consider: the superboss's own revered status in the industry. As a protégé, you know that the superboss's reputation as a talent magnet and innovator is well established. You also know that this Great One has chosen *you*. What could be more meaningful (and scary) than that? As Seth Meyers has said, the *Saturday Night Live* studio felt like a "temple" because of all the greats who came before.[16] For all employees of superbosses, the burden is on *them* to prove they are worthy of the temple in which they work. When they do, they feel even more honored to know they belong. Not only has the superboss inspired them to believe in themselves, but his reputation has lent added credibility to any gesture of support he offers. When he assigns them a tough task or singles them out for their accomplishments, he knows what he's talking about. It's not just lip service. It's real.

In thinking about the creation of cult identities, it's also worth remembering that superbosses actively *preselect* employees for their eagerness to go all in, hiring unusual talent whom they feel have an understanding or at least an affinity for their vision. Former employee Robert Burke has said of Lauren: "Ralph surrounds himself with people who understand his taste level. When he says 'Fred Astaire 1930,' a big picture goes up in your mind. When he says 'Montauk Weekend,' everyone has the same vision."[17] Despite their different backgrounds, protégés of superbosses feel connected the moment they walk in the door because the superboss has ensured that they "get" his defining approach to the business. Lauren's protégés weren't just ordinary employees in their minds, but a unified band of soldiers standing tall in their (very well-tailored) uniforms as they paraded through a conquered village. As Luc Vandevelde, the former Marks & Spencer chairman, remarked of his time working for Michael Miles at Kraft, "We were part of a young generation and clearly were given the feeling that we were going to make it if we developed the company's talent."[18]

The high-performance environments of superboss organizations also naturally reinforce group identities among protégés. Like cast members on *Saturday Night Live,* protégés work long hours together, to the point where work seems to blend into personal lives. "The job and their personal life were kind of inseparable," said former Chiat/Day creative director Bob Dion. "Best friends were also business associates and employees."[19]

The superboss's rejection of hierarchy, noted earlier, also comes into play here. As Michael Milken once observed, "People are much more productive when they feel they're part of a team. It should be a collective force. No one should stand on top of someone else."[20] In most traditional organizations, hierarchy constitutes a formidable barrier to teamwork. It's hard to give yourself over to the group when you're constantly being reminded that you and your colleagues are *not* the same. Thanks to egalitarian policies as well as the open layout common to many superboss work spaces, team members receive both easy access to one another as well as constant affirmation of their unity. On Jon Stewart's *The Daily Show,* cast members maintained a friendly, supportive, and casual kind of interaction, taking time out to coach one another in an office environment that has been described as having "the offhand feel of a college dormitory lounge."[21] Architecturally as well as philosophically, the team reigns supreme.

Some superbosses go even further and locate their open work spaces in out-of-the-way places, creating a den or haven that greatly cements group cohesiveness. Milken moved his offices to Los Angeles, away from the industry's center of Wall Street. During the early 1980s, George Lucas used money earned from the original *Star Wars* to create Skywalker Ranch, a creative mecca in northern California, away from Hollywood. "The idea for this came out of film school," he once explained. "It was a great environment; a lot of people all very interested in film, exchanging ideas, watching movies, helping each other out. I wondered why we couldn't have a professional environment like that. When you make a movie, it really is a fifteen-hour-a-day thing, and you don't have time to do anything else. You need an environment that gets people excited about things, and they don't do that in Hollywood."[22]

Whether a superboss's headquarters are physically removed or not, the lack of hierarchy, long hours, and shared pursuit and belief in the superboss's vision all contribute to a group culture. Protégés I spoke with described a variety of shared memories, work habits, and even ways of communicating. Director, visual effects expert, and Oscar winner Phil Tippett recalls an intuitive "language" that evolved among Lucas protégés: "You develop a language that is almost telepathic where your understanding of film history and your references and the kinds of things that had inspired you in the past kind of become a touchstone. In the context of any particular discussion, you can cut through hours and hours and hours of description by saying, 'Yeah, well, it's gotta feel more like the third-act battle in *The Wild Bunch*' and immediately you know what that means."[23] Imagine understanding your colleagues so well and feeling so close to them that your communication is "almost telepathic." Some married couples don't even enjoy that kind of intimacy, yet among employees of superboss-run companies, it's far from unusual.

The "No Jerks" Rule

As of 2015, the San Antonio Spurs have been the most successful professional basketball franchise in the National Basketball Association for the previous seventeen years. They have made the play-offs every season since 1997–1998, and in 2014, they won their fifth championship in that time span.[24] Their winning streak has taken place not only on the court; the team has also become a factory of talent for the rest of the league. Former assistants have become head coaches and/or general managers for the Atlanta Hawks, New Orleans Pelicans, Oklahoma City Thunder, Orlando Magic, Philadelphia 76ers, and Utah Jazz.[25]

Such talent creation reflects the management approach of the two superbosses at the helm: head coach Gregg Popovich and general manager R. C. Buford. The two emphasize strong teamwork among management, particularly when it comes to decision making. Whereas other teams might marginalize assistants and front-office staff, Popovich and Buford would treat them as integral parts of the leadership team by involving them in decision making and *expecting* them to have good ideas.[26]

Coach Bill Walsh deployed a similar approach with his teams. He believed in creating a "sense of belonging" for his people, and this meant insisting that he, his players, and his coaches overcome their egos and foster an atmosphere of open dialogue and debate. If during studying films of the previous week's game, the lowliest assistant coach saw something Walsh missed, Walsh wanted him to feel comfortable sharing his idea.[27] Walsh even encouraged this type of open environment on the sidelines during games. On Sundays, coaches and players were expected to provide input and feedback in order to make appropriate changes in personnel or in how plays were called. On other occasions, when Walsh analyzed potential recruits, he met with his talent scouts individually and then brought everyone together as a group to hash it out. "We created an atmosphere in meetings in which a scout or a coach was able to express himself completely. If he overstated or understated in any category, he could later change his opinion without being criticized. . . . Everyone was expected to participate."[28]

Hiring specifically for an ability to collaborate is another key technique superbosses deploy to nourish team spirit. "We had a cardinal rule that we weren't going to hire any pricks," Michael Miles told me. "We decided that there were plenty of smart people out in the world, and you could hire smart, nice people as easily as you hire smart, not-nice people. And by doing so, you'd make Kraft into a place where people enjoyed working."[29] Miles's main problem with "pricks" was that their very presence risked creating a "dog-eat-dog environment," and Miles didn't want his protégés to be forced to watch their backs at every turn or aim to succeed at their colleagues' expense.[30]

Another way superbosses instill team spirit is by scrupulously modeling it. Miles Davis and Stan Lee were known for publicly and graciously acknowledging contributions proffered by protégés. "If I was the inspiration and wisdom and the link for this band," Davis remarked, "Tony [Williams] was the fire, the creative spark; Wayne [Shorter] was the idea person, the conceptualizer of a whole lot of musical ideas we did; and Ron [Carter] and Herbie [Hancock] were the anchors. I was just the leader who put us all together."[31]

For coach Bill Walsh, loyalty to the high-performing team and its staff was paramount: "How eager would you be to join an organization that might betray your loyalty?" he asked.[32] Other superbosses placed a high premium on loyalty as well, especially in situations where members of the team were in trouble or in need of protection. Chez Panisse had an informal policy of helping employees personally and professionally. "You [as an employee] have the sense that people will take care of you," manager Gilbert Pilgram said. "If you get into a bit of personal trouble, the restaurant will step in—observing your privacy, of course—to help you."[33] In superboss organizations, "team" isn't an empty slogan. It means something, because the leader of the organization insists on it.

As my interviews revealed, a superboss's team-oriented behavior made a profound impact on protégés. Clayton McWhorter, Frist's onetime president and COO at HCA who went on to found and run Health-Trust, told me that he and his colleagues "really believed that if we performed good service, that the patient came first, that we attracted good people to work with us, then we would be supported in the community as being good citizens in the community. Employees were always number one."[34] Don Suter, a senior executive who worked for Bill Sanders, told me that he had been so impressed with Sanders's ethic of teamwork that he was trying to incorporate it into his own organization. The essence of this model was "to treat people with respect . . . so that we can accomplish a lot more together than any one of you superstars can do on your own."[35]

When you look at superbosses as a group, it becomes clear that there is actually much more to their model than "just" treating people with respect or demonstrating loyalty. Good managers with a professional mind-set do that all the time. Superbosses go further, engaging creatively so as to build emotional bonds among teammates. For instance, superbosses promote team identity by purposely nourishing a distinctive culture among their protégés. If you worked for Mary Kay Ash, the superboss who created Mary Kay cosmetics, you'd know that a bumblebee pin worn on a lapel designated someone as a top performer.[36] You'd also know dozens of songs sung within the company, some touting company principles or maxims (e.g., "If you want to be a director, you've got to be perfecter").[37] You'd know the difference between a salesperson who received a Buick Regal as a bonus and one who received a Cadillac, and you'd also know the meaning of the bumper sticker affixed to the Regal that read: "When I Grow Up, I'm Going to Be a Cadillac."[38] You'd know all kinds of expressions used within the company, such as, "The speed of the leader is the speed of the gang."[39] The existence of all these rituals and practices gave substance to the team identity, making it feel meaningful and real.

Unlike most good professional managers, superbosses also build the culture of their teams by emphasizing socialization outside of work, typically with the superboss as ringleader. When the day's teaching sessions were over, Jorma Panula had fun with his conducting protégés, encouraging them to get to know one another as well. "He takes care of the students like they are a brotherhood," one protégé explained. "You eat together. You live together. You go to art exhibitions together. And he's there with you."[40] Julian Robertson would take his team on informal "outward-bound" weekends to mountain locations for the express purpose of relaxing and bonding.[41] As longtime HCA employee Victor Campbell recalls, colleagues at the company played basketball together after work: "A group of us were into basketball and Tommy would be out playing in the Civic Center with us on a Wednesday night. . . . Here he was and his kids in the stands and my little kids in the stands."[42] Jay Chiat socialized so casually and so regularly with colleagues that he created an environment in which, again, personal and work life seemed to blur. "It took me a while to learn," former Chiat/Day creative director Bob Dion remembered, "but Jay wanted to close the doors at the office and meet you at the restaurant for dinner. And call you on the weekend, meet in the downtown streets in Soho and walk around, meet for brunch with the wives and family."[43]

The Cohort Effect

In 1959, songwriter and producer Berry Gordy launched a small, independent record company using eight hundred dollars he borrowed from family members. One of the first acts he signed was William Robinson, a street performer with a melodious voice. Better known by his nickname, Smokey, Robinson and his group, the Miracles, landed a number one hit on the rhythm and blues chart in 1960 with their song "Shop Around." It was the first of many successes for the Motown label, which went on to become one of the most famous labels in music history. Other legendary artists signed by Gordy include the Supremes, Marvin Gaye, the Temptations, the Four Tops, Gladys Knight and the Pips, Martha and the Vandellas, a young Stevie Wonder, and the Jackson 5 (with little Michael Jackson). These performers all possessed raw talent, to be sure, but Gordy's tutelage was instrumental in helping them rise to become superstars.[44]

Like other superbosses, Gordy created a special setting designed to mold and develop raw talent. Everyone on the Motown label was required to meet weekly for "quality control and product evaluation."[45] While its standards were exacting, the atmosphere at Hitsville (as it became known) "allowed people to experiment creatively and gave them the courage not to be afraid to make mistakes."[46] Many young Motown artists lacked social and presentation skills, so Gordy created an in-house finishing school, teaching them table manners, dress, posture, makeup, and even attitude management. With racial tensions running high (the struggles of the civil rights era were already under way), Gordy "packaged" his acts for mainstream audiences, hiring experts in choreography and stage presence, among other things.[47]

As the Motown artists worked hard to perfect their skills and build their careers, they formed the same kind of connections with one another that protégés of other superbosses experienced. Duke Fakir, one of the Four Tops, told *Vanity Fair*, "We were friends; we played basketball together, we played cards together, we ate together. It wasn't like, if I got a hit, somebody else ain't going to get one. Because one after the other, you kept getting hits, and more hits. It just became a wonderful place to make music. There were always sessions going on, 24/7. And the bar just kept getting raised—higher and higher."[48]

Yet all this fun and warmth between artists didn't mean that Gordy's talent didn't compete with one another. Songwriter and record producer Lamont Dozier recalled that as time passed, "competition became fierce, and to stay on top, you had to be on top of your craft."[49] The drive to claim popularity, attention, and financial success was real, although it never became excessive or destructive. As Stevie Wonder reflected, "The competition at Motown was not the competition that said, 'I don't like you.' It was more like the Brill Building:[50] It was a challenge to come up with great music, great songs. And to me, that was cool. I love Berry to pieces—Berry Gordy was, for my life, a blessing."[51]

We've already seen that superbosses defy easy categorization. They are uncompromising *and* open. They are virtual micromanagers *and* extreme delegators. To these paradoxes, we add one more: superbosses encourage teamwork *and* they also deliberately encourage sharp competition among their intensely unified teams. This combustible mixture of collaboration and competition—what I call the 2-C principle—dramatically boosts the performance of individual team members. It is a phenomenon seldom seen among even the best traditional bosses.

Larry Ellison might not have always gotten the collaboration part right, but he had no trouble with competition. According to one protégé, "he used to set up people in a competing development project. He thought that internal competition was an interesting idea."[52] Many other superbosses, though, aimed for and achieved true 2-C working environments. Lorne Michaels wanted a sense of family to prevail at *SNL,* but he also specifically encouraged competition by hiring more cast members than could perform regularly on the show. The result was an intense but subtle jostling each week as individuals tried to get scenes they had written actually produced and performed. Likewise, at those lunchtime sessions at Tiger Management, there was only a limited opportunity for "airtime," those moments when ambitious analysts could dazzle Julian Robertson in front of their peers. Analysts competed accordingly. "There were always fifty people around the table at different times, and you were competitive with them in that you were fighting for capital, fighting for attention, for being the best person at the firm, the most profitable person in your age group," Chase Coleman told me. "That is the internal competition that occurs . . . but we all want to make the pie grow, because that is in all of our best interests."[53]

One superboss who harnessed competition especially well while still ensuring collaboration was Gene Roberts. He told me he would frequently split off the "all-stars" to form a group of their own. This enabled them to shine without the lower performers dragging them down, creating competition between groups and sending a message to the entire organization that excellence is possible. Teamwork was part of this mix. In managing his people, Roberts created "a sense of collaboration in which everyone recognizes that just a handful of people can't put out a great newspaper—or probably a great anything else. People may on the one hand compete with each other, but on the other hand they have a sense of each other's work."[54]

One reason healthy, balanced competition is so valuable for organizations is that it generates a "cohort effect" when it comes to talent: the more you help people become better, the more they help *one another* get better. As Paul McCartney said of John Lennon, "If I did something good, he'd want to do something better. It's just the way we worked."[55] When asked what he learned from his year at the Nick Bollettieri Tennis Academy, tennis champion Jim Courier replied: "Nick gave us balls, rackets, and damn good players. We went on the back courts and duked it out."[56] Bollettieri put it this way about the tennis lab he created for talented youngsters around the world: "We have a lot of good players at the same place. You put the good against the good and you get excellent players, and eventually that becomes the best."[57] Healthy competition also drives excellence in so-called technology clusters or geographic hubs such as Silicon Valley, where a critical mass of companies exists side by side and talent pushes other talent, causing new ideas to percolate.

While the 2-C principle is central to how so many superbosses think about their protégés as a group, let's go back to the world of comedy for the perfect visual. In his fascinating book about the Los Angeles comedy scene, William Knoedelseder describes how "comics would be gathered at the bar [in the famed Improv at Forty-fourth Street and Ninth Avenue in New York] running lines, critiquing, feeding off one another, jotting down ideas on cocktail napkins."[58] These comics, which in the 1970s included Jay Leno, Richard Lewis, Elayne Boosler, Andy Kaufman, Jimmie Walker, and Richard Belzer, were very much focused on getting their time on stage, yet they were *also* helping one another get better in a maelstrom of creativity. Knoedelseder similarly chronicles how two ti-tans of late-night comedy, Jay Leno and David Letterman, were virtually inseparable in their early years in Los Angeles, forming "a mutual admi-ration society, watching and learning from each other. Night after night at the Comedy Store, when they weren't onstage, they were standing to-gether in the back, taking it all in, studying everything."[59] Another clas-sic example of cooperation and competition at work.

By mobilizing both "Cs," superbosses create their own "talent hubs" marked by intellectual and social ferment. Some protégés, like visual ef-fects expert and director Mark Dippé, explicitly compared their experi-ence to attending a competitive graduate school. Said Dippé: working at Lucas's Industrial Light and Magic was "the best film school for me."[60] Both consciously and unconsciously, superbosses create a kind of caul-dron in which ideas collide, prompting new ideas to arise. This cauldron in turn becomes an engine, powering exceptional performance. The co-hort effect enables superbosses to take all the techniques they use to motivate individuals and *turbocharge* them. It's a powerful formula: indi-vidual employees can grow beyond their wildest dreams; teams and orga-nizations can add value that far exceeds the sum of their parts.

Team Building like a Superboss

Superbosses approach the task of team building in a less structured, more intuitive, and more potent way than traditional good bosses. Some of what they do is deliberate, but the greater part flows organically from the rest of their playbook. Team building doesn't have to take place away from the everyday life of an organization at some five-star retreat; it can be baked right in and take place incrementally. Conversely, work doesn't have to be distancing or alienating; it can be the space in which some of life's most meaningful relationships take root and flower.

Organizations realize considerable benefits from the approach super-bosses take, above and beyond the existence of high-performing teams. The cohort effect is one of the strongest levers we have for developing talent, and it enables superbosses to become magnets for future talent. What supremely talented person wouldn't want to go to an organization where he or she would have a chance to brush up against and learn from other supremely talented peers? The cohort effect also enables businesses to become more entrepreneurial places. Jay Last, who started Teledyne after working with Bob Noyce at Fairchild, recalled the creative fusion that existed at the latter: "There was one bar in particular where everybody seemed to congregate on Friday night, and here you would be talking to people that you would work with one week, and the next week you were business rivals."[61] Imagine what that was like, hanging with Gordon Moore and Bob Noyce. When you bring together big-time talent and position them to collaborate and compete with one another, you produce the kind of creative energy visible at the most dynamic start-ups. It can't help but boost innovation and growth.

So the superboss playbook is critical, not just for what it does for talent spotting, motivation, creativity, and managerial development but also because of how it can help turn groups of individuals into high-powered, take-no-prisoners teams. You can jump-start the cohort effect in your organization by rethinking how you organize talent. If Gene Roberts likes to put his "all-stars" together, why not try that in your own organization or department? Dartmouth economist Bruce Sacerdote's research into primary and secondary education has confirmed that such clustering may be quite useful. As Sacerdote has found, one of the best ways to foster growth and development in children is by putting the stars with the stars and the laggards with the laggards.[62] Managers might fear that doing this within a company will create a class system, but in fact marginal performers get better, too, since they are no longer discouraged by much more capable peers. Think about it: How much fun would it be as a runner to have to train with Olympic marathoners, when you struggle to make a ten-minute mile? Even worse, how good would it be for the Olympians? Talent systems in professional sports are *all* based on clustering. Professional baseball teams don't lump people of different talent all together in one place; they have a system of minor league teams— single "A," double "AA," triple "AAA," followed by "major league" teams. In most areas of life, people of similar capability will naturally serve to push one another higher. Superbosses intuitively take advantage of this principle, and as a manager, you can *consciously* do that.

Many of the team-building techniques used by organizations today are designed to reunite colleagues who have otherwise become dispersed. What if we prevented such dispersal from happening in the first place? Your company's broader culture might not lend itself to the specific techniques that Mary Kay cosmetics uses to build team cohesiveness, but why not notice and celebrate specific rituals—such as quirky vocabulary or inside jokes—that have naturally emerged at work? Why not build team identity and collaboration by delegating more, sharing the credit, and modeling devotion and commitment to the team? Why not structure work so as to *spur* competition? Why not create forums in your organization where bosses and employees mingle to share ideas, and publicly recognize top performers? Be sure, of course, to emphasize both competition *and* collaboration in equal measure. And if geography feels like a barrier, know that technological solutions can make up for a lack of physical proximity, allowing enough contact for meaningful collaboration and competition to occur and for a strong team identity to gel.

Managers aren't the only ones who can benefit from understanding how superbosses approach teams and team building. If you think you may be working for a superboss, then you should realize the importance of peer relationships and do something about it. While it's important to manage up and down the organizational hierarchy, as the protégé of a superboss, you should embrace "managing across" as well. Your peers will be a source of inestimable learning, so it's important to make the most of these relationships. The best business schools create a highly interactive culture that prompts students to engage with, and learn from, not to mention push, classmates. Under these circumstances, they can't help but get better when thrown into a dynamic cohort of talent.

There's one more important lesson to consider. With the two Cs— collaboration and competition—we find superbosses once again embracing contradiction. Superbosses intuitively know that success depends on balancing and integrating opposite goals, on giving up the linear thinking that assumes that because something is good, we want as much of it as possible. Most bosses shrink from seemingly illogical tensions, but superbosses derive immense value from courageously opening themselves to them. Welcome in *all* of life at once, they implicitly tell us, not just the particular side of it that we find easiest or most comforting. The more we can sustain tension between opposites, the more we can deepen our engagement with both sides over time, and the more in tune we'll be with how people, markets, and organizations actually behave.

Given the shared identity and intense emotional bonds that emerge among protégés, you might expect them to stick around in superboss organizations forever. If you're already a member of the "chosen people," and you've gone to battle time and again with your trusted colleagues, how could you possibly go anywhere else? Add in the many other benefits that come from working for a superboss, including the unparalleled opportunities for learning and advancement, and it's not surprising that many protégés I studied did in fact stick around for years, even decades. Others did leave for any number of reasons, including the chance to start their own businesses and claim big opportunities elsewhere. Yet in most cases their allegiance and camaraderie persisted, as they became active participants in their superboss's professional network. Few bosses and organizations today expend much effort maintaining relationships with former employees, but superbosses do because they regard those relationships as vital to their personal and organizational success. As we'll see in the next chapter, superboss networks are always growing, expanding the opportunities available to everyone in the network, including the superboss. It just goes to show: you can leave a superboss, but a superboss never truly leaves you.

CHAPTER EIGHT

Networks of Success

For years you've been a valued employee at your organization. You've gained valuable experience, made friends, even had fun, and learned more than you ever thought possible. But now you sense it's time to move on. You approach your boss, whom you've come to admire and respect. You're a little nervous because you're not sure how she'll respond. Will she try to persuade you to stay, laying on the guilt and enticing you with a bonus? Will she become angry, accusing you of betraying the organization that has given you so much? Will she brush you off, not caring whether you stay or leave? Or will she understand and respect your needs, wish you well, and do everything possible to help you succeed?

Back in 1990, after almost five years of working as a cook at Chez Panisse, Joanne Weir decided it was time for a change. "I was ready to leave but didn't want to go. I knew if I didn't leave then, I might never leave. There were chefs that had been there for 10 even 15 years. I didn't want to be what I called a 'lifer'!"[1] When Weir told Alice Waters of her plans, Waters surprised her with an invitation to her house for a glass of wine. During the ensuing conversation, Weir explained that she felt she needed to leave Chez Panisse but didn't want to burn any bridges and in fact wanted to stay connected in some capacity. Waters came up with the perfect solution, a new transitional job tasting the food at Café Fanny, an establishment Waters co-owned. Getting paid to taste magnificent food and consult with cooks was too enticing to turn down, so Weir accepted the offer and stayed at Café Fanny for a short while before beginning a highly successful career as an author, television personality, and restaurateur.

In recalling this episode, Weir was struck that a famous, busy woman like Waters would take time to talk with her about her career. After all, Weir was only one of many in Chez Panisse's kitchen. But this was only a preview of even greater support and encouragement Waters would give. Weir went on to author numerous cookbooks and magazine articles and appear on such PBS series as *Joanne Weir's Cooking Class* and *Joanne Weir's Cooking Confidence*.[2] Her honors include a James Beard Award (of course!) and an appointment by Hillary Clinton to the American Chef Corps, a group charged with using food to build cross-cultural ties.[3] Some bosses might have been jealous of their former protégés' tremendous success—or at best watched from a distance—but not Waters. Upon publication of Weir's first book, Waters featured her as a guest chef at Chez Panisse. She appeared on Weir's TV show. For Weir's 2012 book *Joanne Weir's Cooking Confidence,* Waters wrote a ringing endorsement: "As a cook, as a teacher, and as an author, Joanne Weir has never strayed from her firm and unassailable convictions that cooking should be pure and simple and that ingredients should be pure and fresh."[4] The endorsement of the book was, in reality, no less an endorsement of Waters's own uncompromising vision of what good food is, another indication of the synergistic benefits of the superboss playbook that accrue to superboss and disciple alike. Weir, of course, has thanked Waters repeatedly in her cookbooks and continues to stay in touch, visiting Chez

Panisse whenever she can. "I just have to get a dose of it, even just to get dinner, just to be there."[5]

Weir is hardly the only former employee who has retained a relationship with Waters and Chez Panisse after moving on. When Sally Clarke was celebrating the thirtieth anniversary of her Clarke's restaurant in London, Waters visited for four days to prepare the menus, while two other prominent former Chez Panisse employees, David Lindsay and Clair Ptak, helped out in the kitchen.[6] Back in America, Waters helped Michael Tusk celebrate the tenth anniversary of his Michelin two-star restaurant Quince by serving as a guest chef.[7] Weir says that Waters is "extraordinarily supportive and will be forever supportive of the people who worked with her."[8]

Beyond any direct help Waters might provide, the Chez Panisse brand continues to connect former protégés with one another and propel them forward, functioning much like an Ivy League degree would for job-seeking graduates. Weir has called Chez Panisse "the Harvard of restaurants," and although she was referencing the quality and passion of her colleagues, the moniker clearly fits from a reputational standpoint.[9] "You go anywhere and somehow, someone knows somebody that worked there or they've heard of Alice or one of the cookbooks," Lippert said. "It even opens doors when you want to go cook in other countries."[10]

For protégés of other superbosses I studied, the experience of leaving is very similar. Protégés may move on for any number of reasons and in a variety of ways, some bearing little relation to the superboss per se. Certainly many protégés I studied did wind up staying for long stretches of their careers. However, I did notice a striking pattern that held for most employees: When they departed, they didn't ever *really* leave. Instead, they become permanent members of the superboss's club—an "extended family" of former protégés as well as customers, suppliers, and other hangers-on. As time passes, club members continue to feel close to the superboss and to one another. They stay in touch. They show intense loyalty. They revel in being industry insiders. And drawing on the tremendous resources offered by other club members, they craft resounding careers and become key players in their industries, much as the superboss did.

How important are superboss networks in boosting careers? Dan Halgin, a professor at the University of Kentucky, did his Ph.D. dissertation on exactly this question. He collected data on all 282 coaching changes in Division I basketball from 2001 to 2007 and statistically assessed the odds of a head coach's being offered a new head-coaching position at a more prestigious school. Dan looked at such things as the "cumulative winning percentage of each coach over his career" (whether as head coach or as an assistant), the "cumulative number of postseason NCAA tournament appearances of each coach" (again whether as head coach or as an assistant), and "whether the coach was either a head coach or an assistant coach of a team that went to the NCAA tournament in the year prior to switching positions." Now, all of these indicators are solid ways to capture a coach's track record, yet none turned out to be as important as this simple question: Is the coach a member of a well-known "coaching tree" headed by a superboss-type figure?[11] Being part of the right network, it turns out, was more helpful in predicting who would get the job than anything else—even more than track record.

What about you? Do you benefit from being a member of an elite, clublike alumni network thanks to a job you've had under a particular boss? While the notion of creating a network of protégés is not a new one, when you look closely, you realize that few companies and few bosses have taken full advantage of the upside of connecting with departing talent over an entire career. By contrast, virtually every superboss I studied made this a priority, reflecting superbosses' radically different assessment of employee retention. Nobody likes it when their best employees leave, but as we saw in chapter 2, superbosses don't fear attrition. On the contrary, most regard the departure of their very best talent as a natural stage of growth and something to be accepted, if not warmly embraced. It makes sense that superbosses would see alumni networks as an opportunity and an asset for both themselves and their organizations.

The Story of Jayday

It's your second day on the job. And by "the job," I mean your *first* real job—ever. While standing at a urinal (if you're not male, please humor me), you strike up a conversation with a guy in the next urinal. He introduces himself as the founder of your organization but, thankfully, he doesn't offer to shake hands.

This was how Steve Alburty, an eighteen-year veteran of Chiat/Day, recalls meeting his superboss, Jay Chiat, back in 1977: "That first meeting always summed up for me the contradictory nature of Jay's personality. His presence could make you feel simultaneously welcome and awkward. Whenever you encountered Jay, you never quite knew if he was going to praise or predigest you." Alburty has described Chiat and the larger culture of his organization as a "confusing amalgam of hot and cold, yin and yang, hate and love." For Alburty, Chiat was "the quintessential Jewish mother, dispensing guilt and favor with equal abandon."[12]

Unlike Joanne Weir and Alice Waters, Alburty and Chiat did not part on the best of terms. Near the end, Alburty told me, Chiat approached then CFO Adelaide Horton and asked her to fire Alburty for reasons he would not divulge. Horton refused, reminding Chiat that Alburty was Chiat/Day's longest-serving employee. She did, however, agree to revise Alburty's duties. When Alburty got wind, he wrote Chiat "the letter from hell"; Chiat grew furious, and Alburty quit. "I got talked into coming back, but I couldn't take it, the place was no longer the place I loved. I asked him for a meeting, knowing he would go into a rage. He did, I grabbed my coat and walked out and never returned. To me, it felt like a betrayal by my father."[13]

All this happened almost twenty years ago. You might expect an employee like Alburty to harbor at least some resentment about how he was treated, or perhaps to have moved on, but here's the crazy part: today, Alburty doesn't just remember Chiat fondly, he maintains a website in his honor (http://www.jayday.org). As a header on the site relates, the site "is dedicated to the vision, energy, and irritability of Jay Chiat and to all the alumni who had the good fortune and patience to work for him."[14]

When I interviewed Alburty, he seemed hard-pressed to explain the website. As I spoke with other protégés, I realized that such mystery and attachment surrounding the superboss-protégé relationship were precisely the point. Superboss networks are founded on deep, emotional connections former protégés retain for their superbosses, years or even decades after their last day on the job. Former employees don't always have wholly positive experiences of their superbosses, but somehow a bond endures that fuels loyalty to and participation in the network. Protégés revere superbosses as godfathers or godmothers—the sort of person who serves as a person's second parent, guiding that person's career and spiritual development. That makes sense, because as we've seen, that's exactly what superbosses are.

In my research, one obvious sign of protégés' affection was their total willingness to speak with me about their superbosses. When you perform research with busy professionals, it's not easy to secure participation; people often won't spare the time. So I was pleased to find that the vast majority of former protégés I contacted quickly returned my calls when they understood I was interested in talking about their superbosses. When we sat down to talk, they eagerly recounted their experiences and expressed how meaningful these bosses were to them. More than a few protégés I spoke with even told me that they "loved" their superboss and regarded him or her as an "inspiration"—again, this was often decades after they had left the superboss's organization. Jeffrey Banks, the award-winning menswear designer who got his start as a design assistant to Ralph Lauren, shared feelings that were typical; his relationship with Ralph Lauren "was almost like having a second father. He cared about me; he cared about my development as a person."[15]

Protégés express their enduring affection in other ways. Filmmaker Jonathan Demme won't make a movie without giving his superboss Roger Corman some kind of cameo role—he played the head of the FBI in Demme's *Silence of the Lambs,* Mr. Secretary in *The Manchurian Candidate* and Mr. Laird in *Philadelphia.* And he's not alone. Protégé Francis Ford Coppola cast Corman as a U.S. senator in *The Godfather Part II;* Ron Howard gave him a cameo as a congressman in *Apollo 13.*[16] When Corman receives honorary awards (he received an Academy Award for Lifetime Achievement in 2009 and has been awarded a "star" on Hollywood Boulevard), luminaries who worked for him at one time or another also happily come out to celebrate their hero.[17]

We can understand why protégés of Nurturers or even Iconoclasts would continue to feel close years later, but why would protégés of Glorious Bastards also feel a connection? The answer is that *all* superbosses impact the lives of their protégés—all serve as godparents. Mike Seashols told me that he left Oracle because he and Larry Ellison were "no longer compatible," and that "I wouldn't consider ourselves friends."[18] Yet Seashols still felt a tug, going on to say: "I would love to get together with Ellison because it would be fun to sort of reminisce . . . and view life and all the passages that we've been through."[19] Alburty told me that Chiat "had a bigger impact on my life and value system than my own parents did. He was an incredibly impacting person, and I consider myself fortunate to have worked with him."[20] Jean-Pierre Moullé, a longtime Chez Panisse chef who was fired by Alice Waters (and who has since taught cooking classes in Bordeaux and published a book), put it this way: "Her employees will give and do anything for her. But sometimes they can be annoyed . . . like when your mother tells you over and over to clean up your room, clean up your room, clean up your room. And she's right. So that's it."[21]

The emotional bond between superbosses and protégés remains strong in part because it's a two-way street. As Alice Waters told me, citing but one of her illustrious offspring: "Nothing makes me more proud than to see somebody like Steve Sullivan [Acme Bread Company] baking all organic bread at Berkeley and inspiring a whole group of bakers across the country and having him being a part of the Bakers Guild that is educating people about traditions in bread making."[22] Larry Ellison, the consummate Glorious Bastard, has had strained relationships with a number of protégés, yet he, too, has expressed similar sentiments: "Even when I'm fighting them," he has said, "I feel proud of these guys."[23]

Superbosses often make an effort to stay in touch with their disciples, even years after they've left. When award-winning designer John Varvatos completed his first collection, he received a congratulatory note from his superboss Ralph Lauren. Ken Segall, former creative director at Apple, told me that although he worked with Jay Chiat for only a year and a half during the mid-1990s, he made a practice of calling Chiat whenever he changed jobs—for years: "I would call Jay and usually within two or three hours at the most, I would get a call back. He would consult with me and advise me. He was that kind of guy."[24]

Superbosses happily participate in or sponsor events that allow them to stay current with their protégés' careers. Alice Waters hosts an elaborate party for Chez Panisse alumni every five years; Gene Roberts brought *Philadelphia Inquirer* staff together for a memorable 2008 reunion party; Bill Sanders and his protégés held a well-attended reunion in 2003 in Las Vegas; and Lorne Michaels has put together many anniversary celebrations and parties for *Saturday Night Live* alumni. Superbosses also check in with protégés on a casual basis. Rick Berman told me in 2006 (when Norman Brinker was still alive) that he still counted him as one of his great friends: "I spoke to him yesterday and I just called him up; well, he had called me up just to see how I was doing."[25] Tommy Frist's alumni network is concentrated in a specific geographic locale (Nashville, Tennessee), allowing for an unusual degree of casual contact: "The social community around here, the arts, the various things that we do to support human service organizations here . . . we all show up at the same places and we all associate with each other."[26] It's certainly not the norm for a boss to call up a former employee just to say hello, nor is it common for former colleagues to continue socializing with one another, but superbosses and protégés have been through so much together; both are more attuned to reinforcing their relationship than letting it slide.

"The fraternity is clear," another Tommy Frist protégé told me. "Once you have been a part of this family, you are always a part of it. Everyone who has been a part of it can call on one another. That is just part of the philosophy of the family."[27] Former Hershey CEO Richard Lenny described the impact and functioning of the Michael Miles alumni network this way: "It's not as though we have a secret handshake, but there are enough of us around that it helps with networking, it helps with connectivity."[28] Comedian Bill Murray remarked that he and his fellow *Saturday Night Live* alumni are "friends for life," will "always be connected," and "are sort of working together all the time."[29] A network of all-stars.

Such powerful sentiments bring to mind Henry V's famous St. Crispin's Day speech in Shakespeare's play *Henry V,* which commemorates the English army's defeat of the far more numerous French: "We few, we happy few, we band of brothers. / For he today that sheds his blood with me / Shall be my brother."[30] Though superbosses might not cast their protégés as members of an underdog army, the bonds formed on superboss-led teams are no less stirring. Protégés evoked for me the deep emotions they felt so many years later, relating how even the slightest trigger—the theme song from *Saturday Night Live,* in the case of Lorne Michaels' protégés—brought back a flood of warm memories. And in interviews, it didn't take long to have superboss progeny give voice to all manner of names and slogans that defined their alumni networks: the "Brinker Boys"; Michael Miles's "Cheez Whiz Kids;" the "Tiger Cubs." Still others talked about "Brinker University," and the "Drexel Diaspora."

Such potent emotional ties in the workplace are, of course, rare. So often we work at jobs, leave to go somewhere else, and never see or talk to our former colleagues again. Think of how heartening it must be to be part of a true band of brothers and sisters—to have a network of people around the country or even the world who care about you and want to see you succeed. One superboss network, OracAlumni, has boasted more than four thousand members and helped create at least one hundred start-ups. As Dominic Castriota of Rhodes Associates remarked of the Drexel Diaspora, "Working at Drexel is like having a degree from an Ivy League university. The network stands you in good stead for the rest of your life."[31] It was a sentiment I heard time and again. When you're a protégé of a superboss, you're no longer left on your own to sink or swim. You have a godparent and your "siblings" behind you backing you up. It's a bond that can last forever; there is no expiration date.

Hillaryland

Perhaps the most meaningful thing superbosses do to show affection is actively promote protégés' careers. Behaving like benevolent godparents, all the superbosses[32] I studied have recommended protégés for new jobs or even made phone calls on their behalf to inquire about job opportunities elsewhere. Bill Walsh is well known for this. If he heard that a college was seeking a football coach, he "wouldn't just make one call; he would make ten or fifteen. Lots of coaches are the exact opposite—they will not be looking out for the best interests of their people."[33]

A shining example of superbosses who catapult former protégés into new jobs are Bill and Hillary Rodham Clinton. The Clintons are known for spawning dozens, even hundreds, of prominent figures in politics and government. Many superboss networks are informal in nature, but the Clintons' was at least partially codified during Hillary's 2008 presidential campaign, taking the form of an Excel spreadsheet that charted both supporters and traitors to the cause.[34] The Clintons have not hesitated to vigorously support politicians and others who have supported them, including many former employees who have gone on to seek political office or other positions on their own. Leaving politics aside, there's no question this network creates value for superbosses and protégés alike.

Terry McAuliffe, for instance, chaired Hillary's 2008 election campaign. As the Clintons' chief fund-raiser, he was so loyal that he gave them a $1.3 million personal loan for the purchase of their Chappaqua, New York, home. When McAuliffe later approached Bill Clinton with plans to run for governor of Virginia, Bill supported him, even though his chances of winning were slim. McAuliffe did end up losing that year, but he won in 2013.[35] Another close Hillary aide, Cheryl Mills, served as White House press secretary under Bill Clinton and has been described as Hillary's "voice of reason." Thanks to her position in Hillaryland, as Hillary's core network of advisers have been called,[36] Mills later received an opportunity to become the nation's chief protocol officer under President Obama—a position that comes with a reserved seat on Air Force One whenever the president is traveling.[37] Usually, this post is given to one of the president's friends; in this case, it went to a friend and associate of Hillary's.

Many of Bill Clinton's staff went on to serve with Hillary during her time as New York State senator and as U.S. secretary of state. Subsequently, they became leaders of the Clinton Foundation, which suggests an important practice of superbosses: not only do they seek jobs for protégés outside their networks but they also frequently rehire employees who have left the fold. The only thing more remarkable than Jay Chiat's habit of hiring people he had previously fired was their willingness to work for him again. And, of course, Lorne Michaels frequently brings back former cast members as performers and guest hosts on *SNL*. Who could forget Tina Fey returning during the presidential campaign of 2008 to satirize Sarah Palin?[38]

"More Aha Moments Than We Could Count"

You know how some affluent parents buy their children new cars for their sixteenth birthdays or new homes as wedding gifts? Well, in lieu of helping protégés get jobs, some superbosses create completely new businesses for them to run. Superbosses spin off these companies, maintaining contact, if not some control, over operations. Because of this, over time, a network emerges that consists of entrepreneurial ventures, not merely individuals.

It's almost as if superbosses, in these instances, leverage the "platforms" or "operating systems" they've honed over their careers—the perspectives on the industry they've developed as well the business models they've established. Just as Apple's iOS operating system creates opportunities for app developers, protégés leaving the superboss start companies that are akin to specific "applications," or articulations, of the platform. Take Julian Robertson's "tiger seeds," each of whom managed his funds as independent businesses but deployed Robertson's capital, expertise, and even his office space at 101 Park Avenue. To some extent, *Saturday Night Live* stands as another example: once the original show was established, *SNL* gave rise to a number of independent movie projects featuring *SNL* alumni and characters from the show. Many of these films were produced in a studio built by Michaels and associated with *SNL*. Michaels is also the executive producer of NBC's *Late Night with Seth Myers* and *The Tonight Show Starring Jimmy Fallon*, both helmed by veterans of *SNL*. Of course, *SNL* also gave rise to other entertainment vehicles that were not direct applications of the platform, but that benefitted nonetheless from Lorne Michaels's support or involvement in some form. The hit show *30 Rock* is one such example: although Michaels served as executive producer, the show was in fact an independent creation of *SNL* star Tina Fey.

Yet another example comes from Oprah Winfrey. Highly influential, charismatic, and powerful, Oprah was the longtime host of *The Oprah Winfrey Show*, the most successful talk show in television history. Born into very humble circumstances (as a girl she famously wore dresses made of potato sacks), she has gone on to win numerous awards, including an honorary doctorate from Harvard and the Presidential Medal of Freedom.[39] Early in her career, Winfrey made the bold move of creating a vertically integrated entertainment business; that is, she not only starred in *The Oprah Winfrey Show* but eventually came to own the studio and the production company, Harpo Productions, a setup that put her in the perfect position to launch talent. She could host personalities on her show, and if they excelled, she could develop their talent and offer them the opportunity to produce their own shows through her studio. This is the path that stars like Dr. Phil, Rachael Ray, Suze Orman, Martha Beck, and Dr. Oz took to fame and commercial success.[40]

Here's how Dr. Phil came into her orbit. In 1996, Oprah became embroiled in what the press dubbed the "Dangerous Foods Lawsuit" in Amarillo, Texas. Oprah had commented on air about mad cow disease; the beef industry responded by accusing her of defamation. Oprah's legal team then hired Dr. Phil McGraw to consult on jury selection. McGraw had already earned a Ph.D. in clinical psychology, run a series of successful self-help seminars with his partner, Thelma Box, and proved that he possessed extraordinary charisma before an audience. To Oprah, though, he was an unknown. Oprah's trial in Texas was, in effect, a type of audition for the man who would become "Dr. Phil."[41]

Their early interactions were tense. As McGraw recalled in a 2011 interview, he initially felt that Oprah was not taking her case seriously enough.[42] At one point, when Oprah was attempting to limit their time together to ten minutes, McGraw reportedly shouted, "It's not my ass being sued!" and demanded she give him as much time as needed.[43] She relented. More recently, McGraw has referred to the trial as an incredibly important bonding time for him and Oprah: "During the trial a small group of us lived together in a bed-and-breakfast out on the edge of town for almost two months. And so she's my ex-roommate . . . And I really got to know her well and we became very dear friends, as we are today."[44]

Oprah eventually won the trial and McGraw soon began appearing on the show in a segment called "Tell It Like It Is, Phil." He did a range of specials for Oprah; in one series, he performed live, on-air therapy with participants, helping them lose weight, mend their relationships, and go back to school. "He gave us more aha moments than we could count," Oprah has said of him.[45]

Oprah promoted Dr. Phil's speaking tours and supported his second book, *Relationship Rescue,* by structuring a series of shows around the content and giving the book to audience members.[46] When Dr. Phil launched his show in 2002, working as both the host and executive producer, it quickly rose to the number two spot in the country—right behind *The Oprah Winfrey Show.*[47] Oprah has also given Dr. Phil a regular column in her magazine. In return for all this assistance, Dr. Phil has made no secret of his gratitude and admiration for his godmother. "Have you ever heard anybody be more enthusiastically supportive of what you have to say?" McGraw has said of Oprah, "[She] is the gold standard in television."[48] She is also the creator of one of the most significant platform-style networks in entertainment, one that as of 2015 continues to grow.[49]

Network Building Beyond the Platform

Not all superbosses treat their organizations as platforms, spinning off new companies specifically for individual protégés—and of those that do, some take other steps to build their networks. A number of superbosses I studied maintained more fluid relationships with protégés, collaborating with former employees on occasion and at other times helping them find opportunities elsewhere. These relationships were largely informal, ongoing, and unending (at least until the superboss dies). Superbosses became the center of an array of star performers, all lingering in the superboss's general vicinity. At Chez Panisse, chefs would pass through for periods of time and then leave. This pattern, which has continued for decades, has made Chez Panisse the center of a locally sourced, organic food constellation in the restaurant business. Other superbosses who have built similarly informal networks include the Clintons, Miles Davis, and Robert Noyce.

Still other superbosses I studied seemed even less strategic or deliberate about fostering networks—but no less committed to playing a godparent-style role. Figures such as Norman Brinker, Jay Chiat, Roger Corman, Ralph Lauren, Michael Miles, and Jorma Panula actively thought about networks and were interested in expanding them, but they tended to rely on other parts of their playbook to mold protégés into all-star talents, at a certain point freeing them to leave and fulfill their potential elsewhere. Over time, networks tended to form naturally around these superbosses, with few formal business ties and relatively little systematic effort on the superboss's part. Yet the relationships among superboss and former employees often continued, in various forms, for decades.

In still more cases, the network-building processes constructed by superbosses seemed to result in a hodgepodge of formal and informal relationships that can only be described as idiosyncratic. George Lucas created companies such as Skywalker Sound, THX, and Industrial Light and Magic, then installed or recruited talented individuals to run them (the "platform" approach), but his protégés also often left to pursue their own opportunities. Many, in turn, started their own companies (including EdNET, Digital Domain, Tippett Studio, and Sonic Solutions), which often hired Lucas veterans for projects, sold to and purchased from other Lucas spin-offs, and sometimes relied on other Lucas alums to staff their founding teams.

Tommy Frist helped protégés start their own businesses, sometimes investing in them or providing advice, other times arranging to buy products and services *from* them.[50] In one instance, Frist helped fund Surgical Care Affiliates, a start-up that protégé Joel Gordon had formed. In the end, Frist's HCA owned 17 percent of Surgical Care. Not a bad investment, considering that between 1984 and 1996, Surgical Care had one of the highest percentage stock price increases of any company that went public during that period. "It could not have happened," Gordon attests, "without the personal encouragement and strong financial support that Frist provided Surgical Care Affiliates."[51] Nashville, Tennessee, is now the headquarters of hundreds of health care companies, with Frist and HCA having some influence over, or a direct role in, the majority of them.[52]

"You Can't Keep Good People Down"

As their behavior suggests, superbosses don't conceive of the employer-employee relationship as ordinary bosses do. They don't consider the relationship over the minute the employee walks out the door, and they're not offended, hurt, or even all that surprised when this happens. Well, *almost* all superbosses feel this way. As we've seen, Chiat acrimoniously parted ways with Alburty. Likewise, one very well known manager at

Oracle related that although he and Larry Ellison parted ways amicably, "people tended to not leave Oracle on good terms. There was a sense that either 'you're in this with us or you're against us,' and once you left, you were a bad guy."[53] Another protégé, John Luongo, was instrumental to Oracle's growth; when he left, Ellison reportedly told him, "John, I really hope you are very successful in whatever you do, but if you blindside me I'll ruin your life."[54] But Ellison is the most prominent exception. Most superbosses are more like Tommy Frist, who, as one protégé noted, "was always happy to see people start new ventures and be successful with it. He was never jealous. He was never saying, 'Well, if you leave me, we don't have anything else to do with you.' That was never the attitude."[55]

We can understand Frist's posture as a natural outgrowth of his playbook. Given all that superbosses like Frist do to prepare and pump up their protégés, it stands to reason that the best people might feel compelled to leave when huge opportunities arise in other places. It would be surprising if this *didn't* happen from time to time, or even frequently. To their immense credit, and benefit, superbosses appreciate this. They accept it. They internalize it. They fully "get" the needs of their best people to pursue their dreams. And they translate this understanding into action. Theirs, in essence, isn't just the superboss playbook. It's the *godparent* playbook.

Other superbosses openly expressed their expectations that some employees might leave. Jay Chiat encouraged his employees to reach their greatest potential and follow their passions, even if doing so meant leaving Chiat/Day. Julian Robertson told me that it was "normal" for people to want to pursue their own interests after a while: "We let these people go on an individual basis, and they left with their heads high and with great feelings toward us. It was probably the most successful thing we ever did."[56] Michael Miles echoed this sentiment: "You can't keep good people down, and if they get a really good opportunity that you can't match, it's inevitable you're going to lose them. But that's the price you pay for having really outstanding people."[57]

Even the most nurturing of superbosses are not simply altruistic, however. Superbosses nurture their networks because they view it as in their self-interest to do so. Most obviously, superbosses tap their protégés for business opportunities—just look at Julian Robertson's tiger seeds, Lorne Michaels's *30 Rock,* or Frist's investment in Surgical Care Affiliates. Superbosses often directly invest in their protégés' new ventures. They know their people better than anyone, possessing a kind of insider information (perfectly legal!). Thanks to this information, superbosses are in the ideal spot to get in on the best opportunities as they arise. Protégés, meanwhile, get the benefit of the investment, and also benefit from the superboss's stellar brand, which serves as a sort of "seal of approval" on their venture. As Julian Robertson partner John Townsend put it, "in Tiger you've got this iconic brand name. You couldn't make it up if you tried."[58]

A second way superbosses benefit from ongoing interactions with protégés is by gleaning valuable information from their networks, as well as assistance with specific challenges or projects. Many of the protégés I spoke with were literally waiting by their smartphones, eager for them to ring with requests from their superbosses. Hedge-fund manager Steve Mandel, another billionaire protégé of Julian Robertson's, recommends potential hires to Robertson—and Robertson listens.[59] As another confidant said, "Robertson constantly took calls from this person or that person in search of information. Some were friends, some were former colleagues."[60] Miles Davis would call up his musicians when he had a space to fill in his band, as saxophonist Bill Evans remembers: "Miles asked me, he just said, 'I need a guitar player.'"[61] A similar request eventually yielded the incomparable John Scofield, who has since appeared on Miles Davis recordings and on dozens of other jazz albums over his long career.[62]

More recently, the Clintons made extensive use of their network while launching Hillary's campaign for the presidency in the 2016 election. The Clintons brought in as campaign chairman John Podesta, a loyal aide who had formerly served Bill as White House chief of staff. Robby Mook, tapped as campaign manager, contributed to Hillary's 2008 presidential run. The Clintons looked to Nick Merrill, a longtime press aide to Bill, to work as the Hillary campaign's traveling press secretary, while former Clinton White House staffer Jennifer Palmieri would serve as the campaign's communications director. The deputy policy director for Hillary's 2008 campaign, Jake Sullivan, became senior policy adviser this time around. These are but a few examples; I could cite a number of others. With the Clintons' vast network of proven and loyal talent, imagine the inherent advantage Hillary had over competitors with a weaker talent bench, to say nothing of the usefulness of her network in raising money.[63]

Networks prove so useful to superbosses (as well as to the protégés who call on them for help) not merely because of the trust that exists among their members, but because of the common background, the perspectives on business, and the language that members share. Comedian Wyatt Cenac, a former correspondent on *The Daily Show,* recalls that when he met fellow correspondent Ed Helms, the two hit it off immediately, even though their time on the show never overlapped: "There's this thing where we can already start communicating about, like, 'Hey, have you ever had a field piece where the subject tried to walk out on you?' 'Yes! I know exactly what you're talking about! And then they come back five minutes later.'"[64]

Or let's say you're a protégé who needs outside help for a design project. You check out three firms and find that their policies and philosophies seem uncannily similar to yours. When you look at the senior management, you find that someone who used to work for your previous boss runs each company. When you call up one of these firms, you're put right through to the president without delay. Before you can even explain what you need, she sees where you're headed and asks questions zeroing in on the points you were going to mention—before you've even begun consulting your notes. It's like talking to someone who has already been working with you for years; her whole way of operating seems instantly recognizable, as if she shares the same DNA. *This* is the kind of collaborative experience that members of an alumni network provide superbosses and fellow alumni. Quite a refreshing difference from a typical supplier-customer relationship, don't you think?

The Fountain of Youth

Yet another, extremely important way networks benefit superbosses is by increasing their own prestige and influence. The more superbosses spawn prominent individuals who are recognizably linked to one another, the more superbosses' *own* stature grows. Superbosses become known not merely as innovators in their industries but as preeminent "talent brands," people who know how to develop the industry's next superstars. They become renowned for their role as godfathers and godmothers. Going forward, this in turn allows superbosses to become magnets for even more talent, as bright up-and-coming prospects flock to them, seeking opportunity.

A good example of this dynamic comes from a legendary godmother in the world of food, Julia Child. For decades the most famous chef in America, Child touched the careers of many young chefs, including those who had only brief contact with her. Sara Moulton, former executive chef at *Gourmet* magazine and one of the Food Network's first celebrities, was hired to assist Child with her TV show *Julia Child & More Company.* As a result of this experience, she referred to Child as "my mentor," writing that "Child was an angel to me, helping me to get jobs and pushing me to work hard."[65] James Beard Award winner Jody Adams met Child around 1980, serving as kitchen help for a fund-raiser in which Child was featured. Child helped guide her to a job with renowned chef Lydia Shire, where Adams began to learn the craft of cooking.[66] Over time, as such protégés established themselves and a network grew up, Child became known among restaurateurs and others in haute cuisine as a conduit for talent. This only prompted more up-and-coming chefs to connect with Child in hopes of breaking in. Even Thomas Keller, the first American chef with two Michelin three-star restaurants, contacted Child early in his career for help in finding an apprenticeship in France.[67] The great Jacques Pépin put it this way: "She made it her business to help young chefs."[68]

Superbosses' ability to enhance their reputation and attract talent is not a secondary benefit—it's huge. Roger Corman's biographer wrote that Corman would "far prefer that his graduates go shine elsewhere, trusting that their glory will reflect back on him."[69] This is not simply about glory; it's about longevity, the ability to constantly replenish the workforce and reinvigorate the business with fresh perspectives and enthusiasm. Luc Vandevelde commented that he didn't worry that Kraft would lose its top people; "there was so much talent building up that actually we felt that we were going to conquer the world."[70]

David Swensen, chief investment officer at Yale University, has spawned many of the top names in the nonprofit endowment investing field, including Peter Ammon at the University of Pennsylvania, Paula Volent at Bowdoin College, Anne Martin at Wesleyan University, Seth Alexander at MIT, Robert Wallace at Stanford, Andrew Golden at Princeton University, D. Ellen Shuman at the Carnegie Corporation, Donna Dean at the Rockefeller Foundation, and Lauren Meserve at the Metropolitan Museum of Art.[71] You can't talk to anyone in the business for five minutes before Swensen's name comes up. He went out of his way to help his protégés transition to their new organizations, where they could take on the number one job. As Andrew Golden, president of Princeton University Investment Company, told me, turnover for Swensen created a "natural vibrancy" and was a "great recruiting tool"; it served as a billboard proclaiming to prospects: "Come here and someday have my job, or a job just like mine."[72]

For all superbosses I studied, the existence of thriving alumni networks helped create a virtuous cycle of talent spawning: as their network swelled, membership in it became even more valuable; this, in turn, made young talent even *more* eager to seek out the superboss. What Chris Rock has said about *SNL* applies to all superbosses and their organizations: "*Saturday Night Live* brands you as a professional. No matter what is written about me to this day, *SNL* comes up. Everybody passed through it."[73] In every industry I studied, membership in a superboss's network was a golden ticket to career success. Prospective employers saw it as a diploma, a "certification" of talent and world-class training. But large, impressive networks of alumni were one of the main elements that allowed superbosses to be recognized as the premier place in their industry in the first place. For alumni, having a superboss on your résumé was the gift that kept on giving; for the superboss's organization, the alumni network was the closest thing to a fountain of youth. It's one thing to train the very best, and quite another to train a generation of top performers who identify so strongly with a specific network and continuously show loyalty to it. A thriving network of talent takes on a momentum of its own, with mutual payoffs that reinforce the network time and again.

Building Alumni Networks like a Superboss

For many protégés, leaving a superboss is just as memorable as being selected for a job with one. And for the best of them, it's just as inevitable as well. Managers and leaders should pay attention to the specific ways that superbosses handle this inevitability. The first lesson is one we discussed back in chapter 2: attrition is not nearly as damaging as you think. Follow the superbosses and embrace it as an opportunity. When key people leave, we have a choice: either watch them from the sidelines or participate in their upside. Which would you rather do? Make the development of next-generation leaders a primary activity and expectation for managers, even with the knowledge that, yes, these leaders will likely go elsewhere at some point. You never do know how much departing employees may help you one day. And if you do get angry and cut ties, the opportunity is lost, like leaving money on the table.

When employees leave, don't forget about them or, even worse, see them as traitors. Instead, be smart: act like a concerned godparent and stay in touch with them. Are you keeping track of employees who are leaving the organization or transferring to another department internally? It doesn't take much to occasionally send an email or make a phone call to check in on someone. It's even easier to Google former employees periodically to see where they've landed (and when they feel the *need* to tell you, you know you're on the way to being a superboss). When you're looking to hire someone or you're seeking help with a project or challenge, don't immediately run to people or organizations you don't know. Pause and think about the assets and resources your former employees can offer. Take the initiative and trigger participation in your network. Do your part to sustain the bonds that were built while your former employees were still with you.

As you open up to the possibilities of churn, protect yourself by ensuring succession plans are in place. Large multinational corporations often think about succession planning for the top few hundred executives, but superboss logic beckons us to think about succession wherever we are in an organization. At Dartmouth, where I teach, a very talented undergraduate has started an unusual and much-beloved choir composed of students and community members. As this student was about to start his senior year, I asked him: "What's going to happen to the choir when you leave? Are you training your successor right now?" The student replied that he hadn't thought about it. The same is true of so many managers. The time to start thinking about succession is now, particularly since we should assume that many of our best employees will leave.

When you get right down to it, what this means is that managers should evaluate current employees with an eye toward their eventual departure. Most large companies have standard methods of evaluating talent: they coach or terminate employees who score low on key performance measures and they typically give employees who score high bigger and better jobs. While such an exercise is useful, we need to recognize that some, maybe many, high performers will eventually *need* to leave. So the scoring grids we use—which might normally have three designations: poor, satisfactory/good, and excellent—might need a fourth level: time to go. It's not that we automatically want to see our best people go. In fact, many of them will stay. But we need to improve the relationships we have with top performers who do depart, and one way to do that is to have frank conversations with them about their immense potential and the best ways available for them to pursue it. We also need to alert our organizations as early as possible to the departures that should and will take place.

Lately, some forward-leaning executives have been embracing superboss-style networking practices. When Netflix CEO Reed Hastings published his well-known "culture slides" in 2009, one of the mantras within was a recognition that "Netflix doesn't have to be for life, in which case we should celebrate someone leaving for a bigger job that we didn't have available to offer them."[74] In his 2014 book *The Alliance,* LinkedIn CEO Reid Hoffman argues that the model of lifetime employment is poorly suited to today's more volatile, uncertain, networked age and in fact "is in varying degrees of disarray globally."[75] Let's also not forget that traditional lifetime employment is at odds with the mind-set of millennial employees, who seek growth and purpose through work and will not hesitate to change organizations to find it. Does anyone really think that the millennial generation expects to get a gold watch after working twenty-five or thirty years for the same company? We know that doesn't make sense, but we're still running organizations as if that's going to happen. If we know that millennials embrace free agency more than any generation before them, why would we adopt a system that's all about retention?

As an alternative, Hoffman advocates that companies form "alliances" with employees and think about employment in terms of shorter "tours of duty" that may or may not turn into long-term stays with the same company. Hoffman also emphasizes the importance of alumni networks, which can create a ready source of customers who already know how good your company is after their tour of duty is over. Yet as Hoffman confirms, much potential in this area remains untapped. Although more than 118,000 alumni groups now populate the LinkedIn platform, most are not formally affiliated with their companies, and surveys have found that most companies don't invest in alumni networks.[76]

Long before anyone had ever heard of formal alumni networks or LinkedIn, superbosses were already building some of the most formidable networks around. They've proved that an alternative model emphasizing professional growth and lifelong connection (although not necessarily employment) with an organization or a boss is not only possible but also highly beneficial to both companies and employees. If you're a boss, think of how great it would be to have dozens or even hundreds of top people waiting to take your call, as well as legions of the most unusually talented prospects knocking at your door. If you're an employee, imagine how enriching it would be to be part of a large and committed "band of brothers and sisters" throughout your career—and to have your boss nourishing and affirming this brotherhood, too. Superbosses as diverse as Alice Waters, Lorne Michaels, Oprah Winfrey, Tommy Frist, and Ralph Lauren know that the secret to both a satisfying, lengthy career and a sustainable, perennially "young" business is not especially complicated. It's a counterintuitive but fertile combination of letting go, staying in touch, and helping out. As you think about your own company, department, or team, don't just strive to build a successful organization—aim higher than that. Work to craft a vast and powerful *network* of success.

You have a choice when it comes to talent: hire and develop people who will reach a natural ceiling, and keep them forever; or cultivate a new generation of talent that intends to surpass you, and help them do it. These superperformers will not be satisfied playing second fiddle, so unless you can keep growing at a pace that constantly opens up new opportunities for your stars, you will lose them. I've had more than one CEO tell me that this is nuts; why would we plan to lose our best talent? Here's what they don't get: their star performers will leave no matter what. The best people are constantly looking for more opportunity, more challenge, more accomplishment. The only question is whether you will leverage your best talent to create career-long connections that provide ongoing payback via new opportunities for business transactions, talent acquisition, and investment deals. And this will be even truer as the careers of millennials accelerate.

Look at it this way: Are you better off having an organization full of okay performers who stay for decades, or a company populated by the world's best talent who expressly came to work for you, for a time, because of your track record as a talent magnet; and who, upon leaving, stay in the network, serving as ambassadors for you and your brand? The choice is clear.

CHAPTER NINE

Superbosses and You

One way to appreciate the immense impact superbosses have on employees and organizations is to experience their absence, or to watch someone close to you experience it. I had an opportunity to do the latter in 2014, while I was in the midst of writing this book. My daughter Erica had graduated from college about eighteen months earlier and had gotten a job at a midsize consulting firm in New York City. She was lucky; her first boss was a good one, intuitively exhibiting many of the superboss practices I've been talking about in this book. She took time to understand Erica and give her challenging assignments, and she went out of her way to create opportunities for Erica to interact with clients and the firm's senior management. On many occasions, she taught Erica aspects of the business, and thanks to her open-door policy, Erica always felt free to approach her with informal questions as they arose. On those occasions when Erica took the initiative with an assignment and did more than had been required, this boss was genuinely pleased, leaving Erica with a feeling of satisfaction and a drive to do even more.

Under this boss, Erica learned a lot in a short time and she looked forward to working with her for years to come. But it was not to be. After Erica had been working at the firm for about a year, her boss unexpectedly left the company to pursue a bigger opportunity elsewhere. A new boss came in, a woman I'll call Tracy. Tracy was much different from Erica's former boss—she was actually a weak, even incompetent manager. She seemed to distrust Erica from the beginning, assuming that it was Erica's fault whenever something went wrong. Tracy insisted that Erica write her a detailed email every morning containing an hour-by-hour plan of activities for the day, and she never seemed to be around to coach Erica or handle her questions. In addition, she dictated minute details about how Erica should work, showing little flexibility and offering no opportunities for Erica to demonstrate any personal initiative. When Erica asked to talk about her progress, Tracy would say, "Sure, let's do that, of course," but never followed through. Weeks went by, and there was no interaction between Tracy and Erica aside from those morning emails and the harsh directives.

Erica soon found herself hating her job. At first she couldn't put her finger on it, but over time she realized she didn't like her firm's culture and, bottom line, she didn't like Tracy. She was working twelve-hour days, but nothing Tracy said or did made the effort meaningful for her. She didn't seem to be learning much, nor was she working toward any personal development goals. She came to see herself as unappreciated, downtrodden, pretty much clocking in and clocking out without anyone noticing. But like other bright millennials, Erica was not about to linger and work in a pointless job. Within a matter of months, she began to look for a new position, and found one at a boutique consulting firm. When the offer came in, she didn't hesitate to say good-bye to Tracy. And she didn't look back.

Watching Erica's story play out, I couldn't help but connect it with my work on superbosses. The difference between a superboss-style manager and a fairly inept traditional boss was stark, as were their impacts on

Erica and the organization. The superboss-style boss had energized Erica, galvanizing her to work at her best and to grow. The traditional boss had undone all that, eroding any commitment Erica had. When Erica's initial boss left, the organization experienced what we might call "good" churn due to employee growth and advancement; but when Erica herself left, that was definitely bad churn—the loss of a promising young employee who had become needlessly frustrated. I've remarked on the positive nature of churn and the willingness of superbosses to accept it, but Erica's experience reinforces the notion that superboss-style bosses are actually quite effective at helping organizations retain more of their best talent. Over time, an organization filled with managers like Erica's first boss will become flush with great talent, developing a reputation that attracts even more talent. An organization filled with managers like Tracy will find that the great people it hires constantly slip through its fingers.

Erica's experience brought home to me how urgent it is for more managers to study and learn from superbosses, and also for more senior leaders to identify the superbosses in their organization, encourage them, and find ways to spread their practices. Although many organizations today boast talented and devoted bosses, organizations in which most bosses are superbosses are few and far between, if they exist at all. An up-and-coming employee like Erica can't just jump onto a job-search board, look for open listings, and hope to find a superboss-rich organization to work for—it can be hard enough to find or come across a single, individual boss who is a superboss.

Imagine what it would be like if your company, division, unit, or department were populated from top to bottom by individual bosses who lived the superboss playbook. Think of how innovative the organization would be, how resilient, even dominant. Think of how much fun individual employees would have, how much more productive they'd become, how much more loyalty they would show even years after they'd left the fold. Think how much further and faster employees would progress. Applying superboss practices isn't always easy, but if we actively disseminate them, we can give work the incredible meaning and vitality that it should have but all too frequently does not. Everyone has the potential to be a superboss. And every organization has the potential to become stocked from top to bottom with these extraordinary, talent-generating bosses.

Manage like a Superboss

Let's suppose you're a midlevel manager seeking to become a superboss. You're already a good boss. You keep up to speed on "best practice," and you take care to apply those practices on the job. Still, you want to become even better. How best to proceed? First, study the superboss playbook presented in this book. Learn from it. Challenge yourself to integrate it into your existing management practices. But don't feel that you have to do everything at once. Pick two or three elements and try them out. You might experiment with a "superboss day" in which, for twenty-four hours, you adopt every part of the playbook. Or you could hold a "superboss meeting" or a "superboss business trip" during which you communicate and behave as superbosses would. See how it feels and see what works for you. And see if others around you notice a difference. I bet they will.

As you get started, it's a good idea to pause and take an honest look at who you already are and how you currently operate as a boss. A great tool to try out is what I call the *superboss quotient*. Of course there's no way to gauge with absolute precision whether you are a superboss, much less whether you're an Iconoclast, Glorious Bastard, or Nurturer. But asking several carefully chosen questions, paying close attention to the answers, and even calculating a numerical quotient can help you assess your affinity for superboss practices as well as compare yourself with other bosses.

Here are ten sample questions (or bundles of questions) I've used, corresponding to the main elements in the superboss playbook. Feel free to adjust the language to fit your own style, but do your best to get at each of these critical issues. And, by the way, these questions are not just for seasoned managers; younger, first-time managers can dial into the same benchmarks:

1. *Do you have a specific vision for your work that energizes you, and that you use to energize and inspire your team?*

2. *How often do people leave your team to accept a bigger offer elsewhere? What's that like when it happens?*

3. *Do you push your reports to meet only the formal goals set for the team, or are there other goals that employees sometimes also strive to achieve?*

4. *How do you go about questioning your own assumptions about the business? How do you get your team to do the same about their own assumptions?*

5. *How do you balance the need to delegate responsibilities to team members with the need to provide hands-on coaching to them? How much time do you usually spend coaching employees?*

6. *When promoting employees, do you ever put them into challenging jobs where they potentially might fail? If so, how do you manage the potential risk? And what happens if they do fail?*

7. *How much affection or connection do members of your team feel with one another? Do people tend to spend time out of the office socializing? What is the balance of competition and collaboration on the team?*

8. *Do you continue to stay in touch with employees who have left to work elsewhere?*

9. *Have any former employees of yours gone on to have particularly noteworthy careers, either here or elsewhere? If so, how many? Any examples?*

10. *What is the culture like in your team with respect to how much energy you devote to nurturing or developing individuals versus getting the job done?*

After you frame initial answers to these questions, go back and really think about how "superboss-like" your responses were. Rate your answers using a three-point scale: weak (one point); okay (two points); or strong (three points). As you determine your score, consider other relevant factors that bear on each question, but that the question itself did not directly elicit. Did you happen to think of a former employee who had gone on to great success elsewhere? In talking about vision, did you simply reference the organization's overall vision, or did you also translate or personalize that vision as a motivational tool for your own purposes? How did you handle the delegation versus coaching question? Was it an either/or answer, or did you emphasize the importance of both? Be honest and go as deep as you can. Add up your points. It's hard to be too precise, but there's a big difference between a score of 25 or better (that's a superboss!) and one that comes in closer to 10 (the "anti-superboss").

Self-assessments are helpful, but I'm sure many people are reading this and saying, "Well, what about other points of view?" And that would be exactly right. It might take a little courage, to be sure, but it's no different from any other 360-degree-type feedback many managers are already doing. Superbosses love feedback; you can model this behavior by soliciting multiple perspectives when assessing your superboss quotient, as well as those of your reports who also manage people. Keeping track of superboss quotients is particularly important for senior leaders who know they can't win without building superior teams. Human-resources professionals should also deploy regular monitoring of superboss quotients to track talent in their organizations.

In evaluating yourself, it helps to reflect on the basic compact employees make when working for superbosses. Employees are asked to take a chance on the superboss, work incredibly hard, help the superboss hit it out of the park, and become part of his or her merry band of brothers and sisters. In return, the superboss implicitly pledges to give protégés the "keys to the kingdom," conveying invaluable skills as well as social connections and reputational capital that will open doors to even bigger opportunities. The superboss also pledges to give employees a chance to make a difference—to be part of something bigger, something that matters. Are you *really* offering this kind of deal to your employees? You may be demanding extreme performance, but are you offering enough in return?

Don't fall into the trap of thinking that becoming a superboss is impossible. It's not. Yes, we all have key performance indicators (KPIs) that govern our work lives, but if we spend time on the superboss playbook, our performance will improve. Yes, the superbosses profiled in this book are extraordinary people—forces of nature—but there's no reason any of us can't become at least a little bit more like them. Yes, there are many parts to the playbook, but there's no reason you need to check off every part at once. Yes, the culture of our organizations often seems like a formidable force working against us, but you do still wield considerable influence over your own team—enough to make a real difference.

Put aside the excuses and instead focus on teasing out what fits your personal style and what works best in the context of your organization. Here are some ideas and action items that will get you started on making the superboss playbook happen for you. Pick the ones you like best and try them. As with many things in life, the most difficult step is usually the first one.

- *Design a training-and-development program around the playbook. If you can't do this yourself (i.e., you're not senior enough or it's too complicated or time-consuming), then talk to key people in HR or Learning and arrange to present what you've been doing to peers and other curious co-workers.*

- *When the organization notches a win thanks to the playbook, make a point of celebrating it.*

- *Track your own "genealogical tree," listing former employees and where they've gone. If some of them have also become superbosses, try to track some of the stars that they, too, have developed. Put your genealogical tree on your wall for all to see, updating it regularly.*

- *Share your own version of the superboss playbook, as it emerges, with your peers and your own boss. Explain why you're doing it, and how it's paying off.*

- *Try writing a short "case study" that describes a scenario in which you applied part of the playbook. Share this among your peers and team members.*

- *Set aside ten minutes every day to reflect on whether you really acted like a superboss, and what you could have done that day to bring the playbook alive even more.*

- *As you apply the playbook to your team, teach your reports how to apply it to their own teams as well.*

- *More generally, give yourself time to be a superboss. Every week, make sure you've adopted a new superboss idea or two. You're not going to become a superboss if you don't commit to it.*

The most important task of all is to start to *think* like a superboss on a daily basis. It's amazing what a simple change of mind-set can accomplish, and how it can show up in small ways. For instance, over the course of my time researching superbosses, I've found myself actually becoming more innovative. I'm always thinking of new ways of solving a problem in ways I wasn't before, and in meetings I'm always asking people to give me their craziest idea. I now regularly ask administrative colleagues whom they're developing on their teams who can take over their responsibilities when they're ready to take on a new challenge themselves. When I work with research assistants—and there have been many involved in my research for this book—I spend time ensuring that they understand my vision for the book and feel they are making a difference in how that vision comes to life. I've also noticed that I've become more alert to the importance of inspiring others. When I teach our very demanding first-year course on strategy and leadership to MBA students, not only do I pile the work on but I also tell them they're "chosen people," fully qualified to be in the game, to be great leaders. It might seem logical that a professor would look to energize students, but I had never quite done it the same way before. Yes, I had always maintained high expectations, but I never accompanied those expectations with explicit inspiration, as superbosses do. Now, thanks to my exposure to superbosses, I have become just a little bit more effective in my ability to boost others' development.

Open yourself up to internalizing superboss wisdom. In a business context, whereas ordinarily you might have delegated a small task to a team member and left her entirely alone, you might find yourself gradually stepping a little closer to coach in real time. You might find yourself keeping an eye out for new opportunities that your highest-performing employees might tackle. You might find yourself taking more time to get to know your reports informally or foster collegial relationships between reports. You might find yourself welcoming new thinking and experimentation, and being more forgiving if employees' great new ideas don't exactly work out. You might find yourself articulating your powerful vision for the business more clearly. Whatever the case, just a small shift can produce noticeable results in how employees view you, themselves, and their jobs. Becoming a superboss is a marathon, not a sprint. And a little bit of superboss really does go a long way.

Finding Superbosses in Your Midst

What if you're a senior leader seeking to populate an entire organization with superbosses? The first thing you'll want to do is figure out how many leaders on your roster already practice parts of the superboss playbook, and determine exactly who these leaders are. That way, you'll be in a position to begin to learn from these superboss types, reward them, and celebrate them.

To get a handle on your current stock of superbosses, you might once again deploy the superboss quotient questionnaire, interviewing managers to probe for superboss practices, or if you lead a large organization, having your HR department perform the interviews. You might wish to go further than the questions I presented earlier. After all, if you're hunting for superbosses, you've got to have the right ammunition to bag one. Here are some others to think about posing:

1. *Have you answered the "why do we exist" question for your team? Could all of your team members share this answer with me right now?*

2. *Do you have people on your team who have followed nontraditional paths to their jobs, or do you find yourself attracted to cookie-cutter backgrounds?*

3. *Are people on your team energized to come to work in the morning? How would you even know?*

4. *Do you have deep knowledge of the projects each of your subordinates is working on this month? Are you thinking about how you can effectively delegate to team members at the same time as you're actively coaching them?*

5. *What percentage of your time do you spend in formal meetings or working alone in your office? How does that compare to the percentage of time spent in the trenches, working with team members informally?*

6. *How often do people leave your team to take a job in another part of your company or in another company? Are they leaving for "good" reasons (i.e., they're ready to move on to bigger responsibilities) or "bad" reasons (i.e., they're just not that good or they're plagued with an inept boss)?*

7. *Do you get angry or feel wounded when your people leave?*

8. *How often do potential employees reach out to you directly to see if you're hiring?*

9. *Are you inspiring people to believe that they can achieve great things?*

10. *Are you removing the bureaucratic barriers and hierarchy that get in the way of meaningful interaction and getting the job done?*

11. *How often do you actively teach people how to do something, as opposed to just telling people what to do?*

12. *Are you doing all you can to continue helping former employees in their careers? Are you capitalizing on the power of your network, or have you let it become a nonentity?*

As before, put a little meat on the bones and score managers to gauge how they're doing. Have them focus on their weak areas, and then create a plan to fill in the gaps. Check back in with this test after six months, a year, or two years. Have their superboss quotients improved? Do certain areas remain better or worse than others? It's great if you administer this assessment to many different managers. How do their superboss quotients compare, and how well do certain departments collectively do relative to others? If one manager's or department's score is much lower, why is that, and what should they—or you—do about it? Better for you to find out how your people rank on the superboss quotient than to blindly think everyone is a top-notch boss when they might not be.

When you're assessing the superboss quotient of bosses in your organization, don't fall into the trap of assuming you're looking for a male superboss, not a female one. The number of female superbosses is on the rise, and it should continue to soar as more women gain power in organizations. You can already find important female superbosses in many fields (in politics, for instance, former Texas governor Ann Richards[1] may well have rivaled Hillary Clinton as a godmother). A business leader like Facebook's Sheryl Sandberg has already mentored all-star executives at both Google and Facebook, such as Emily White (who went on from Google and Facebook to become COO at Snapchat), among others. Even Lady Gaga has spoken of her desire "to be the 'grandmother of pop music,' bringing up new bands, nurturing their talents, watching them grow.[2]

Even if bosses you evaluate seem to practice some parts of the playbook, be sure to ask questions of younger colleagues for confirmation. Who in the company has a reputation for putting employees on the fast track? Does anybody? Many companies list job openings. Ever notice that the manager leading one team barely has an opening before it's filled, while the manager of another can't seem to find anyone?

As a leader, make it your business to pay attention. Ask questions. Look for opportunities across the broader ecosystem of the company to converse informally with bosses down the hierarchy. Take your time in performing due diligence; you'll be far more likely to uncover superboss types who operate in plain sight as middle and upper managers. And start your investigations early—in fact, almost immediately upon joining a new company, division, office, or team. Even if your bosses generally manifest strong superboss tendencies at the outset, you might find that opportunities exist for them to do even more, or to spread their practices even further. Every quarter that goes by with specific superboss practices lacking is a quarter in which the organization and its people failed to deliver on their innate potential.

A Superboss Culture

Once you've taken stock of superbosses, there are a number of things you can do to spread their influence throughout the organization, encouraging more managers to embrace what they do. One way to proceed is by taking a single department, function, region, or product division and teaching the *entire* playbook to managers. Alternatively, you can start with one part of the playbook and roll it out across the entire organization. If you choose the latter, the question then becomes which part of the playbook to pick. For many organizations, it might seem easiest or most straightforward to focus first on changing how you spot and hire talent. However, you might want to start instead by having leaders craft a vision. Asking "Why do we exist as a company or organization?" seems obvious, yet many leaders just gloss over the question. Drilling down to the teams that managers have responsibility over is just as important. Are your team leaders inspiring all those people your organization spent so much time hiring? Taking it seriously and spending time on it are powerful ways to begin bringing the superboss's magic into your own organization. Your goal is to energize people to pursue subsequent parts of the playbook while also facilitating execution (it's a lot easier hiring and motivating unusual talent, for instance, when you've already gotten behind a clear, compelling vision).

Whichever path you wind up taking, make sure to point to the super-bosses in your midst as positive role models. Identify them and publicize their methods, much as I did with superbosses in this book. Celebrate their accomplishments openly in your corporate communications. Give them a platform (e.g., webinars, articles, teaching opportunities) to communicate internally, so that other managers can understand what they do. And grant them wide latitude to impact others, remembering that impact is ultimately what superbosses at any level care about most.

In addition, you might wish to make the organization more superboss friendly by creating processes, structures, or cultural norms that in some way embody superboss practices. Early in its history, PayPal was known as a prolific spawner of talent. When studying the company's secrets of success, I noted, among other things, a number of formal and informal policies in place at the company that were designed to erode hierarchy and formality, in turn enabling apprenticeship-style interactions to take place. Everyone at PayPal was encouraged to challenge executives. As VP of Engineering Jeremy Stoppelman[3] remarked, "I was a 22-year-old whippersnapper, and I remember firing off this e-mail that disagreed with the entire executive staff. I didn't get fired—I got a pat on the back."[4] Former PayPal COO David Sacks[5] also implemented a no-unnecessary-meetings policy. He would just walk into a meeting for a few minutes, decide whether anything useful was going on, and if not, end it on the spot.[6]

The top-tier consulting firm McKinsey provides a classic illustration of how an organization can systematize parts of the playbook related to the building of alumni networks. Outgoing people stay on the company payroll for up to three months on full salary and with only light office duties, while they search for a job. One of the big assets McKinsey provides is access to their alums as part of this process. Partners and other colleagues will also often connect departing employees to helpful contacts in their networks. "The amount of love and partnership you get when you say you're leaving is unbelievable," one McKinsey veteran told me. "I got more calls when I said I was leaving the firm than when I got elected partner."[7] McKinsey alums also enjoy support from McKinsey staff and communication resources dedicated to alumni management, which comprises "a large infrastructure to make sure they have the best careers going forward. Everyone who walks out the door could be hiring the firm in the future."[8] Smart, isn't it?

You can go even further by integrating the superboss playbook into any leadership or competency models or frameworks that are already in use. Start to measure how many employees of specific bosses are promoted to bigger jobs, inside or outside the company. Make sure your KPIs are facilitating implementation of the playbook, not getting in the way. Emphasizing people development in your KPIs sends a strong signal to the entire company, and it reduces the odds that you will inadvertently drive away any existing superbosses and would-be superbosses. The bottom line is that if you don't create metrics that measure and reward the playbook, you're going to have a hard time incorporating it into your culture.

Policies, systems, and structures are of course no substitute for creating an influential phalanx of individual superboss-type bosses. So be sure to concentrate on finding ways to nourish superboss-like behavior among managers. And don't forget to take steps to discourage bosses from behaving in decidedly *un*-superboss-like ways. Many companies will tolerate egotistical bosses who run roughshod over their people simply because they are high performers who drive business results. What these companies don't fully account for is the collateral damage that occurs when good people exit the organization because of their interaction with such bosses. In effect, a talent vacuum is created as the alleged "high performer" gets promoted; the traditional boss's former team then stumbles and reverts to poorer performance, erasing all gains—a pattern that continues every time the "high performer" moves up. More broadly, bad bosses erode an organization's talent brand, making it difficult to attract the best people, and preventing the organization from getting the best out of people who do come onboard. It takes guts for senior leadership to remove bad bosses who hit their numbers, but it almost always pays off over the long term; the company can now better groom its next generation of leaders for success, building that success not solely on a single superstar who hogs the spotlight.

Whenever you celebrate individual superbosses and promote their practices, make sure your expectations are realistic. The superboss playbook takes time to implement, and any changes need to be *authentic*. You can't just ask a manager to embrace a vision for her team, department, or division; she has to really believe in it and be willing to align her people around it. You also have to give managers the resources they need to attract the best, most creative people they can find, and give them sufficient room to properly manage them once they're onboard. Beyond that, you need room inside your organization for your people to grow. Superbosses create fast tracks for their protégés, and unless the larger organization can absorb that advancing talent, your managers will lose their all-stars too quickly. Growth solves a lot of problems, including this one. But superboss-driven talent machines will also generate big-time growth, creating a win-win virtuous circle. Superbosses produce great talent, and great talent produces winning, even dominant, business.

In disseminating superbosses and their practices, don't disregard line employees. Since many of them will have worked for traditional bosses, they're going to need to adjust as more superbosses and superboss practices permeate the organization. What should they do to succeed under a superboss? Here are some basics that I would impart to them:

- Soak it in and pay attention to the little things your superboss-style boss does—his or her wisdom is there for the taking.

- Do what you think your superboss wants you to do as part of your job description. And then do more.

- Never *show up unprepared for anything. Once you've lost the superboss's confidence, you won't get it back, and a whole legion of other prospects are waiting in the wings, eager for a position with your boss to open up.*

- Be proactive and bold. Superbosses expect you to suggest new ideas directly to them, and they also expect you to break the rules on occasion to get the job done (obviously don't do anything illegal or unethical, but don't hesitate to take an original approach to solving a problem).

- Don't be afraid to push back when you've got an idea that's not getting heard. If "perfect is good enough," you've got to stand up for what you believe in.

- When opportunities come your way, grab them. Superbosses are particularly attuned to taking risks, and will naturally gravitate toward people who are also comfortable doing so.

- Think about the business as if you owned it. This is one of the best ways to stand out, because that's how superbosses think.

- Learn to read your boss. We've seen that superbosses all have their own ways of communicating—from Panula's grunts to Ellison's tirades. Your superboss won't necessarily be like any other superboss. Get to know him or her.

Employees who've served in the military might find these steps even easier and more natural than the average person. In my teaching of graduate students, I've found that veterans invariably connect with the idea of superbosses. It makes sense, since many elements of the playbook also come up big in military contexts. Like protégés of superbosses, military personnel work extremely hard in high-pressure situations. They form deep bonds with colleagues, if not necessarily with every commander they've worked for. They are given incredible responsibility at a young age, in some cases commanding dozens of battlefield troops before the age of twenty-five. Further, making the cut in elite military units like the Navy SEALs comes down to adaptability, open-mindedness, and creativity—classic superboss attributes. Ask employees who have military backgrounds to think about how some of the practices they've adopted in the service might carry over to serving under a superboss. Of course, that's not to say they're the only employees who can succeed or intuitively understand a superboss system. The steps I've outlined above will give any team member a running start to fast-tracking his or her career and helping the whole organization function better.

One final word of wisdom to leave with employees: they should pay attention to how quickly they're moving up, and to how much attention they're getting from their superboss. Traditional bosses will either give you formal feedback or fire you when you're not doing well. Superbosses are all about giving feedback anywhere and everywhere, and if employees don't get it, they've got a problem. This is one of those situations where no news *isn't* good news.

The Making of a Superstar

In 1984, a nervous young theater actor arrived in Chicago. He had attended college in Virginia, studying philosophy, before transferring to Northwestern University in Chicago because he felt it would benefit his career. Now in need of money, he started working at the box office for Second City, one of the nation's most respected comedy theaters. He enrolled in Second City's comedy classes, which were free for employees. He wound up auditioning and getting selected to join the Second City touring company. He toured with them for two years before being promoted to the company's main stage in Chicago.[9]

From Chicago, our young comedian moved to New York City, where he collaborated on a number of projects with Second City alumni. A series of gigs followed: working as a freelance writer for *Saturday Night Live;* providing the voice for a cartoon character on the short-lived sketch-comedy series *The Dana Carvey Show;* working as a script consultant; and filming a few funny segments for *Good Morning America.*[10] By this point, a couple of years had passed without much financial or professional success. Considering the cost of living in New York City, it would have been understandable if this comedian left town, giving up his dream in order to find a "real" job. As it turned out, he didn't leave town, and he did find a real job. On Comedy Central, as an early correspondent on *The Daily Show with Jon Stewart.* And that's where he stayed until 2005, when he set out with his own show spoofing Fox's *The O'Reilly Factor.*[11] More recently, he has appeared most nights on CBS as heir to one of late-night comedy's great franchises. This comedian (you may have guessed) is Stephen Colbert, creator and host of *The Colbert Report,* host of *Late Show with Stephen Colbert,* and one of the greatest comedic talents of his generation.

In our culture, we tend to think of talent—and certainly all-star talent—as something mysterious and inaccessible. We point to unusually successful or inventive individuals and assume that these people are just "different" from the rest of us. They're born with it (whatever "it" is). They're "geniuses." Their success is inevitable, magical. It is beyond our comprehension. It is even, depending on your beliefs, a gift from the divine.

While such genius no doubt exists, a lot more goes into an all-star career than that. People like Stephen Colbert aren't just born; they're also made. And the secret to success turns out to be something any of us has the potential to access. It's that combination of personal talent, drive, and dedication, coupled with the support, inspiration, guidance, knowledge, wisdom, and professional networks of superbosses—or in Colbert's case, of a superboss-like organization.

Whether it's hedge-fund billionaire Chase Coleman, the legions of jazz greats who worked with and studied under Miles Davis, the food industry CEOs and presidents who came up under Michael Miles, or any of the other hundreds, if not thousands, of protégés whose stories we've examined, top performers in almost every field have achieved greatness thanks to their contact with a boss who had an unusual knack for helping others grow. Under their superboss's tutelage, protégés have worked their absolute hardest to get better at what they do. They've moved up quick. They've attained or even exceeded their greatest professional dreams. And they've achieved the power, as all of us can, to serve as potential superbosses themselves for the next generation.

The essence of the superboss phenomenon is the transfer of knowledge, wisdom, and success from old to young—and not just know-how, but also a way of thinking, even a way of life. At its core is a deep and abiding respect that protégés have for superbosses, an admiration that helps bind together and sustain the superboss's powerful alumni network. Superbosses function as godparents—and protégés appreciate this and feel grateful for it. To me, nothing communicates all of this better than an old, ragged poster I've had hanging in my office for years, long before I entered the world of superbosses. Hockey legend Gordie Howe and the younger hockey great Wayne Gretzky are sitting together on a bench, talking. Howe looks to be in his fifties or sixties, while Gretzky is perhaps in his late twenties or early thirties. The two have just worked out and are dressed in sweaty gym clothes, skates, and protective gear. Howe, probably on the way to the shower, has a white towel slung around his neck. This is how it happens: an old master taking the time to bring a younger colleague—even an especially talented one—along with the knowledge that one day, that younger colleague may well surpass him.

Superbosses serve as models for how any of us can better lead, inspire, and nurture others. And they yield a framework for making today's organizations—which are for the most part grossly imperfect—at least a little bit better. Superbosses prove that we don't have to settle for mediocrity in our careers *or* in the teams and companies we lead. We can find workplaces that don't push us down or smother our own spark of genius. And if we're in leadership positions already, we can help create workplaces like that, too. Our organizations will be more innovative, more sustainable, more influential, and, frankly, more fun—not to mention much more successful. The key to organizational vitality is, after all, the ability to constantly regenerate talent. Superbosses help solve the most fundamental challenge all organizations face: how to survive and thrive, year after year.

Bringing superboss wisdom into our careers and organizations takes effort and a dose of open-mindedness. Much of what superbosses do is counterintuitive, so all of us who are not currently superbosses, but who want to be, will have to learn to behave differently. Those of us looking to work for superbosses will also have to be more proactive in searching them out, and once we find them, we have to be willing to inject everything we've got to make it work—we have to go "all in." Are you up for the challenge?

Crafting Your Legacy

On May 16, 2007, I helped lead a daylong strategy retreat at the global beer, wine, and spirits powerhouse Constellation Brands, owner of dozens of brands from Robert Mondavi wine to Svedka vodka. The event was held at Robert Mondavi's ranch in California, and sixty to seventy of the company's top executives had flown in from around the world for the occasion. It was a long day, full of heated discussion about the company's future. The executives in the room cared about the company and had taken off the gloves as they critiqued one another's ideas and presented ideas of their own.

At the end of the day, we all attended a barbecue dinner at the ranch, and I was seated across from Mr. Mondavi and his wife, Margrit. Mr. Mondavi, who died one year after I met him, is widely remembered as a pioneer in the wine industry, the man who helped produce the flowering of the U.S. wine industry. He is also remembered as one of the greatest talent spawners in the industry. The Robert Mondavi Winery became known as "Mondavi University" because it produced the country's best winemakers, including those whose wines won the legendary "Judgment of Paris" tasting in 1976, signaling the arrival of California wines on the international scene.[12]

By 2007, as he sat at our table, Mondavi was already in physical decline. He sat in a wheelchair; he couldn't, or wouldn't, speak; and his wife helped him with his meal. He was still handsome, though, and dressed neatly in a well-tailored suit. As I made small talk with a few other tablemates, I saw an unforgettable sparkle in his eye. He seemed to be paying attention to our conversation.

About halfway through the dinner, people from other tables started coming up to greet Mr. Mondavi. Many of these hard-boiled executives were former Mondavi protégés, while others hadn't directly worked for him but had still been strongly influenced by him. At first, they came up one or two at a time. Then a whisper went around the room and more people got up, standing in line for their turn to speak to him. They knelt down and touched him on the arm, a gesture of reverence and love. "Thank you so much, Mr. Mondavi, for everything you've done for me and for the wine business. It's an honor and a privilege to be here with you."

I was taken aback. None of this was planned. It was organic and authentic. Here was a man who had touched many people, and so many years later, they were *still* immensely grateful. Robert Mondavi hadn't just made wines. He had made people. He had crafted careers. And now, in his old age, he had something to show for it. He had a legacy. He was, simply put, someone who *mattered*.

My thoughts drifted to myself. What am I accomplishing in my own career? When I'm in a wheelchair, will anyone line up to greet me?

Every single one of us has the chance to impact the world for the better. We all spend an incredible amount of time in organizations. Not just at work, but also in social and voluntary organizations, in schools, in religious institutions. What is that actually like? Do these organizations really work well? Is the immense potential of the people who dedicate their lives to the creation and ongoing operation of these organizations being met, let alone surpassed? And what are we doing about it?

Superbosses have cracked the code on how to make organizations work better by designing a playbook that helps people accomplish more than they ever thought possible in their careers, or their lives. By studying the superbosses and what they do, we now know how genuinely unusual talent comes to populate an organization. We know how to motivate and inspire people, how to energize people, and how to give people the confidence to believe they can make things happen. We know how to unleash the creative potential of people at work—or in any organization—and understand the great things that happen when you do so. We know how to create an organization that is built to change. We know how to craft a different type of relationship between bosses and employees, one that is built on apprenticeship, opportunity spotting, and learning. We know how to fashion teams that are like bands of brothers and sisters, and not just transactional work units. And we know what it takes to become a talent magnet whose network of protégés continues to create social and economic value long after they've moved on to new challenges.

In the end, studying these superbosses gives us a master class in how each of us can make an impact in what we do. Superbosses show us a markedly different and innovative path, one that unites the success of an organization with the people charged with accomplishing that success. From Alice Waters to Gene Roberts, Ralph Lauren to Jay Chiat, superbosses I examined have all thrived by helping those around them get better at what they do. And they have obtained immense satisfaction not just from the companies they've built, the awards they've won, or even the wealth they've amassed, but from building a legacy.

Robert Mondavi was certainly deeply satisfied that evening. I knew this not because of anything he said. In fact, as his protégés came up to see him, he never uttered a single word. But his eyes, redolent with wisdom and experience—they sparkled the entire time.

ACKNOWLEDGMENTS

Imagine a world where the work you do really matters. Where the person whom you call your boss changes your life by helping you accomplish more than you ever thought possible. Where your own opportunities would multiply in ways you may have been afraid to even dream of. That's the world this book is about, the world of superbosses and the incredible yet often disarmingly simple things they do to make all this happen.

I've been unbelievably fortunate to be at a place that nurtures and promotes the type of research and thinking that a project such as this entails. Even if it takes ten years to go from idea generation to publication, as this book has. The Tuck School of Business at Dartmouth College is an oasis in the frozen north: one that brings genius students and alumni to campus all year round, affords consistent access to CEOs and other leaders, surrounds you with curious colleagues, and gives you the time and money to do what you need to do to answer the questions you want answered.

As a professor at Tuck, I've been able to call on and learn from such colleagues as Ron Adner, Ella Bell, Connie Helfat, Steve Kahl, Adam Kleinbaum, Tom Lawton, Margie Peteraf, and Alva Taylor at Tuck, and Fred Haas, Chris Jernstedt, and Aaron Kaplan at Dartmouth, among many others. I've spoken about the ideas behind *Superbosses* to many MBA classes and Tuck alumni groups, generating both excitement to reinforce my focus and questions to push me to dig a little deeper.

There have been so many MBA and undergraduate students, student partners, and others who have contributed to the research at various times, and they deserve thanks. These include Bob Batt, Kelly Blewett, Matt Bolduc, Scott Borg, Cristen Brooks, Jamesa Brown, Will Buell, Jessica Burke, Louisa Carter, Fern Chaddad, Kevin Demoff, Noah Dentzel, Brian Flaherty, Eric Francis, Lauren Fraser, Matthew Goldfine, Catie Griggs, Andrew Grimson, Sarah Guinee, Evan Hacker, Alison Hillas, Vernita Irvin, Ramsey Jay, Juhi Kalra, Katherine King, Ore Koren, Britt Krivicich, Margot Lalonde, Ben Magnano, William Olgiati, Alex Olshonsky, Daiana Petrova, Brian Recht, John Rutigliano, Joseph Santo, Rebecca Savage, Jeffrey Shaffer, Mary Sieredzinski, Julie Skaff, Amy Sweeney, Cristina Tejeda, Scott Turco, Craig Urch, Mary Vargas, Betsy Wakeman, Sara Weeks, Sarah Williams, Sarah Austrin-Willis, and Chris Zablocki.

Working with Seth Schulman helped bring *Superbosses* to fruition and was incredibly valuable. Beyond talent, a pleasure to work with. Thank you, Seth.

The time and money to help pay for all these people, and even more important, the energy and interest among the team of deans at Tuck—Paul Danos, Bob Hansen, and Matt Slaughter—were essential. At Dartmouth, both former president and head of the World Bank Jim Yong Kim as well as current Dartmouth president Phil Hanlon were influential in crafting a university that lives many of the superboss virtues.

We conducted easily more than two hundred interviews with superbosses and their protégés, too many to list all of them here. Suffice it to say that thanks go to the literally dozens of CEOs and numerous other people who worked for a superboss and wanted to share their experiences with me, as well as the many superbosses themselves who fielded my questions about what they did and why they did it. I'd especially like to thank Lorne Michaels of *Saturday Night Live* for the two interviews he did with me, as well as encouraging several performers and writers to talk to me as well. Thanks to him, and to other leaders whom we talked to, including Joseph Abboud, Julius Blank, Lee Clow,

Doug Conant, Mickey Drexler, Tommy Frist, Sid Ganis, Steve Hayden, Thomas Keller, Jim Kilts, Max Levchin, Gordon Moore, Elon Musk, Lou Neeb, Eric Ripert, Julian Robertson, Esa-Pekka Salonen, Bill Sanders, Mike Seashols, Wayne Shorter, David Swensen, Luc Vandevelde, Jean-Georges Vongerichten, and Alice Waters.

Numerous friends listened to what I was up to, seldom giving voice to my "scintillating" pace but instead doing the one thing that has continued with virtually everyone I talk to about the research. They'd bring up their own superboss—that influential person they worked for, at some point in their lives, who made a difference. To see their eyes when they described these people is to see the incredible impact that one person, one boss, can have on others. So to friends like Ephi Eyal, David Garrison, Larry Hoffer, Michael Johnson, Ilene Kahn, Joel Krasnow, Blair LaCorte, Nigel Leeming, Joel Litwin, Melinda Muth, the late Kirby Myers, Cathy Nieman, Mara and Rich Weissmann, and Harry Zelnick, thank you.

This is the second time around with my publisher, Portfolio, and the team has come through again. My editor, Natalie Horbachevsky, was spot-on with guidance, and the power team of Adrian Zackheim and Will Weisser demonstrated why they're at the top of the business. I thank my agent, Lorin Rees, for bringing me back to Portfolio and providing feedback when it was most needed. I had many conversations with Helen Rees about this book long before a word was written, a testament to her influence and presence for me, and so many other authors. She is, and will continue to be, very sorely missed.

I'm particularly fortunate to be able to draw on an amazing team of individuals to spread the word about *Superbosses*. At Tuck, Gina des Cognets, Anne Linge, Justine Kohr, and Jen Johnson; at Portfolio, Margot Stamas; and my own team of Kiki Keating and my daughter, Erica Finkelstein.

Various sections and drafts of this book were completed in coffee shops. For a foodie and coffee snob, this was as it should be. At places like Caffe Medici in Austin, Primo Passo Coffee and Intelligentsia in Los Angeles, Stumptown and Joe in New York, Coutume in Paris, and the Dirt Cowboy and Market Table in Hanover, baristas did their thing and left me alone. As it should be.

Over the course of ten years life goes on, and sometimes you see someone you love dealt the worst of hands yet somehow demonstrate extreme courage and wondrous inspiration throughout. Even when ill, my niece now in heaven, Jacqui, would ask me about my "new book."

You also watch as your daughter grows into a strong and talented young woman. The connections between husband and wife turn deeper and richer. The love and support of Erica and Gloria are as sure as anything can be.

This book is dedicated to my mother, certainly the first superboss I ever experienced. Despite, or perhaps because of, an unsparing life, my mother was a tower of strength, both to me and my older brothers, Simon and Arthur. I couldn't help but think of her as I learned how superbosses inspired others to do more than they ever thought possible, how closely involved superbosses were with their protégés, and how in the end they prepared their offspring to move forward to bigger opportunities. She passed some time ago, but you never forget a superboss.

NOTES

INTRODUCTION

1. Seen Lippert, interview, April 24, 2006.
2. Thomas Keller, chef-owner of the French Laundry, interview, May 1, 2006.
3. Eberhard Muller, interview, March 28, 2006. Muller's culinary credits include the Michelin three-star Paris restaurant L'Archestrate and the *New York Times* four-star restaurant Le Bernardin, among others.
4. According to a recent study, the top priorities for leaders both now and in the future are succession management, leadership development, and talent acquisition and retention. See Rebecca L. Ray, Charles Mitchell, Amy Lui Abel, Patti Phillips, Emily Lawson, Bryan Hancock, Allison Watson, Brooke Weddle, *The State of Human Capital 2012, Research Report R-1501-12-RR*, Report by McKinsey & Company and the Conference Board, 2012. McKinsey's War for Talent created quite a stir when it was launched in 1998, but the effects of this war remain ambiguous. Eight years after that initial report, McKinsey published a follow-up lament. Interviews with senior leaders, including CEOs, revealed that more than half were unhappy with the attention paid to talent development in their organizations. Consider this quote from the article: "Senior managers don't see the point of managing people and getting the best out of them." (M. Guthridge, A. B. Komm, and E. Lawson, "The People Problem in Talent Management," *McKinsey Quarterly* 2 [2006], 6–8.)
5. *BlackRock Investor Forum*, October 23, 2014.

CHAPTER 1: ICONOCLASTS, GLORIOUS BASTARDS, AND NURTURERS

1. Gail Shister, "Inquirer Leaves Good and Bad Memories at 400 North Broad Street," *Philadelphia*, June 26, 2012, http://www.phillymag.com/news/2012/06/26/inquirer-leaves-400-north-broad-street/#DDYK4vjIArpZrIvd.99 (accessed December 27, 2014).
2. Alan Heavens, "Inquirer Sells Its Building," *Philly.com*, July 29, 2011 (accessed December 27, 2014).
3. Bob Andelman, "Roberts' Rules of Leadership," *Poynter Online*, September 3,

2002, http://www.poynter.org/content/content_view.asp?id=46544 (accessed October 14, 2010).

4. Rich Heidorn, "Is There Life After the Newsroom? The Philadelphia Inquirer Reunion," *Tree House Media Project*, July 17, 2008, http://treehouse-media.net/blog/is-there-life-after-the-newsroom-the-philadelphia-inquirer-reunion/2008/ (accessed October 14, 2010).

5. Jim Naughton, interview, September 30, 2010. Naughton was the past president emeritus of the Poynter Institute and longtime associate managing editor–news editor under Roberts.

6. Ibid.

7. Ibid.

8. Don Barlett, interview, September 30, 2010. A longtime investigative reporter at the *Philadelphia Inquirer,* Barlett won two Pulitzer Prizes for National Reporting while at the paper.

9. Rich Heidorn, "Is There Life After the Newsroom?"

10. John H. McManus, "Who's Responsible for Journalism?" *Journal of Mass Media Ethics: Exploring Questions of Media Morality* 12 (1) (1997), 8.

11. Even though "engaged workers are the lifeblood of their organizations," the Gallup (2012) report "State of the American Workplace: Employee Engagement Insights for U.S. Business Leaders" found that 70% of surveyed workers are unhappy at work (20% reported as actively disengaged, and another 50% uninspired by their work or their managers).

12. Alfred Lubrano, "A Final Farewell, but the Tower's Stories Live On," *Philly .com,* July 2, 2012 (accessed December 26, 2014).

13. Ibid.

14. Ibid.

15. Gene Roberts, interview, October 1, 2010.

16. "The Press: Philadelphia Story," *Time,* September 3, 1973, http://www.time .com/time/magazine/article/0,9171,910757-2,00.html (accessed October 14, 2010).

17. Gene Foreman, interview, September 20, 2010. Retired Larry and Ellen Foster Professor of Journalism at Pennsylvania State University, he was managing editor under Roberts; Alicia Shepard, "The Inquirer's Midlife Crisis," *ajr .org,* January/February 1995 (accessed December 26, 2014).

18. John Carroll, former editor of the *Baltimore Sun* and *Los Angeles Times,* and the metro editor under Gene Roberts, interview, October 1, 2010.

19. Gene Roberts, interview, October 1, 2010.

20. Julia Cass, "Roberts Transformed Newspaper," *Philly.com,* August 1, 1990,

http://articles.philly.com/1990-08-01/news/25931660_1_eugene-l-roberts
-journalism-investigative-reporter (accessed December 27, 2014).

21. Data on coaches, coaching changes, and coaching trees was accessed on May 9,
2014, from a variety of sources: *The Huddle,* http://www.thehuddle.com/2014/nfl/
coaching-changes.php; http://coachingroots.com/football/coaches; http://www
.sports-central.org.

22. *Bloody Mama* also starred Bruce Dern, the 2013 Academy Award winner for
Best Actor in *Nebraska.*

23. "A Mile High Is a Sweet Spot for REITs: Real Estate Investment Trusts Like
to Call Denver Home," *ColoradoBiz,* March 1, 2008, http://goliath.ecnext.com/
coms2/gi_0199-7628145/A-mile-high-is-a.html (accessed May 2010).

24. Gerald H. Tolson and Michael J. Cuyjet, "Jazz and Substance Abuse: Road
to Creative Genius or Pathway to Premature Death," *International Journal of
Law and Psychiatry* 30 (2007), 530–38; John Tucker, interview with author,
April 9, 2008.

25. "Alumni Life: Passings," *Northwestern* magazine, http://www.northwestern
.edu/magazine/spring2014/alumnilife/passings.html (accessed December 26,
2014).

26. John Tucker, interview, April 9, 2008.

27. Miles Davis with Quincy Troupe, *Miles: The Autobiography of Miles Davis*
(New York: Simon & Schuster, 1989), 311.

28. Alice Waters, interview, July 26, 2006.

29. Phoebe Eaton, "Fashion's Number One: Ralph Lauren Is the Biggest-Selling
Designer in the World. He's Created Some of Fashion's Greatest Hits, and
his Influence Can Be Felt Around the World. On the Eve of his 40th Anniversary Year, He Reveals the Secret of his Staggering Success," *Harper's
Bazaar,* March 1, 2006, 46, http://www.lexisnexis.com (accessed October 1,
2008).

30. Davis and Troupe, 196.

31. Quincy Troupe, *Miles and Me* (Berkeley and Los Angeles: University of California Press, 2000), 45.

32. In "Talking Jazz," *The Miles Davis Companion: Four Decades of Commentary,*
ed. Gary Carner (London: Omnibus Press, 1996), 196, as cited in Paul Tingen, *Miles Beyond* (New York: Billboard Books, 2001), 24.

33 Davis and Troupe, 273.

34. Ibid.

35. Interview with Bill Evans, Grammy-nominated saxophonist, September 22,
2006.

36. Stuart Lauchlan, "Interview: Steve Garnett, Chairman and Co-president EMEA, Salesforce.com," *Mycustomer.com,* July 10, 2007, http://www.my customer.com/cgi-bin/item.cgi?id=133118 (accessed November 2009).

37. This point was made in virtually all of the interviews I did with former Oracle employees.

38. Mike Seashols, interview, November 3, 2006. Seashols, who was the first VP for sales and marketing at Oracle, went on to become chairman, CEO, or president of nine other high-tech companies after leaving Oracle.

39. Matthew Symonds, *Softwar* (New York: Simon & Schuster Paperbacks, 2003), 290.

40. Ibid.

41. Gary Bloom, interview, May 24, 2007.

42. Cheryl Hall, "Dallas Restaurateur Norman Brinker Dies," *Dallas Morning News,* June 11, 2009, http://www.dallasnews.com/sharedcontent/dws/bus/stories/061009dnbusbrinkerobit.62c468c5.html (accessed January 20, 2010).

43. Richard Feloni, "Why Oracle Founder Larry Ellison NEEDS To Have The World's Greatest Competitive Team," *Business Insider,* http://www.business insider.com/larry-ellison-yacht-racing-2014-10 (accessed January 2, 2015).

44. He competed in equestrian competition at the Helsinki Summer Olympics in 1952. "William Grimes, Norman Brinker, Casual Dining Innovator, Dies at 78," *New York Times,* June 9, 2009, http://www.nytimes.com/2009/06/10/business/10brinker.html?r=0 (accessed June 15, 2015).

45. Leslie Berlin, *The Man Behind the Microchip: Robert Noyce and the Invention of Silicon Valley* (New York: Oxford University Press, 2006).

46. Howard Rudnitsky, Allan Sloan, Richard L. Stern, and Matthew Heller, "A One Man Revolution," *Forbes,* August 25, 1986, http://www.factiva.com (accessed April 2010).

47. Leslie Berlin, *The Man Behind the Microchip,* 2.

48. Joyce Goldstein, another James Beard Award–winning chef who worked at Chez Panisse, interview, August 17, 2005.

49. Marty Staff, former president and CEO of Hugo Boss, interview, May 28, 2008.

50. Charles Prince, interview, October 23, 2006.

51. Sandy Lutz, "Frist 'Family Tree' Has Roots Firmly Planted in Nashville," *Modern Healthcare,* September 11, 1995, 46.

52. Victor Campbell, senior vice president, Health Corporation of America, interview, October 16, 2008.

53. Atso Almila, interview with author, May 2, 2006.

54. Bob Andelman, "Roberts' Rules of Leadership," *Poynter Online,* September 3,

2002, http://www.poynter.org/content/content_view.asp?id=46544 (accessed October 14, 2010).

55. Paul Tingen, *Miles Beyond,* 15.
56. http://www.forbes.com/profile/ralph-lauren/ (accessed April 14, 2015).
57. "Grammy Hall of Fame: Past Recipients." Grammy.org, http://www.grammy .org/recording-academy/awards/hall-of-fame (accessed December 26, 2014); "Lifetime Achievement Award," Grammy.org., http://www.grammy.org/recording -academy/awards/lifetime-awards (accessed December 26, 2014).
58. http://www.forbes.com/profile/larry-ellison/ (accessed August 1, 2015).

CHAPTER 2: GETTING PEOPLE WHO "GET IT"

1. Melissa Kelly, interview, December 12, 2006.
2. "Chef Melissa Kelly of Primo—Biography," *Star Chefs,* September 2013, http:// www.starchefs.com/cook/chefs/bio/melissa-kelly (accessed December 2014).
3. Mclissa Kelly, interview, December 12, 2006.
4. Meredith Goad, "Chef Melissa Kelly: 'It Just All Felt Very Surreal,'" *Portland Press Herald,* May 6, 2013, http://www.pressherald.com/2013/05/06/maine -chef-wins-prestigious-james-beard-award/ (accessed December 2014).
5. http://www.primorestaurant.com (accessed August 2, 2015).
6. Joseph Hayes, "Salad Days," *Orlando Magazine,* February 2013, http://www .orlandomagazine.com/Orlando-Magazine/February-2013/Salad-Days/ (accessed July 1, 2014).
7. Don Barlett, longtime investigative reporter at the *Philadelphia Inquirer,* inter- view, September 30, 2010.
8. Marty Staff, former president and CEO, Hugo Boss, interview, May 28, 2008.
9. Lorne Michaels, producer, *Saturday Night Live,* interview, March 7, 2008.
10. Lee Clow, chairman, TBWA/Media Arts Lab, interview, July 15, 2005.
11. Rick Berman, former senior executive at Steak and Ale restaurant chain, in- terview, May 2, 2006.
12. R. Scot Sellers, chairman and CEO, Archstone, and former VP for Sanders at Security Capital, interview, September 15, 2008.
13. Mike Wilson, *The Difference Between God and Larry Ellison* (New York: Wil- liam Morrow and Company, 1997), 9.
14. Shades of billionaire Peter Thiel, the PayPal veteran and early Facebook in- vestor who is funding fellowships for young people who choose to skip univer- sity in favor of some scientific, social, or business endeavor.
15. "Interview: Larry Ellison Founder, Oracle Corporation," Academy of Achieve- ment, May 22, 1997, http://www.achievement.org/autodoc/page/ell0int-1 (ac- cessed November 2009).

16. Bill Barber, *We Were Champions: The 49ers Dynasty in Their Own Words*. (Chicago: Triumph Books, 2002), 36.
17. Miles Davis with Quincy Troupe, *Miles: The Autobiography* (New York: Simon & Schuster, 1989), 263.
18. Constance Moore, president and CEO, BRE Properties, interview, December 18, 2008.
19. Stevan Alburty, former director of information systems, Chiat\Day, and the creator and keeper of JayDay.org, the website dedicated to the memory of Jay Chiat, interview, June 3, 2005.
20. James M. Naughton, 46 Frogs: Confessions of a Media Scamp (unpublished manuscript, 2010), 222.
21. John Tucker, interview, April 9, 2008.
22. John Griffin, founder and president, Blue Ridge Capital, interview, October 15, 2012.
23. Ibid.
24. "Interview: Larry Ellison Founder, Oracle Corporation," *Academy of Achievement,* May 22, 1997, http://www.achievement.org/autodoc/page/ell0int-1 (accessed November 2009).
25. C. Ronald Blankenship, president and CEO, Verde Realty, interview, January 8, 2009.
26. Davis with Troupe, *Miles: The Autobiography,* 286.
27. William Ruhlmann, "Artist Biography," *All Music,* http://www.allmusic.com/artist/john-coltrane-mn0000175553/biography (accessed December 2014).
28. Lauren Collins, "Burger Queen," *New Yorker,* November 22, 2010, http://www.newyorker.com/magazine/2010/11/22/burger-queen (accessed February 1, 2015).
29. Michael Gross, *Genuine Authentic* (New York: HarperCollins Publishers, 2003), 263.
30. Joyce Goldstein, interview, August 17, 2005.
31. Joanne Weir, James Beard Award–winning cookbook author and chef, interview, July 26, 2005.
32. Marc Chiat, artist-director, interview, September 14, 2005.
33. Bill Sanders, interview, January 20, 2009.
34. Roy Bukstein, one of the first employees at Oracle, quoted in Mike Wilson, *The Difference Between God and Larry Ellison* (New York: William Morrow and Company, 1997), 93.
35. Seen Lippert, interview, April 24, 2006.
36. David Kamp, *United States of Arugula: How We Became a Gourmet Nation* (New York: Clarkson Potter, 2006), 164.

37. Tom Shales and James Andrew Miller, *Live from New York: An Uncensored History of* Saturday Night Live (Boston: Little, Brown and Company, 2002), 40.

38. Mark Dippe, interview, October 27, 2006.

39. Seen Lippert, interview, April 24, 2006.

CHAPTER 3: MOTIVATING EXCEPTIONAL PEOPLE TO DO THE IMPOSSIBLE

1. Paul Goldberger, "Architecture View: 25 Years of Unabashed Elitism," *New York Times,* February 2, 1992, http://www.nytimes.com/1992/02/02/arts/architecture-view-25-years-of-unabashed-elitism.html?sec= (accessed February 2010).

2. Joseph Abboud, *Threads* (New York: HarperCollins Publishers, 2004), 104.

3. Salvatore Cesarani, part-time assistant professor, course bio (New York: Parsons School of Design), http://www.newschool.edu/parsons/faculty.aspx-?id=4f44-5178-4d51-3d3d (accessed December 31, 2014).

4. Sal Cesarani, interview, July 31, 2008.

5. Ibid.

6. Ibid.

7. Ibid.

8. Ibid.

9. Ron Marston, interview, January 30, 2009.

10. Michael Gross, *Genuine Authentic* (New York: HarperCollins Publishers, 2003), 219.

11. *Deloitte Millennial Survey,* January 2014, http://www2.deloitte.com/global/en/pages/about-deloitte/articles/2014-millennial-survey-positive-impact.html (accessed January 3, 2015); *Telefónica Global Millennial Survey,* November 2014, http://survey.telefonica.com/survey-findings/ (accessed January 3, 2015).

12. C. Ronald Blankenship, president and CEO, Verde Realty, interview, January 8, 2009.

13. Victor Campbell, interview, October 16, 2008.

14. Andy Samberg, 2014 Golden Globe winner for the sitcom *Brooklyn Ninety-Nine,* interview, April 30, 2008.

15. Technology executive, interview, June 10, 2009.

16. Carmen Policy, former president and CEO of the San Francisco 49ers and Cleveland Browns, interview, May 26, 2006.

17. Don Suter, CEO of M3 Capital Partners, interview, September 24, 2008.

18. Ibid.

19. Constance Moore, president and CEO, BRE Properties, interview, December 18, 2008.

20. Andy Samberg, interview, April 30, 2008.

21. Chase Coleman, interview, October 15, 2012.

22. Lee Clow, chairman, TBWA/Media Arts Lab, interview, July 15, 2005.

23. David Lipke, "Polo U; There Are No Classrooms, No Professors and No Ivy on the Walls, but Polo Ralph Lauren Has Long Been a Training Ground for the Men's Wear Industry," *Daily News Record*, July 22, 2002.

24. David A. Vise, "Michael Milken: A Dream-Maker's Rude Awakening," *Washington Post*, November 20, 1988, http://www.lexisnexis.com (accessed April 2010).

25. C. Ronald Blankenship, interview, January 8, 2009.

26. David Lipke, *Daily News Record*, July 22, 2002.

27. Connie Bruck, *The Predators' Ball: The Inside Story of Drexel Burnham and the Rise of the Junk Bond Raiders* (New York: Penguin Books, 1988), 56.

28. David Carr, "101 Secrets (and 9 Lives) of a Magazine Star," *New York Times*, June 29, 2008, http://www.nytimes.com/2008/06/29/business/media/29bonnie.html?_r=1&oref=slogin.

29. Megan Hamill, "Celebrity, Spanish, Teen Categories Break the Mold," *Circulation Management*, 2005, http://www.circman.com/viewmedia.asp?prmMID=1807.

30. Myrna Blyth, "How About a Bit Less?," *National Review*, April 17, 2006, http://www.nationalreview.com/article/217342/how-about-bit-less-myrna-blyth (accessed August 2, 2015).

31. http://finance.groups.yahoo.com/group/isurvivedbonnie/.

32. John Griffin, founder and president, Blue Ridge Capital, interview, October 15, 2012.

33. R. Scot Sellers, interview, September 15, 2008.

34. Clearly employees are getting burned out. According to the 2014 *Deloitte Global Human Capital Trends* report, 79 percent of respondents reported that engaging and retaining employees were "important" or "urgent" problems. See http://d2mtr37y39tpbu.cloudfront.net/wp-content/uploads/2014/03/Global HumanCapitalTrends_2014.pdf.

35. Gallup, *State of the American Workplace: Employee Engagement Insights for U.S. Business Leaders*, 2012.

36. Doug Hill and Jeff Weingrad, *Saturday Night: A Backstage History of Saturday Night Live* (San Francisco: Untreed Reads, 2011), e-book.

37. Howard Roffman, interview, December 19, 2007. It's also worth noting that Lucas was exactly right. Sixteen years after *Return of the Jedi*, the so-called prequel trilogy movies started to hit the screens (generating global box-office receipts of $2.5 billion). And at the end of 2015, the seventh film (*Star Wars: The Force Awakens*), this time directed by J. J. Abrams, was released.

38. David Harris, *The Genius: How Bill Walsh Reinvented Football and Created a Dynasty* (New York: Random House, 2008), 86.
39. Tom Shales and James Andrew Miller, *Live From New York: An Uncensored History of Saturday Night Live* (Boston: Little, Brown and Company, 2002), 22.
40. R. Scot Sellers, interview, September 15, 2008.
41. Howard Kazanjian, interview, October 3, 2007.
42. Ibid., December 19, 2007.
43. Michael Rubin, interview, January 30, 2007.
44. Miles Davis with Quincy Troupe, *Miles: The Autobiography* (New York: Simon & Schuster, 1989), 205.
45. Thomas McNamee, *Alice Waters and Chez Panisse* (New York: Penguin Books, 2007), 227.
46. Shales and Miller, 571.
47. Linda Lewis, chief financial officer, Broadway Real Estate Partners, interview, September 9, 2008.
48. Phil Tippett, interview, August 14, 2007. Tippett won an Academy Award for Best Visual Effects for *Jurassic Park* in 1994.
49. Sheila Barry, "Tribute to Robert Mondavi," *Napa Valley Vintners,* member post, May 21, 2008, 3:05:30 p.m., http://www.napavintners.com/robert_mondavi/in_memory.asp (accessed July 30, 2008).
50. Joyce Goldstein, interview, August 17, 2005.
51. Protégé Chase Coleman, for example, was named in 2011 to *Forbes*'s "Youngest Billionnaires in the World" list at the age of thirty-six: "Youngest Billionaires in the World," *Forbes,* http://www.forbes.com/pictures/eimh45lhg/no-15-chase-coleman/ (accessed December 31 2014).
52. Again, the connection to the millennial generation jumps out. Remarkably, almost all of the superbosses profiled in this book rose to prominence before anyone even knew what the word *millennial* came to mean, yet the superboss playbook—both here when it comes to motivation and continuing in subsequent chapters as I share other elements of the playbook—seems tailor-made for the workplace challenges of our era.
53. Tom Carroll, chairman, TBWA Worldwide, interview, July 18, 2005.
54. Jeffrey A. Trachtenberg, *Ralph Lauren: The Man Behind the Mystique* (Boston: Little, Brown and Company, 1988), 154.

CHAPTER 4: UNCOMPROMISINGLY OPEN

1. Valerie J. Nelson, "Bebe Barron: Her Pioneering Score for 'Forbidden Planet' Helped Popularize Electronic Music," *Los Angeles Times,* April 27, 2008, Obituaries.
2. Geeta Dayal, "Ben Burtt on *Star Wars, Forbidden Planet* and the Sound of Sci-Fi," *Wired,* May 5, 2012, http://www.wired.com/2012/05/ben-burtt-sci-fi-sound-effects/ (accessed December 29, 2014).
3. Ibid.
4. "'The Sounds of Star Wars,' Now at Fans' Fingertips," National Public Radio, *Weekend Edition,* Sunday, December 12, 2010, http://www.npr.org/2010/12/12/131968222/-the-sounds-of-star-wars-now-at-fans-fingertips (accessed December 30, 2014).
5. Ibid.
6. Ben Burtt, sound designer at Lucasfilm, interview, November 29, 2007.
7. Ibid.
8. Ibid.
9. Ibid.
10. Academy Awards Database—Academy of Motion Picture Arts and Sciences (AMPAS), http://awardsdatabase.oscars.org/ampas_awards/BasicSearchInput.jsp (accessed December 30, 2014).
11. Susan King, "Ben Burtt on the Sound of 'Raiders,' 'ET' and Spielberg's Inspiration," *Hero Complex* (blog), *Los Angeles Times,* October 2, 2012, http://herocomplex.latimes.com/movies/ben-burtt-on-the-sound-of-raiders-et-and-spielbergs-inspiration/ (accessed December 30, 2014).
12. Animation Sound Design: Ben Burtt Creates the Sounds for Wall-E (Part 2 of 2) (Walt Disney Pictures, Special Feature on the DVD release of *Wall-E,* 2008), https://www.youtube.com/watch?v=eySh8FOUphm (accessed December 30, 2014).
13. Seen Lippert, interview, April 24, 2006.
14. Thomas McNamee, *Alice Waters and Chez Panisse* (New York: Penguin Books, 2007), 49.
15. Alice Waters, interview, July 26, 2006.
16. Lindsey Shere, winner of the James Beard Award for Outstanding Pastry Chef, interview, February 20, 2006.
17. Interview with Joanne Weir, James Beard Award-winning cookbook author and chef, July 26, 2005.
18. Seen Lippert, interview, April 24, 2006.
19. Ibid.
20. Alice Waters, interview, July 26, 2006.

21. Kyle Craig, interview, March 29, 2006.
22. Ken Sugiura, "The West Coast Offense Is Born: Walsh's Scheme; Innovative Coach Took Limited Passer and Created an Offensive Philosophy," *Atlanta Journal-Constitution,* September 5, 2004, http://www.lexisnexis.com (accessed March 2010).
23. *2014 Official NFL Record & Factbook* (National Football League, 2014), 552.
24. Ken Sugiura, "The West Coast Offense Is Born."
25. Bill Walsh, "West Coast Offense 101," *Sporting News,* January 19, 1999, http://www.sportingnews.com/archives/sports2000/trends/135237.html (accessed March 2010).
26. Scott Hume, "Norman Brinker: Casual Dining's Trailblazer Reflects on His Career with Pride and Satisfaction," *Restaurants & Institutions* (accessed October 2004).
27. Top 10 Memorable Movie Eating Scenes, *Time,* January 6, 2012, http://www.entertainment.time.com/2012/01/06/top-10-memorable-movie-eating-scenes/slide/tom-jones/ (accessed December 30, 2014).
28. Norman Brinker and Donald T. Phillips, *On the Brink: The Life and Leadership of Norman Brinker* (Irving, TX: Tapestry Press, 2002), 83–84.
29. Ibid., 86.
30. Lou Neeb, former Chairman and CEO, Burger King, interview, July 26, 2006.
31. Jim Sullivan, "What You Say Is What You Get: Quotable Quotes 2005," *Nation's Restaurant News,* July 18, 2005, http://findarticles.com/p/articles/mi_m3190/is_29_39/ai_n14819910/ (accessed January 2010).
32. Kyle Craig, interview, March 29, 2006.
33. Adelaide Horton, former senior vice president and chief operating officer, Chiat\Day, interview, July 6, 2005.
34. Scott Ross, interview, April 19, 2007.
35. Kyle Craig, interview, March 29, 2006.
36. Stevan Alburty, former director of information systems, Chiat\Day, and the creator and keeper of JayDay.org, the website dedicated to the memory of Jay Chiat, interview, June 3, 2005.
37. Character actor Dick Miller, quoted in Beverly Gray, *Roger Corman: An Unauthorized Life* (Los Angeles: Renaissance Books, 2000), 51.
38. Clive Thompson, "End the Tyranny of 24/7 Email," *New York Times,* August 28, 2014 (accessed December 31, 2014). Thompson cites the research of Jennifer Deal at the Center for Creative Leadership on email practices in the workplace.
39. John Griffin, founder and president, Blue Ridge Capital, interview, October 15, 2012.

40. Miles Davis, with Quincy Troupe, *Miles: The Autobiography* (New York: Simon & Schuster, 1989), 273.
41. Tom Shales and James Andrew Miller, *Live from New York: An Uncensored History of Saturday Night Live* (Boston: Little, Brown and Company, 2002), 345.
42. Jennifer Armstrong, "The Evolution of 'SNL,'" *EW.com*, September 22, 2006, http://www.ew.com/ew/article/0,1537658,00.html (accessed January 2010).
43. Alice Waters, interview, July 26, 2006.
44. David Murphy, interview, June 16, 2005.
45. Sal Cesarani, interview, July 31, 2008.
46. Sam Merrill, "A Candid Conversation with Roone Arledge, Sports Broadcasting Visionary," *Playboy*, January 30, 2014, http://playboysfw.kinja.com/a-candid-conversation-with-roone-arledge-sports-broadc-1511880255 (accessed December 30, 2014).
47. Ibid.
48. Kyle Craig, interview, March 29, 2006.
49. Marj Charlier, "Maverick of Dinner Houses Faces Spaghetti Shoot-Out," *Wall Street Journal*, January 29, 1990, B1.
50. Michael Barrier, "Entrepreneurs Who Excel," *Nation's Business* (August 1996), http://findarticles.com/p/articles/mi_m1154/is_n8_v84/ai_18522633/ (accessed January 2010).
51. Eivind Aadland, interview, October 13, 2006.
52. Ibid.
53. Beverly Gray, *Roger Corman: An Unauthorized Life*, 214.
54. Ibid.
55. Lou Neeb, former chairman and CEO, Burger King, interview, July 26, 2006.
56. Sid Ganis, senior VP at Lucasfilm during the early 1980s, interview, April 5, 2007. Ganis went on to produce more than a dozen movies, and in 2005 was elected president of the Academy of Motion Picture Arts and Sciences.
57. John P. Kotter, *Leading Change* (Boston: Harvard Business Review Press, 2012).
58. The term *undiscussable* was coined by the late management theorist Chris Argyris. For more, see his classic book, *Overcoming Organizational Defenses: Facilitating Organizational Learning* (Englewood Cliffs, NJ: Prentice Hall, 1990).

CHAPTER 5: MASTERS AND APPRENTICES

1. Dario A. Covi, *Andrea del Verrocchio: Life and Work* (Florence: Leo S. Olschki, 2005), 251.
2. Ibid., 14.
3. Ibid., 15.
4. Liletta Fornasari, "Andrea del Verrocchio and the Workshops of Tuscany," in *Verrocchio and the Renaisance Atelier,* trans. Susan Herbstritt (Firenze: Pagliai Polistampa, 2001), 15.
5. Ibid.
6. Patricia Rubin and Alison Wright, *Renaissance Florence: The Art of the 1470s* (London: National Gallery Press, 1999), 104.
7. Jill Dunkerton, "Leonardo in Verrocchio's Workshop: Re-examining the Technical Evidence," *National Gallery Technical Bulletin* 32, 15.
8. Rubin and Wright, 97.
9. Biography Online, "Top 10 Artists/Painters of All Time," http://www.biogra phyonline.net/artists/top-10-painters.html (accessed January 2, 2015).
10. Tamar Jacoby, "Why Germany Is So Much Better at Training Its Workers," *Atlantic,* October 16, 2014, http://www.theatlantic.com/business/archive/2014/10/why-germany-is-so-much-better-at-training-its-workers/381550/ (accessed January 3, 2015).
11. United States Department of Labor Employment and Training Administration, http://www.doleta.gov/oa/data_statistics.cfm (accessed January 2, 2015).
12. Lois Therrien, "Marlboro Man, Meet the Master of Mayo," *Business Week,* October 31, 1988, http://www.lexisnexis.com (accessed February 2010).
13. Richard Gibson and Robert Johnson, ". . . And Richman's Acumen May Prove Kraft's Undoing," *Wall Street Journal,* October 19, 1988, http://www.factiva .com (accessed February 2010).
14. John Tucker, interview, April 9, 2008.
15. Ibid.
16. Ibid.
17. Paul Batalden, interview, October 20, 2006.
18. Juhani Poutanen, Finnish violinist, interview, June 23, 2006.
19. John Carroll, former editor of the *Baltimore Sun* and *Los Angeles Times,* and the metro editor of the *Philadelphia Inquirer* under Gene Roberts, interview, October 1, 2010.
20. Samuel Howard, chairman and CEO of Phoenix Holdings, Inc., and Xantus Corporation, interview, August 12, 2008.
21. Connie Bruck, *The Predators' Ball: The Inside Story of Drexel Burnham and the Rise of the Junk Bond Raiders* (New York: Penguin Books, 1988), 87.

22. "Brinker International: The Personal Touch," *Financial World* 162 (12) (June 8, 1993), 38.
23. Eivind Aadland, chief conductor and artistic leader, Trondheim Symphony Orchestra, interview, October 13, 2006.
24. Sid Ganis, senior vice president at Lucasfilm, and former president of the Academy of Motion Picture Arts and Sciences, interview, April 5, 2007.
25. Thomas Keller, chef-owner of the French Laundry, interview, May 1, 2006.
26. Noyce filed U.S. Patent 2,981,877 in 1959. In 1980, Jack Kilby, who worked at Texas Instruments, was awarded the Nobel Prize in physics for the invention of the integrated circuit, an honor Noyce would have shared with him had he not died ten years earlier. No less a pioneer in integrated circuits than Julius Blank, one of the original "Traitorous Eight" who left Shockley Semiconductor to go to Fairchild at the very beginning of the revolution that created Silicon Valley, believes Bob Noyce would have won a Nobel Prize had he been alive when Jack Kilby was so honored. He told me, "Absolutely. I know Jack and I think he did a great job, but nobody makes that device the way he did it. Kilby's invention is unmakeable; you couldn't manufacture it without what Noyce did" (Julius Blank, interview, June 15, 2006).
27. Robert Slater, *Portraits in Silicon* (Cambridge, MA: MIT Press, 1989), 153.
28. Charles E. Sporck and Richard L. Molay, *Spinoff: A Personal History of the Industry That Changed the World* (Saranac Lake, NY: Saranac Lake Publishing, 2001), 3.
29. Tom Wolfe, "The Tinkerings of Robert Noyce," *Esquire*, December 1983, 346–74, http://www.factiva.com (accessed November 12, 2008).
30. Gordon Moore, cofounder of Intel, interview, August 17, 2006.
31. Ibid.
32. Tom Wolfe, "The Tinkerings of Robert Noyce."
33. Tim Jackson, *Inside Intel* (New York: Dutton, 1997), 37.
34. John Griffin, founder and president, Blue Ridge Capital, interview, October 15, 2012.
35. Open offices have come under fire in recent years, with critics regarding them as too loud and unsuitable for introverts. I would note that the downsides to open offices tend to arise when leaders operate out of a desire to cut costs and stuff more people into the same space, and when they promote a false egalitarianism. In the case of superbosses, open offices reflect a genuine attempt to embrace egalitarianism, and employees tend to have a far more positive experience.
36. Stevan Alburty, former director of information systems, Chiat\Day, and the

creator and keeper of JayDay.org, the website dedicated to the memory of Jay Chiat, interview, June 3, 2005.

37. Chris Blackhurst, "Exclusive MT Interview: Archie Norman," *Management Today*, September 3, 2007, http://www.managementtoday.co.uk/search/article/735030/exclusive-mt-interview-archie-norman/ (accessed October 15, 2008).

38. It should come as no surprise then to find that the most structured and bureaucratic companies tend to be the least fruitful hunting grounds for corporate recruiting firms (Dean Foust, "Where Headhunters Fear to Tread," *Business Week*, September 14, 2009, 42–44).

39. Tom Carroll, chairman, TBWA Worldwide, interview, July 18, 2005.

40. David Curtis, interview, November 8, 2006.

41. Ibid.

42. Ibid.

43. Ibid.

44. John Carroll, interview, October 1, 2010.

45. Luc Vandevelde, interview, January 21, 2008.

46. John Carroll, interview, October 1, 2010.

47. Scott Ross, interview, April 19, 2007.

48. Bill Evans, Grammy-nominated saxophonist, interview, September 22, 2006.

49. Mary Sue Milliken, co-owner-chef of Border Grill (Santa Monica and Las Vegas) and Ciudad, interview, September 9, 2005. Several other female chefs we interviewed made a point of remarking that Alice Waters was a particularly poignant role model for them because she was such a prominent woman in a business still dominated by men. And this was even more true when Waters was just starting out.

50. "Ed Stack Resigns Behavioral Healthcare CEO Post," *Nashville Post*, February 2, 2001, https://www.nashvillepost.com/news/2001/2/2/ed_stack_resigns_behavioral_healthcare_ceo_post (accessed December 27, 2014).

51. Edward Stack, interview, October 22, 2008.

52. Beverly Gray, *Roger Corman: An Unauthorized Life* (Los Angeles: Renaissance Books, 2000), 107.

53. Ibid., 224.

54. "The Best Advice I Ever Got," *Fortune*, July 6, 2009, 45, http://archive.fortune.com/galleries/2009/fortune/0906/gallery.best_advice_i_ever_got2.fortune/7.html (accessed January 2, 2015).

55. Gayle Ortiz, interview, September 2, 2005.

56. Richard Lenny, interview, April 1, 2008.

57. Doug Conant, interview, October 4, 2007.

58. John Griffin, founder and president, Blue Ridge Capital, interview, October 15, 2012.
59. Esa-Pekka Salonen, principal conductor of the Philharmonia Orchestra in London, and past music director of the Los Angeles Philharmonic, interview, May 31, 2006.
60. David Curtis, interview, November 8, 2006.
61. John Griffin, interview, October 15, 2012.
62. David Murphy, interview, June 16, 2005.
63. Sir Michael Barber, Fenton Whelan, and Michael Clark, *Capturing the Leadership Premium* (McKinsey&Company, November 2010), http://mckinseyon society.com/capturing-the-leadership-premium/ (accessed January 2, 2015).
64. Motoko Rich, "As Apprentices in Classroom, Teachers Learn What Works," *New York Times,* October 10, 2014, http://www.nytimes.com/2014/10/11/us/as-apprentices-in-classroom-teachers-learn-what-works.html?hp&action=click&pgtype=Homepage&version=HpSum&module=first-column-region&region=top-news&WT.nav=top-news&_r=0 (accessed December 27, 2014).

CHAPTER 6: THE HANDS-ON DELEGATOR

1. "Tiger Global's Chase Coleman: With This Reclusive Billionaire, Actions Speak Louder Than Words," *iBillionaire,* June 2, 2014, http://ibillionaire app.tumblr.com/post/87625160543/tiger-globals-chase-coleman-with-this-reclusive (accessed January 2, 2015).
2. Gary Weiss, "What Really Killed Robertson's Tiger," *Business Week,* April 17, 2000, http://www.businessweek.com/archives/2000/b3677111.arc.htm (accessed January 8, 2009).
3. Daniel A. Strachman, *Julian Robertson: A Tiger in the Land of Bulls and Bears* (Hoboken, NJ: John Wiley and Sons, 2004), 169.
4. "How Julian Robertson Turned $8.8 Million into $21 Billion," *Dan Strachman Interview,* http://www.tradingmarkets.com/recent/how_julian_robertson_turned_88_million_into_21_billionthe_dan_strachman_interview-656158.html (accessed December 30, 2014).
5. "Profile/Biography on Hedge Fund Legend Julian Robertson (Tiger Management)," *Market Folly,* June 3, 2009, http://www.marketfolly.com/2009/06/profilebiography-on-hedge-fund-legend.html (accessed January 2, 2015).
6. Jennifer Karchmer, "Tiger Management Closes," *CNN Money,* March 30, 2000, http://money.cnn.com/2000/03/30/mutualfunds/q_funds_tiger/ (accessed January 2, 2015).
7. Julian Robertson, interview, November 11, 2008.

8. Chase Coleman, interview, October 15, 2012.

9. Email communication from Gil Caffray, chief investment officer, Tiger Management LLC, July 15, 2015.

10. Ibid.

11. "Chase Coleman, III," *Forbes*, http://www.forbes.com/profile/chase-coleman-iii/ (accessed August 1, 2015).

12. Email communication from Gil Caffray, chief investment officer, Tiger Management LLC, August 5, 2015. As of 2012, out of the $2 trillion or so invested by hedge funds around the world, fully 20 percent of them—tiger cubs and tiger seeds alike—either currently work for or have worked for Julian Robertson (John Townsend, interview, October 15, 2012).

13. Anthony Effinger, Katherine Burton, and Ari Levy, "Top Hedge Fund Returns 45% With Robertson's 36-Year-Old Disciple," Bloomberg, January 9, 2012, http://www.bloomberg.com/news/articles/2012-01-10/chase-coleman-channels-ancestor-stuyvesant-with-45-robertson-like-return.

14. Brian O'Keefe, "Tiger's Julian Robertson Roars Again," *Fortune*, January 29, 2008, http://money.cnn.com/2008/01/28/news/newsmakers/okeefe_tiger.fortune/index.htm (accessed January 8, 2009).

15. "Julian Robertson, Jr." *Forbes*, http://www.forbes.com/profile/julian-robertson-jr/ (accessed August 1, 2015); Mebane Faber, "Grab a Tiger's Tail," *Forbes*, April 27, 2010, http://www.forbes.com/2010/04/27/apple-visa-google-intelligent-investing-julian-robertson.html (accessed January 2, 2015).

16. Beverly Gray, *Roger Corman: An Unauthorized Life* (Los Angeles: Renaissance Books, 2000), 151.

17. Gary Bloom, an executive vice president under Ellison who went on to become chairman and CEO of Veritas, which was sold to Symantec in 2005, interview, May 24, 2007.

18. David Murphy, interview, June 16, 2005.

19. Curry Kirkpatrick, "Now Pacing Sideline, Pitino Protégés," *New York Times*, February 18, 1997, B12.

20. Jared Diamond, "Iowa: The Harvard of Coaching," *Wall Street Journal*, December 21, 2011, D5.

21. Ken Plume, "An Interview with Stephen Colbert," *IGN*, August 11, 2003, http://jerriblank.com/colbert_filmforce.html (accessed July 4, 2008).

22. Public service employees are among the worst example of this type of lockstep promotion system, where tenure is more important than talent. Despite banalities that people come first, however, aspects of the tenure system remain in place at most for-profit companies even today, creating what might

be the single most important competitive advantage for Silicon Valley–type companies that refuse to play by these outmoded bureaucratic rules. And academic institutions, especially universities, may well be the most egregious example of the dangers of valuing tenure above competence.

23. Jared Diamond, "Iowa: The Harvard of Coaching," D5.
24. Karen Southwick, *Everyone Else Must Fail* (New York: Crown Business, 2003), 65.
25. Chase Coleman, interview, October 15, 2012.
26. David Harris, *The Genius: How Bill Walsh Reinvented Football and Created a Dynasty* (New York: Random House, 2008), 84.
27. Jeff McLaughlin, ed., *Stan Lee: Conversations* (Jackson: University Press of Mississippi, 2007), 36.
28. Jordan Raphael and Tom Spurgeon, *Stan Lee and the Rise and Fall of the American Comic Book* (Chicago: Chicago Review Press, 2003), 152.
29. Gene Roberts, interview, October 1, 2010.
30. Richard Frank, longtime CEO of Chuck E. Cheese, interview, April 5, 2006.
31. Rob Gilbert, interview, March 21, 2007.
32. Arja Ropo and Erika Sauer, "The Success Story of Finnish Conductors: Grand Narratives and Small Stories on Global Leadership" (paper presented at the 7th AIMAC Conference, Milan, June 2003), 7–8.
33. R. Scot Sellers, interview, September 15, 2008.
34. Richard Frank, interview, April 5, 2006.
35. Michael Miles, interview, January 21, 2008.
36. Sal Cesarani, interview, July 31, 2008.
37. Richard Rapaport, "To Build a Winning Team: An Interview with Head Coach Bill Walsh," *Harvard Business Review*, January–February 1993, 117.
38. Tom Wolfe, "The Tinkerings of Robert Noyce," *Esquire*, December 1983, 346–74, http://www.factiva.com (accessed November 12, 2008).
39. Jim Naughton, interview, September 30, 2010.
40. Jeffrey A. Trachtenberg, *Ralph Lauren: The Man Behind the Mystique* (Boston: Little, Brown and Company, 1988), 53.
41. Ibid., 94–95.
42. Curry Kirkpatrick, "Now Pacing Sideline, Pitino Protégés."
43. Stanley Gellers, interview, June 17, 2008.
44. Andy Samberg, interview, April 30, 2008.
45. Michael Sullivan, interview, March 27, 2006.
46. Jeff Campbell, who was promoted to CEO of Burger King by Brinker in 1983, interview, April 12, 2006. This sentiment dovetails nicely with superbosses' tendency to hire smart as well.

47. Ted Leland, interview, June 5, 2008.

48. Personal communication with former Ellison employee who requested anonymity.

49. Mark Leckie, interview, March 11, 2008. Leckie got his start under Michael Miles, worked closely with former Gillette CEO Jim Kilts (whom Miles also hired at Kraft), and after a few moves ended up CEO of the Gillette division of P&G after that acquisition.

50. Karl VanDevender, interview, February 20, 2009.

51. Gordon Moore, cofounder of Intel, interview, August 17, 2006.

52. Gary Bloom, former CEO, Veritas, interview, May 24, 2007.

53. Ibid.

54. Miles Davis with Quincy Troupe, *Miles: The Autobiography* (New York: Simon & Schuster, 1989), 273.

55. Former manager at Polo Ralph Lauren, interview, July 29, 2008.

56. Chase Coleman, interview, October 15, 2012.

57. Gayle Ortiz, interview, September 2, 2005.

58. Former Oracle senior manager who went on to become CEO and board member at several Silicon Valley companies, interview, February 19, 2007.

59. Del Jones, "Some Firms' Fertile Soil Grows Crop of Future CEOs," *USA Today*, January 9, 2008, B1; Monica C. Higgins, *Career Imprints: Creating Leaders Across an Industry* (San Francisco: Jossey-Bass, 2005). Higgins's fabulous book is the first to analyze "career imprinting," the notion that where someone worked leaves lasting effects that enhance, or detract, from his or her ability to shift jobs. She studied the "Baxter Boys," the dozens of managers who left Baxter to become senior executives—often CEOs—of emerging biotech firms.

60. Jeff Campbell, interview, April 12, 2006.

CHAPTER 7: THE COHORT EFFECT

1. Rachel Dratch, *Girl Walks into a Bar . . . Comedy Calamities, Dating Disasters, and a Midlife Miracle* (New York: Gotham Books, 2012), 14.

2. *SNL* has won forty Emmy awards, and counting, http://www.emmys.com/shows/saturday-night-live (accessed January 4, 2015).

3. SaturdayNightLive.com, cast bios, http://www.saturday-night-live.com/snl/castbios/racheldratch.html (accessed January 2, 2015).

4. Rachel Dratch, interview, April 3, 2007.

5. Lorne Michaels, interview, March 7, 2008.

6. Jim Downey, *SNL* writer, interview, April 24, 2008. Downey worked with Lorne Michaels for almost the entire span of the show, until retiring in 2013.

Comedian Dennis Miller called Downey the second most important person in the history of *SNL*.

7. Tom Shales and James Andrew Miller, *Live from New York: An Uncensored History of* Saturday Night Live (Boston: Little, Brown and Company, 2002), 420.

8. Ibid., 546.

9. Michael Gross, *Genuine Authentic* (New York: HarperCollins Publishers, 2003), 219.

10. Ibid., 246.

11. Teri Agins, *The End of Fashion* (New York: HarperCollins Publishers, 1999), 91.

12. Quoted in Richard Rapaport, "To Build a Winning Team: An Interview with Head Coach Bill Walsh," *Harvard Business Review*, January–February 1993, 116.

13. Thomas McNamee, *Alice Waters and Chez Panisse* (New York: Penguin Books, 2007), 320.

14. Stan Lee and George Mair, *Excelsior!: The Amazing Life of Stan Lee* (New York: Simon & Schuster, 2002), 154.

15. Mark Evanier, *Kirby: King of Comics* (New York: Abrams, 2008), 16.

16. Rebecca Leung, "Michaels: Lip-Sync an 'SNL' No-No," *60 Minutes* (New York: CBS, October 28, 2004), http://www.cbsnews.com/stories/2004/10/28/60minutes/main652196.shtml (accessed February 1, 2015).

17. David Lipke, "Polo U: There Are No Classrooms, No Professors and No Ivy on the Walls, but Polo Ralph Lauren Has Long Been a Training Ground for the Men's Wear Industry," *Daily News Record*, July 22, 2002.

18. Luc Vandevelde, interview, January 21, 2008.

19. Bob Dion, interview, June 27, 2005.

20. Connie Bruck, *The Predators' Ball: The Inside Story of Drexel Burnham and the Rise of the Junk Bond Raiders* (New York: Penguin Books, 1988), 84.

21. Eric Deggans, "For Aasif Mandvi, Cultural Irreverence on 'The Daily Show,'" May 31, 2008, http://www.tampabay.com/features/media/for-aasif-mandvi-cultural-irreverence-on-the-daily-show/545843 (accessed February 1, 2015).

22. Jean Vallely, "The Empire Strikes Back and So Does Filmmaker George Lucas With His Sequel to Star Wars," *Rolling Stone*, June 12, 1980, quoted in *George Lucas Interviews*, ed. Sally Kline (Jackson: University Press of Mississippi, 1999), 94.

23. Phil Tippett, Academy Award winner, interview, August 14, 2007.

24. NBA.com, San Antonio Spurs, http://www.nba.com/spurs/history/spurs_history.html, (accessed January 3, 2015).

25. Miles Wray, "The Tree of Popovich and Buford," *HP Basketball Network* (blog), http://hardwoodparoxysm.com/2014/06/19/coaching-tree-popovich-buford-spurs/ (accessed January 4, 2015).

26. Nate Taylor, "A San Antonio Graduate Program That Churns Out N.B.A. Coaches," *New York Times*, June 16, 2013, http://www.nytimes.com/2013/06/17/sports/basketball/a-san-antonio-graduate-program-that-churns-out-nba-coaches.html?emc=eta1&_r=0.

27. Ray Didinger, *Game Plans for Success* (New York: McGraw-Hill, 1996), 188.

28. David Harris, *The Genius: How Bill Walsh Reinvented Football and Created a Dynasty* (New York: Random House, 2008), 72.

29. Michael Miles, interview, January 21, 2008.

30. Ibid.

31. Miles Davis with Quincy Troupe, *Miles: The Autobiography* (New York: Simon & Schuster, 1989), 273.

32. Bill Jamison, "The Bill Walsh Way," *Washington Post*, September 4, 2009, http://views.washingtonpost.com/leadership/guestinsights/2009/09/the-bill-walsh-way.html (accessed December 30, 2014).

33. Thomas McNamee, *Alice Waters and Chez Panisse*, 289.

34. R. Clayton McWhorter, former CEO, HealthTrust, interview, November 26, 2008.

35. Don Suter, CEO of M3 Capital Partners, interview, September 24, 2008.

36. Mary Kay Ash, *Mary Kay* (New York: Harper & Row, 1981), 159.

37. Ibid., 40.

38. Ibid., 49.

39. Ibid.

40. Atso Almila, interview, May 2, 2006.

41. Julian Robertson, interview, November 11, 2008.

42. Victor Campbell, interview, October 16, 2008.

43. Bob Dion, interview, June 27, 2005.

44. Motown Museum, "Motown: The Sound That Changed America," http://www.motownmuseum.org/story/motown/ (accessed January 3, 2015).

45. "Berry Gordy: Sweet Soul Music, Growth Strategies," *Entrepreneur*, October 9, 2008, http://www.entrepreneur.com/article/197634 (accessed January 3, 2015).

46. Ibid.

47. Larry Schweikart, "Berry Gordy Jr. and the Original 'Black Label,'" *Ideas on Liberty*, May 2003, http://fee.org/files/docLib/schweikart0503.pdf (accessed January 3, 2015).

48. "It Happened in Hitsville," *Vanity Fair*, December 2008, http://www.vanity

fair.com/culture/features/2008/12/motown200812 (accessed January 31, 2013).

49. Ibid.

50. The Brill Building in Manhattan was the epicenter of popular music in America for decades, housing music publishers (Leo Feist), composers (Carole King), and bands (the Glen Miller Orchestra).

51. "It Happened in Hitsville," *Vanity Fair.*

52. Former senior executive at Oracle, interview, September 29, 2006.

53. Chase Coleman, interview, October 15, 2012.

54. Gene Roberts, interview, October 1, 2010.

55. Quoted in John Colapinto, "When I'm Sixty-Four: Paul McCartney Then and Now," *New Yorker,* June 4, 2007, 63.

56. Matthew Futterman, "Questions for Nick Bollettieri," *Wall Street Journal,* August 27, 2008, http://online.wsj.com/article_print/SB121912927628652603.html (accessed August 28, 2008).

57. Ibid. The academy is now known as the IMG Academy.

58. William Knoedelseder, *I'm Dying Up Here: Heartbreak and High Times in Stand-Up Comedy's Golden Era* (New York: Perseus Book Group, 2009), 22.

59. Ibid., 55.

60. Mark Dippé, award-winning visual effects expert, director of *Spawn,* interview, October 27, 2006.

61. Jay Last, interview, June 13, 2006.

62. Bruce Sacerdote, "Peer Effects in Education: How Might They Work, How Big Are They and How Much Do We Know Thus Far?," *Handbook of Economics of Education* (Amsterdam: North Holland, 2010).

CHAPTER 8: NETWORKS OF SUCCESS

1. Joanne Weir, "Millet Muffin Recipe," *Food Wine Travel,* January 14, 2011, http://joanneweir.blogspot.com/2011_01_01_archive.html (accessed January 4, 2015).

2. PBS.org, *Food,* http://www.pbs.org/food/chefs/joanne-weir/ (accessed January 4, 2015).

3. Paula Forbes, "US State Department Reveals the American Chef Corps," *Eater,* September 10, 2012, http://www.eater.com/2012/9/10/6547279/us-state-department-reveals-the-american-chef-corps (accessed January 4, 2015).

4. Alice Waters, foreword to *Joanne Weir's Cooking Confidence,* by Joanne Weir (Newtown, CT: Taunton Press, 2012), https://itunes.apple.com/us/book/joanne-weirs-cooking-confidence/id577932785?mt=11 (accessed January 4, 2015).

5. Joanne Weir, James Beard Award–winning cookbook author and chef, interview, July 26, 2005.

6. Catherine Hanly, *Hot Dinners Gastroblog*, September 30, 2014, http://www .hot-dinners.com/Gastroblog/Latest-news/chez-panisse-chef-alice-waters-joins-clarke-s-restaurant-anniversary-celebrations (accessed January 4, 2015). Add Chez Panisse alums Lindsay (head chef to the US ambassador in Bern, Switzerland) and Ptak (chef and founder of the East London bakery Violet Cakes) to the list of successful Alice Waters progeny.

7. Jay Barrman, *SFist* (SF food blog), November 15, 2013, http://sfist.com/2013 /11/15/quince_rings_in_ten_years_with_big-.php (accessed January 4, 2015). Michael Tusk is a good example of how the superboss influence can rub off on subsequent generations. He credits Alice Waters and former Chez Panisse chef Paul Bertolli for helping to shape his culinary philosophy. The 10th anniversary celebration of Tusk's restaurant Quince included a special dinner prepared by his own protégés, now running their own restaurants as head chefs.

8. Joanne Weir, interview, July 26, 2005.

9. Joanne Weir, "Chez Panisse through the Eyes of the People behind the Stoves, Weir: It's the Only Kitchen I'll Work In," *San Francisco Chronicle*, August 22, 2001, http://www.sfgate.com/restaurants/article/Chez-Panisse-through-the-eyes-of-the-people-2887163.php (accessed January 4, 2015).

10. Seen Lippert, interview, April 24, 2006.

11. Daniel Halgin, "The Effects of Social Identity on Career Progression: A Study of NCAA Basketball Coaches," *Academy of Management Best Paper Proceedings* (2009).

12. Stevan Alburty, *Chiat's Day and Night* (blog), http://home.earthlink.net/ ~alburty/chiat.htm (accessed January 4, 2015).

13. Stevan Alburty, former director of information systems, Chiat\Day, and the creator and keeper of JayDay.org, the website dedicated to the memory of Jay Chiat, interview, June 3, 2005.

14. http://www.jayday.org.

15. Jeffrey Banks, interview, July 2, 2008.

16. IMDb, Roger Corman (actor), http://www.imdb.com/name/nm0000339/?ref _=fn_al_nm_1 (accessed January 4, 2015).

17. Susan King, "Hollywood Star Walk: Roger Corman," *Los Angeles Times*, August 20, 2006, http://projects.latimes.com/hollywood/star-walk/roger-corman/ (accessed January 4, 2015).

18. Mike Seashols, interview, November 3, 2006.

19. Ibid.

20. Stevan Alburty, interview, June 3, 2005.

21. Jean-Pierre Moullé, interview, August 17, 2005.

22. Alice Waters, interview, July 26, 2006.

23. Chris Taylor, "Eat . . . Or Be Eaten," *Time,* June 23, 2003, http://www.time .com/time/magazine/article/0,9171,1005055,00.html (accessed November 2009).

24. Ken Segall, interview, June 24, 2005.

25. Rick Berman, interview, May 2, 2006.

26. Jack Bovender, interview, November 20, 2008. Bovender worked closely with Tommy Frist at HCA, becoming CEO of that company himself in 2001. *Institutional Investor* magazine recognized Bovender as "Best CEO in America" for health care facilities in 2003, 2004, and 2005. Bovender retired as chairman of HCA in 2009.

27. Sylvester L. Reeder III, former VP of HCA and more recently CEO at two different health care companies, interview, August 13, 2008.

28. Richard Lenny, interview, April 1, 2008.

29. Tom Shales and James Andrew Miller, *Live from New York: An Uncensored History of* Saturday Night Live (Boston: Little, Brown and Company, 2002), 498.

30. William Shakespeare, *Henry V,* act 4, scene 3, http://shakespeare.mit.edu/ henryv/henryv.4.3.html (accessed January 30, 2015).

31. "Milken's Minions," *Institutional Investor,* February 1997, http://proquest .umi.com/pqdweb?did=11129436&Fmt=3&clientId=4347&RQT=309&V Name=PQD (accessed April 2010).

32. Yes, even Larry Ellison was, at least on occasion, supportive of some of his people moving on . . . as long as they didn't compete directly with him.

33. Ted Leland, former director of athletics at Stanford University, interview, June 5, 2008.

34. Jonathan Allen and Amie Parnes, *HRC: State Secrets and the Rebirth of Hillary Clinton* (New York: Crown Publishers, 2014).

35. Ibid.

36. Lois Romano, "Gatekeepers of Hillaryland," *Washington Post,* June 21, 2007, http://www.washingtonpost.com/wp-dyn/content/article/2007/06/20/ AR2007062002567.html (accessed January 4, 2015).

37. US Department of State, What Does the Office of the Chief of Protocol Do?, http://www.state.gov/s/cpr/51328.htm (accessed January 4, 2015).

38. Catalina Camia, "Sarah Palin Speaks about Tina Fey and Being Depicted as an 'Idiot,'" *USA Today,* August 20, 2014, http://onpolitics.usatoday.com/2014/08/20/ sarah-palin-tina-fey-saturday-night-live/ (accessed January 4, 2015).

39. Kitty Kelley, *Oprah: A Biography* (New York: Crown Publishers, 2010); Janet

Lowe, *Oprah Winfrey Speaks: Insight from the World's Most Influential Voice* (New York: John Wiley & Sons, 1998).

40. Lauren Effron, "Oprah-Made: 8 Stars Who Shot to Fame Thanks to Winfrey," *ABC News Go,* October 15, 2012, http://abcnews.go.com/Entertainment/oprah-made-stars-shot-fame-winfrey/story?id=17236783#2 (accessed July 24, 2014).

41. Dr. Phil McGraw, biography, http://www.biography.com/people/dr-phil-mcgraw-9542524 (accessed on January 4, 2015). Also another interesting example of how superbosses find talent in unusual places.

42. Kitty Kelley, *Oprah: A Biography,* 322.

43. Ibid., 227.

44. "Dr. Phil: Oprah Is 'The Gold Standard In TV,'" *Tell Me More,* National Public Radio, May 23, 2011, http://www.npr.org/2011/05/23/136579294/dr-phil-talks-oprahs-legacy (accessed July 24, 2014).

45. Ibid.

46. Mark Donald, "Analyze This," *Dallas Morning Observer,* April 13, 2000, http://www.dallasobserver.com/2000-04-13/news/analyze-this/full (accessed July 24, 2014).

47. CBS Television press release, February 5, 2008, https://www.cbspressexpress.com/cbs-television-distribution/releases/view?id=17864 (accessed February 2, 2015).

48. "Dr. Phil: Oprah Is 'The Gold Standard In TV,'" *Tell Me More,* National Public Radio.

49. Other protégés of Oprah's, as of this writing, include Nate Berkus, Iyanla Vanzant, Gayle King, and Bob Greene.

50. Paul Batalden, interview, October 20, 2006.

51. Joel Gordon, interview, October 1, 2008.

52. Ibid.

53. Anonymous senior executive, interview, September 12, 2006.

54. John Luongo, interview, February 19, 2007.

55. Ron Marston, former senior executive, interview, January 30, 2009.

56. Julian Robertson, interview, November 11, 2008.

57. Michael Miles, interview, January 21, 2008.

58. John Townsend, interview, October 15, 2012.

59. Julian Robertson, interview, November 11, 2008.

60. Daniel Strachman, *Julian Robertson: A Tiger in the Land of Bulls and Bears* (Hoboken, NJ: Wiley, 2004), 47.

61. Bill Evans, Grammy-nominated saxophonist, interview, September 22, 2006.

62. Marc Myers, "Interview: John Scofield," *JazzWax* (blog), March 28, 2012,

http://www.jazzwax.com/2012/03/interview-john-scofield.html (accessed January 4, 2015).

63. Katie Glueck, "The Power Players behind Hillary Clinton's Campaign," *Politico,* April 12, 2015, http://www.politico.com/story/2015/04/hillary-clintons-power-players-116874.html#ixzz3ZUTaZIBl (accessed May 13, 2015).

64. Bradford Evans, "Talking to Wyatt Cenac about 'The Daily Show,' Writing for 'King of the Hill,' and What's Next for Him," *Splitsider,* September 19, 2013, http://splitsider.com/2013/09/wyatt-cenac-interview/ (accessed February 1, 2015).

65. Sara Moulton, "How Meryl Streep Nailed Her," *Daily Beast,* August 4, 2009, http://www.thedailybeast.com/blogs-and-stories/2009-08-04/how-meryl-streep-nailed-her/ (accessed September 24, 2009).

66. Katie Workman, "Jody Adams Talks About Julia Child and the Movie *Julie and Julia,*" *NY Food Examiner,* August 14, 2009, http://www.examiner.com/x-8456-NY-Food-Examiner~y2009m8d14-Jody-Adams-talks-about-Julia-Child-and-the-movie-Julia-and-Julia (accessed September 24, 2009).

67. Sam Gugino, "Thomas Keller—A Love for French Food," *Wine Spectator,* September 30, 2009, 52.

68. Owen Dugan, "Jacques Pépin—Cooking French in America," *Wine Spectator,* September 30, 2009, 58.

69. Beverly Gray, *Roger Corman: An Unauthorized Life* (Los Angeles: Renaissance Books, 2000), 137.

70. Luc Vandevelde, interview, January 21, 2008.

71. Geraldine Fabrikant, "For Yale's Money Man, a Higher Calling," *New York Times,* February 18, 2007, http://www.nytimes.com/2007/02/18/business/yourmoney/18swensen.html (accessed September 2008); Sophie Gould, "Investments Office Alumni Excel," *Yale Daily News,* April 18, 2013, http://yaledailynews.com/blog/2013/04/18/investments-office-alumni-excel/ (accessed January 11, 2015).

72. Andrew Golden, president, Princeton University Investment Company, interview, September 18, 2008.

73. Shales and Miller, *Live from New York,* 422.

74. Reed Hastings, "Freedom & Responsibility Culture (Version 1)," *Slideshare,* http://www.slideshare.net/reed2001/culture-1798664, Slide 115 (accessed February 1, 2015).

75. Reid Hoffman, Ben Casnocha, Chris Yeh, *The Alliance: Managing Talent in the Networked Age* (Boston: Harvard Business Review Press, 2014), 5.

76. Reid Hoffman, "Four Reasons to Invest in a Corporate Alumni Network," *Tal-*

ent (blog), http://talent.linkedin.com/blog/index.php/2014/09/four-reasons-to
-invest-in-a-corporate-alumni-network (accessed January 7, 2015).

CHAPTER 9: SUPERBOSSES AND YOU

1. Jan Reid, *Let the People In: The Life and Times of Ann Richards* (Austin: University of Texas Press, 2012).
2. Brendan Sullivan, "Lady Gaga: The Grandmother of Pop," *Esquire,* May 2010, http://www.esquire.com/entertainment/a7223/lady-gaga-bio-and-pics-0510/ (accessed August 2, 2015).
3. Now the founder of Yelp.
4. Rachel Rosmarin, "The PayPal Exodus," *Forbes,* July 12, 2006, http://www.forbes.com/2006/07/12/paypal-ebay-youtube_cx_rr_0712paypal.html (accessed January 1, 2015).
5. Founder and former CEO of Yammer.
6. Jeffrey M. O'Brien, "Meet the PayPal Mafia," *Fortune,* November 26, 2007, http://money.cnn.com/2007/11/13/magazines/fortune/paypal_mafia.fortune/index.htm.
7. Anonymous McKinsey principal, interview, February 4, 2009.
8. Anonymous McKinsey alumnus, interview, January 30, 2009.
9. Adam Sternbergh, "Stephen Colbert Has America by the Ballots," *New York* magazine, October 16, 2006, http://nymag.com/news/politics/22322/ (accessed July 11, 2007).
10. Ken P., "An Interview with Stephen Colbert," *IGN,* http://www.ign.com/articles/2003/08/11/an-interview-with-stephen-colbert (accessed January 7, 2015).
11. Jacques Steinberg, "'Daily Show' Personality Gets His Own Platform," *New York Times,* May 4, 2005.
12. "California Wine: A Buyer's Guide," *Guardian,* July 24, 2008, http://www.theguardian.com/robertmondavi/guide.to.californian.wine (accessed January 4, 2015).

INDEX

Page numbers in *italics* refer to a table.

Abboud, Joseph, 62, 64, 153
accessibility of superbosses, 108–10
accountability, 137–38
adapting organizations to new talent,
    51–53
advancement of employees, 7, 131–33,
    143, 201
adversity, reframing of, 154–55
African Americans, 23
Alburty, Steve, 93, 115, 175–76, 177,
    186
alumni networks, 171–96
    benefits of, 188–92, 195–96
    building, 192–96
    and Chez Panisse, 171–74
    degrees of formality in, 185–86
    of McKinsey, 210–11
    and new ventures, 182–84, 188
    as priority
        for superbosses, 174
    and promotion of protégés' careers,
        180–82
    and superboss-protégé relationship,
        175–80
    and superboss quotient, 202, 207
    and talent spawning, 192
apprentices. *See* master-apprentice
    relationships
Arledge, Roone, 95–96
arrogance, reputation for, 51
Ash, Mary Kay, 29, 161
authenticity, as superboss attribute,
    31–32

autonomy, granted by superbosses,
    136–37

Bertolli, Paul, 57
Big Personality paradox, 141–42
Blankenship, C. Ronald, 20, 65, 68
Bossy Bosses, 6–7, 31, 47
Brinker, Norman
    and advancement of employees, 148
    alumni networks of, 185
    autonomy cultivated by, 136–37
    confidence of, 30
    and customer feedback, 96
    and employee retention, 54
    failures of, 93
    flexibility emphasis of, 44
    hands-on style of, 111
    and hiring practices, 43
    innovative approach of, 89, 90–92,
        97
    and intelligence, 42, 50
    and leadership opportunities, 142
    as Nurturer, 29
    relationships with protégés, 178–79
    superboss status, 5
    as teacher, 120, 122
bureaucracy, 116, 124, 207

Campbell, Victor, 32, 65, 162
career development, commitment to,
    134
career ladders, 134, 146
Cesarani, Sal, 62–63, 64, 79, 95

change, demand for, 98–101
character traits of superbosses, 30–33
Chez Panisse
  alumni network of, 174, 178, 185
  and employee departures, 171–73
  and interviews, 57
  magnetism of, 55–56
  talent fostered at, 1–3
  trial runs at, 39–41, 55
Chiat, Jay
  and adaption of company to new
    talent, 52
  and advancement of employees,
    131
  and Alburty, 175–76, 177, 186
  alumni networks of, 185
  and bureaucracy, 116
  and departures of employees, 187
  drive to improve, 95
  egalitarian style of, 115
  and employee retention, 54
  expectations of, 67, 144
  and hiring practices, 43, 47
  influence of, 123
  innovative approach of, 92, 93
  management style of, 27
  motivational skills of, 76
  relationships with protégés, 177,
    178
  search for talent, 45–46
  superboss status, 5
  and team cultivation, 162
Child, Julia, 190–91
"chosen people" group identity, 154
churn, employee, 53–54, 58, 193, 199
Clinton, Bill, 181–82, 189
Clinton, Hillary, 5, 181–82, 189, 208
clustering effect, 167–68
cohort effect, 162–66, 167
Colbert, Stephen, 20–21, 214–16

Coleman, Chase, 67, 127–31, 134, 145,
  164
collaboration, 151, 152, 159, 164–65,
  169, 201
Collins, Jim, 99
Coltrane, John, 26, 50–51
common characteristics of superbosses,
  25–26
communication, 125, 213
compensation, 55, 75
competitiveness
  and collaboration, 152, 169
  cultivation of, 168
  in Motown, 163–64
  on *SNL* set, 150–51
  of superbosses, 30
  and superboss quotient, 201
confidence, 30, 49, 50, 69–71
Corman, Roger, 19–20
  alumni networks of, 185
  and arrogance, 51
  flexibility emphasis of, 44
  forward thinking of, 97
  and high turnover, 53
  and hiring practices, 43, 45, 46
  and Howard, 133–34
  management style of, 27
  relationships with protégés, 177
  and success of employees, 191
  superboss status, 5
  as teacher, 120, 122
  trust in employees, 93
creativity, 25, 43
criticism of superbosses, 69
curiosity, 95
customer feedback, 96

Daily Show, The, 20–21, 132, 157, 189, 215
Davis, Miles
  ability to share the spotlight, 141

acknowledgement of others'
contributions, 160
and adding new talent, 52–53
alumni networks of, 185, 188
childlike fascination of, 25
and drive to improve, 94
fearlessness of, 93
focus of, 33
as Iconoclast, 25–26
interview techniques of, 46–47
and learning from younger musicians,
144
personality of, 23–24
success of, 34
and success of Coltrane, 50–51
superboss status, 5
and tailoring management, 134
talent cultivated by, 22
as teacher, 119
vision of, 73
delegation
Hands-On Delegators, 140–41
importance of, 136–37, 147
and superboss quotient, 201, 207
and team cultivation, 168
departures of employees
attitudes toward, 53–54, 174,
187–88, 193, 207
positive nature of, 53–54, 199
and succession plans, 193–94
and superboss quotient, 201, 207
and turnover in companies, 53–54
See also alumni networks
diversity
racial, 10
of superbosses, 24
Drexler, Mickey, 96–97

egalitarianism, 113–17, 139, 157
egos, in superbosses vs. Bossy Bosses, 31

Ellison, Larry
and advancement of employees, 131,
133
and challenging employees, 49
and committment of employees,
144
competitiveness of, 27
confidence of, 30, 49
and high turnover, 53
and hiring practices, 42, 43, 44, 45,
47, 51
integrity of, 31
and internal competition, 164
magnetism of, 55
management style of, 27–28
motivational skills of, 65
relationships with protégés, 177, 178,
187
success of, 34
and success of employees, 142
superboss status, 5
evaluations of employees, 194
Evans, Bill, 26, 119, 134, 188
expectations of superbosses, 65–69,
213
expertise, 18, 112

failure, 92–94, 136–37, 138, 201
fearlessness, 30, 93, 135
flexibility, 44, 52
football, 3–4, 16–17, *17*
Frist, Tommy
accessibility of, 110
and advancement of employees, 131,
133
alumni network of, 179, 186, 195
authenticity of, 32
expectations of, 65
as godparent of alumni, 187
hands-on style of, 111

Frist, Tommy (*cont.*)
  loyalty to, 64
  as Nurturer, 29
  superboss status, 5
  teaching by example, 120
Fry, Hayden, 132, 133
Fuller, Bonnie, 27, 68–69

Gladwell, Malcolm, 146
Glorious Bastards, 26–28, 50, 107, 177
goals, 65, 139, 143, 201
godparent role of superbosses, 177, 180,
    185, 187, 193, 208, 216
Gordy, Berry, 162–63
Gretzky, Wayne, 216–17

Halgin, Dan, 174
Hambrick, Don, 78
Hancock, Herbie, 26, 46–47, 119
Hands-On Delegators, 127–48
  methods of, 140–41
Hastings, Reed, 194
hierarchy, 113–17, 124, 157, 207
hiring practices
  and ability to "get it," 42, 45
  and adapting to new talent, 51–53
  and already-successful candidates,
    51
  at Chez Panisse, 39–41
  creativity emphasis in, 43
  finding unusual talent, 42, 49–50, 58,
    98, 121, 156
  first-tier prospects passed by, 48
  and flexibility, 44
  and high turnover, 53–54
  and intelligence, 42–43
  and interview techniques, 37–38, 43,
    45–46, 58
  opportunism in, 46
  and qualifications, 45

and searching for candidates, 45–46
and superboss culture, 209
Hoffman, Reid, 194, 195
Howard, Ron, 20, 133–34, 177
Howe, Gordie, 216–17

Iconoclasts, 25–26
identification of superbosses, 18–19
improvement, constant drive for, 94–98
industry trends, 21
innovation and openness
  central importance of, 88
  creating safe environments for, 92–94
  cultivation of, 84, 98–101
  and "cult" work culture, 156
  and demand for change, 98–101
  and drive to improve, 94–98
  encouraging risk taking, 88–92
  expectations of, 81–83
  Lucas's demand for, 82–83
  and solicitation of opinions, 88
  and vision, 84, 85
instant replay technology, 95–96
integrity, 31
intelligence, 42–43, 44, 50
interview techniques, 37–38, 43, 45–46,
    58

job descriptions, 52, 57–58

Keller, Thomas, 2, 51, 112, 191
Kraft, 108–9, 115, 142, 156, 159, 191

Lauren, Ralph
  alumni network of, 196
  background of, 24
  and "cult" work culture, 153–54, 156
  and hiring practices, 42, 46, 52
  as Iconoclast, 25
  and intelligence, 42

and learning from protégés, 144
loyalty to, 61–63, 64
micromanagement of, 140
motivational skills of, 67, 79
and opinions of others, 138–39
passion of, 68
relationships with protégés, 177, 178
and remaining current, 95
single-mindedness of, 79
success of, 33
superboss status, 5
talent spawned by, 4
as teacher, 119, 121
as visionary, 31
Leading Change (Kotter), 98–99
Lee, Stan, 5, 135–36, 155, 160
legacies, 217–19
Leno, Jay, 166
Leonardo da Vinci, 104–5
Letterman, David, 166
Lippert, Seen, 1, 57, 87–88, 173
listening skills, 138
loyalty, 61–64, 160
Lucas, George
  accessibility of, 111
  alumni networks of, 185–86
  autonomy cultivated by, 137
  confidence of, 70–71
  expectations of, 82–83
  fearlessness of, 93
  hands-on style of, 112
  and high turnover, 54
  as Iconoclast, 25
  and innovation, 82–83
  and job descriptions, 52
  magnetism of, 56
  micromanagement of, 140
  superboss status, 5
  vision of, 73, 74
  work environment of, 157

McGraw, Phil, 183–84
McKinsey, 8, 210–11
managers, development of, 106, 206–9
Mary Kay cosmetics, 168
master-apprentice relationships, 103–26
  and accessibility of mentors, 108–10
  benefits of, 123
  declining opportunities for, 105
  and Glorious Bastards, 107
  and hands-on style of leadership,
    111–12
  implementation of, 124–26
  and performance results, 107
  reciprocity in, 145
  and subject-matter expertise, 112
  and teaching style, 117–23
  of Verrocchio, 103–5
  and West Coast–style management,
    113–17
meetings, attitudes toward, 116, 207, 210
memos, banning or retention of, 116
Michaels, Lorne
  alumni network of, 178, 195
  careers launched by, 149–50
  confidence of, 70
  and drive to change/improve, 94
  expectations of, 65
  hands-on delegation of, 141
  as Iconoclast, 25
  and intelligence, 42–43
  and internal competition, 164
  interview techniques of, 46
  magnetism of, 56
  micromanagement of, 140
  office hours of, 68
  and returning cast members, 182
  and roles of employees, 52
  superboss status, 5
  talent spawned by, 21
  and ventures of protégés, 188

Michaels, Lorne (*cont.*)
  vision of, 73, 74
  and work environment, 150
micromanagement, 140
midlevel superbosses, 19
Miles, Michael
  accessibility of, 108–10
  alumni network of, 179, 185
  and departures of employees,
    187–88
  egalitarian style of, 115
  and eliciting/limiting skills, 119
  as Nurturer, 29
  passion of, 68
  personality of, 22–24
  recruitment tactics of, 48
  and success of employees, 142
  superboss status, 5
  talent spawned by, 22
  as teacher, 121
  and team cultivation, 159–60
  on tolerance of mistakes, 138
military veterans, 213–14
Milken, Michael
  competitiveness of, 30
  expectations of, 67–68
  management style of, 27, 111
  superboss status, 5
  and teams, 157
  work environment of, 157
millennial(s), 8, 64, 195, 196, 198, 233n
mistakes, tolerance of, 138
Mondavi, Robert, 74, 217–19, 220
Moore, Constance, 20, 47, 66–67
motivating employees, 61–79
  as core skill of superbosses, 77
  and desire for impact, 73
  and inspiring self-confidence, 69–71
  and loyalty, 61–64
  with money, 75

  and perfectionism, 65–69
  role of passion in, 78–79
  with success, 75–76
  with vision, 71–74, 76–77
Motown record label, 162–63

New York Times, 17–18
Nicholson, Jack, 20, 44, 120
Norman, Archie, 29, 115–16
novelty, passion for, 95
Noyce, Bob
  alumni networks of, 185
  and cohort effect, 167
  competitiveness of, 30
  confidence of, 30
  egalitarian style of, 113–15
  expectations of, 144
  as Iconoclast, 25
  listening skills of, 138
  superboss status, 5
Nurturers, 28–29, 65

openness. *See* innovation and openness
opinions of employees, 88, 138–39
opportunity spotting of superbosses,
    131–33
Oracle, 27–28, 131, 133, 142, 146, 187
Outliers (Gladwell), 146

Panula, Jorma
  accessibility of, 110
  alumni networks of, 185
  authenticity of, 32
  autonomy cultivated by, 137
  forward thinking of, 97
  as Iconoclast, 25
  integrity of, 31, 122
  micromanagement of, 140
  subject-matter expertise of, 112
  superboss status, 5

as teacher, 117–18, 122
and team cultivation, 161
passion, 6, 25–26, 78–79
PayPal, 210
perfectionism, demand for, 65–69
performance measurements, 7
personalities of superbosses, 23–24
Philadelphia Inquirer
alumni network of, 178
culture of, 11–14, 33
employee retention at, 54
recruitment tactics at, 51
success of, 15–16
talent spawned at, 13–14, 17–18
Pitino, Rick, 131–32, 139
Popovich, Gregg, 29, 159

qualifications, unconventional, 45

rehiring employees, 182
Renaissance Italy, 103–5
resignations. *See* departures of
employees
retention, talent, 54, 174–75, 195, 199,
225n
Richards, Ann, 208
risk taking, 88–92, 123, 213
Roberts, Gene
ability to attract talent, 18
accessibility of, 110
alumni network of, 178
autonomy cultivated by, 136
background of, 24
and bureaucracy, 116
and collaboration, 164–65
flexibility emphasis of, 44
and hiring practices, 42, 46
and ideas of employees, 93–94
listening skills of, 138
personality of, 33

recruitment tactics of, 47–48, 51
and resignations, 53
and salaries, 55
success of, 15–16
superboss status, 5
talent spawned by, 12–14, 17–18
as teacher, 119, 120
vision of, 73
Robertson, Julian
accessibility of, 111
and challenging employees, 49
and competition, 164
and departures of employees, 187
expectations of, 67, 69
and learning curves, 145
and learning from employees, 144
management style of, 27
and success of employees, 182
superboss status, 5
and tailoring management, 134
talent spawned by, 4–5
as teacher, 121–22
and team cultivation, 161–62
and ventures of protégés ("tiger
seeds"), 129–30, 131, 144, 182,
188
roles of employees, 52
rules, breaking, 88–92

Sacerdote, Bruce, 167
Sacks, David, 210
Samberg, Andy, 65, 67, 141
San Antonio Spurs, 158–59
Sandberg, Sheryl, 208
Sanders, Bill
alumni network of, 20, 178
autonomy cultivated by, 137
expectations of, 65, 68, 69
and hiring practices, 44, 47
and knowledgeable employees, 50

Sanders, Bill (*cont.*)
 motivational skills of, 75
 perfection, demands for, 65–66
 recruitment tactics of, 47
 and salaries, 55
 superboss status, 5
 and team ethic, 160–61
 vision of, 73, 74
Saturday Night Live
 alumni network of, 178, 179, 180,
  192, 215
 competition/collaboration in, 149–51,
  152, 164
 and "cult" work culture, 156, 157
 and drive to improve, 94
 and Michaels's confidence, 70
 pressure experienced in, 65
 projects associated with, 182–83
 and returning cast members, 182
Second City, 214–15
self-assessment, 200–203
self-confidence, 69–71
Sellers, R. Scot, 20, 69, 73, 137
sports broadcasting, 95–96
Star Wars film series, 70–71, 73, 81–83,
  111, 157
Steak and Ale, 90–91
Stewart, Jon, 20–21, 29, 132, 157
succession plans, 147–48, 193–94
superboss culture, 209–14
superboss effect, 13–14, 34
superboss quotient, 200–203, 206–8
Swensen, David, 5, 29

talent magnets, 54–56, 156, 190
talent spawners, 13, 16–22, *17*, 27, 29,
  192
talent spotting, 38–39, 41–42
teachable practices of superbosses, 34,
  57

Teach for America, 123
teaching, 28–29, 117–23, 134, 207. *See
  also* master-apprentice relationships
teams and teamwork, 149–70
 and clustering effect, 167–68
 and cohort effect, 162–66, 167
 and "cult" work culture, 153–58
 language of, 158
 poor teamwork, 152
 and productivity, 157
 on *Saturday Night Live*, 149–50, 152
 team building, 166–70
 and 2-C principle, 164
 and work environments, 157–58
technology, communication, 125
ten-thousand-hour rule, 146
30 Rock (television series), 183, 188
Tiger Management, 127–30, 164
Trachinger, Bob, 95–96
Trump, Donald, 6, 48
Tucker, John, 23, 48, 109
2-C principle, 164–65
types of superbosses, 25–29, 50

urgency, creating a sense of, 98

Vandevelde, Luc, 119, 156, 191
Verrocchio, Andrea del, 103–5, 116
vision and visionaries, 71–74
 and "cult" work culture, 153
 and innovation, 84, 85
 and performance results, 76–77
 and superboss culture, 209–10
 superbosses' expectations for, 85
 and superboss quotient, 201, 206
 and teaching, 121
 as trait of superbosses, 30–31

walking around, managing by,
  123–24

Walsh, Bill
  and adversity, 154
  commitment to employees, 135
  confidence of, 71
  and employee retention, 54
  and hiring practices, 45
  innovative approach of, 89–90
  internship program of, 45–46
  and loyalty, 160
  as Nurturer, 29
  passion of, 65
  and positions of players, 52–53
  and promotion of protégés' careers,
    180–81
  search for talent, 45–46
  success of, 33
  and success of employees, 142
  superboss status, 5
  talent spawned by, 3–4, 16, 17
  teaching style of, 118–19
  and team cultivation, 138, 159, 160
Waters, Alice
  alumni network of, 178, 195
  background of, 24
  and departures of employees, 171–73
  drive to improve, 95
  and employee retention, 54
  and guest chefs, 51
  hands-on delegation of, 141
  and high turnover, 54
  and hiring practices, 39–41, 45, 47,
    57
  as Iconoclast, 25
  innovative approach of, 86–88
  magnetism of, 55
  micromanagement of, 140
  passion of, 30–31
  public promotion of employees, 155
  relationships with protégés, 177–78
  superboss status, 5
  talent spawned by, 1–3
  as teacher, 120, 121
  vision of, 73
West Coast–style management, 113–17
Winfrey, Oprah, 5, 183–84, 195
women superbosses, 208

SYDNEY FINKELSTEIN is the Steven Roth Professor of Management at the Tuck School of Business at Dartmouth College and the director of Tuck's Center for Leadership. He is a consultant and speaker to senior executives around the globe, as well as an executive coach, focusing on talent development, corporate governance, learning from mistakes, and strategies for growth. He has published eight previous books, including the *Wall Street Journal* bestseller *Why Smart Executives Fail*. He is listed in Thinkers50, the world's most prestigious ranking of leadership gurus.